DATE DUE

11-22-2016	
	PRINTED IN U.S.A.

Cambridge Medieval Textbooks

THE HUNDRED YEARS WAR

Cambridge Medieval Textbooks

This is a new series of specially commissioned textbooks for teachers and students, designed to complement the monograph series 'Cambridge Studies in Medieval Life and Thought' by providing introductions to a range of topics in medieval history. The series will combine both chronological and thematic approaches, and will deal equally with British and European topics. All volumes in the series will be published in hard covers and in paperback.

Already published

Germany in the High Middle Ages *c.* 1050–1200
HORST FUHRMANN
Translated by Timothy Reuter

The Hundred Years War: England and France at War *c.* 1300–*c.* 1450
CHRISTOPHER ALLMAND

Other titles are in preparation

THE HUNDRED YEARS WAR

England and France at war c. 1300 – c. 1450

CHRISTOPHER ALLMAND
Reader in Medieval History, University of Liverpool

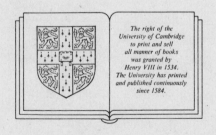

The right of the
University of Cambridge
to print and sell
all manner of books
was granted by
Henry VIII in 1534.
The University has printed
and published continuously
since 1584.

CAMBRIDGE UNIVERSITY PRESS

Cambridge

New York   New Rochelle   Melbourne   Sydney

Published by the Press Syndicate of the University of Cambridge
The Pitt Building, Trumpington Street, Cambridge CB2 1RP
32 East 57th Street, New York, NY 10022, USA
10 Stamford Road, Oakleigh, Melbourne 3166, Australia

First published 1988

Printed in Great Britain
by the University Press, Cambridge

British Library cataloguing in publication data
Allmand, C. T.
The Hundred Years War: England and France at war,
c.1300 – c.1450. – (Cambridge medieval textbooks).
1. Hundred Years' War, 1339–1453
I. Title
944′.025   DC96

Library of Congress cataloguing in publication data
Allmand, C. T.
The hundred years war.
(Cambridge medieval textbooks)
Bibliography: p.
Includes index.
1. Hundred Years' War, 1339–1453.   2. France–History,
Military–1328–1589.   3. Great Britain–History,
Military–Medieval period, 1066–1485.   I. Title.
II. Series.
DC96.A44 1987   944′.025   87-13251

ISBN 0 521 26499 5 hard covers
ISBN 0 521 31923 4 paperback

For
Bernadette

CONTENTS

PREFACE

This book is the product of a way of presenting the subject which has been forming in my mind since I began to teach the subject a good many years ago. I am not the first nor, I suspect, shall I be the last to have found the writing of a 'general' book more of a challenge than I had anticipated when I took it on. Only the reader will be able to tell how useful and successful the experiment will have been.

The preface is usually the last part of a book to be written. By the time that stage is reached, the writer knows to whom he is indebted. To the many Liverpool students who, over the years, have stopped me in my tracks by telling me that what seemed clear to me was not so to them, I owe a debt of gratitude. I am grateful, too, to the Syndics of the Cambridge University Press for inviting me to write this book, to Mrs Betty Plummer for typing the text, and to Kay McKechnie for carrying out her work as the Press's subeditor with such efficiency.

To an old friend, James Sherborne, I owe a particularly warm word of thanks. A dozen or more years ago he organised a very successful conference at Bristol on the theme of this book. When I asked him if he would read my draft, he accepted and completed the work with speed. He saved me from a number of errors of both fact and interpretation, while also making valuable suggestions how to improve the text. None the less, as the person whose name appears on the title page, I accept full responsibility for what is contained in the chapters which follow.

Christopher Allmand

ABBREVIATIONS

A.H.R.	*American Historical Review*
A.B.	*Annales de Bourgogne*
A.Est	*Annales de l'Est*
A.M.	*Annales du Midi*
B.I.H.R.	*Bulletin of the Institute of Historical Research*
Econ.H.R.	*Economic History Review*
E.E.T.S.	Early English Text Society
E.H.R.	*English Historical Review*
H.T.	*History Today*
J.E.H.	*Journal of Ecclesiastical History*
J.Med.H.	*Journal of Medieval History*
J.W.C.I.	*Journal of the Warburg and Courtauld Institute*
M.A.	*Le Moyen Age*
M.M.	*Mariner's Mirror*
P.B.A.	*Proceedings of the British Academy*
P&P	*Past & Present*
R.H.	*Revue Historique*
R.S.	Rolls Series
S.H.F.	Société de l'Histoire de France
T.R.Hist.S.	*Transactions of the Royal Historical Society*

1 France in 1337

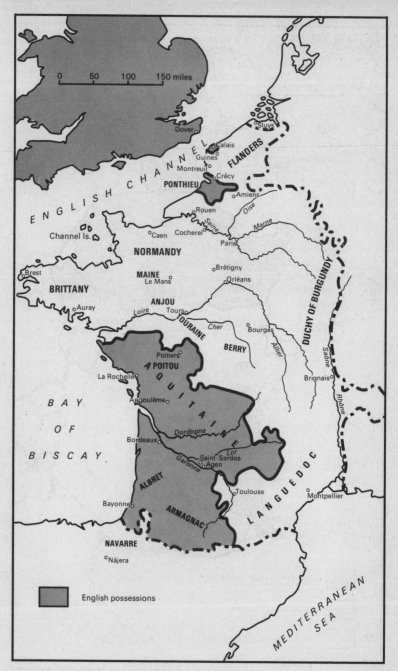

Scale: 0, 50, 100, 150 miles

ENGLISH CHANNEL

Dover
Sluys
Calais
Guines
Montreuil
Crécy
FLANDERS
PONTHIEU
Amiens
Rouen
Oise
Seine
Marne
Channel Is.
Caen
Cocherel
Paris
NORMANDY
Brest
MAINE
Le Mans
Brétigny
Orléans
BRITTANY
ANJOU
Auray
Loire
Tours
TOURAINE
Cher
Bourges
Allier
DUCHY OF BURGUNDY
Saône
BERRY
Poitiers
POITOU
La Rochelle
AQUITAINE
Brignais
Angoulême
BAY
Rhône
OF
Dordogne
BISCAY
Bordeaux
Lot
Saint-Sardos
Garonne
Agen
ALBRET
Toulouse
LANGUEDOC
Montpellier
Bayonne
ARMAGNAC
NAVARRE
Nájera

English possessions

2 France in 1360

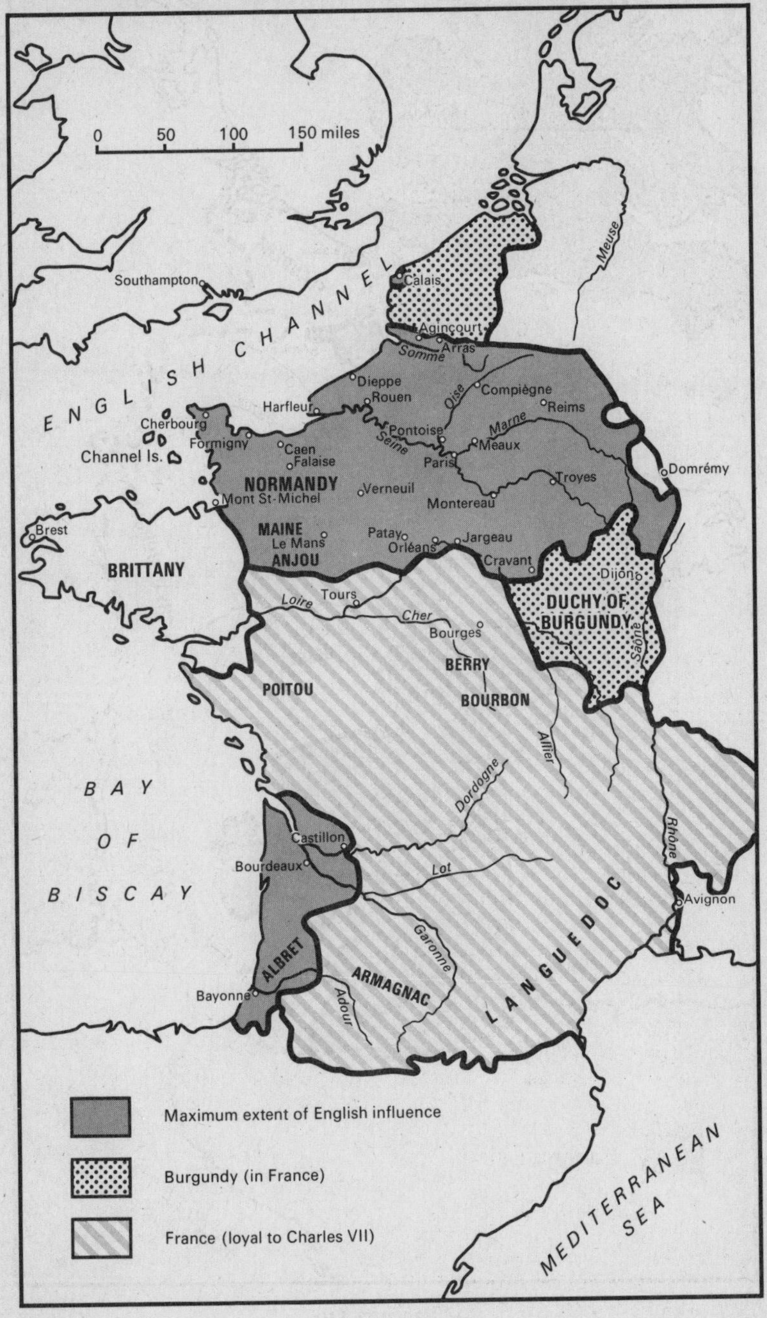
0 50 100 150 miles
ENGLISH CHANNEL
Southampton
Calais
Agincourt
Arras
Somme
Meuse
Dieppe
Rouen
Harfleur
Oise
Compiègne
Reims
Cherbourg
Formigny
Channel Is.
Caen
Falaise
Pontoise
Seine
Marne
Meaux
Paris
Domrémy
NORMANDY
Verneuil
Troyes
Mont St-Michel
Montereau
Brest
MAINE
Le Mans
ANJOU
Patay
Orléans
Jargeau
Cravant
BRITTANY
Dijon
Tours
Loire
Cher
Bourges
DUCHY OF BURGUNDY
Saône
BERRY
POITOU
BOURBON
Allier
BAY OF BISCAY
Dordogne
Rhône
Castillon
Bourdeaux
Lot
Avignon
LANGUEDOC
Garonne
ALBRET
ARMAGNAC
Bayonne
Adour
Maximum extent of English influence
Burgundy (in France)
France (loyal to Charles VII)
MEDITERRANEAN SEA

3 France in 1429

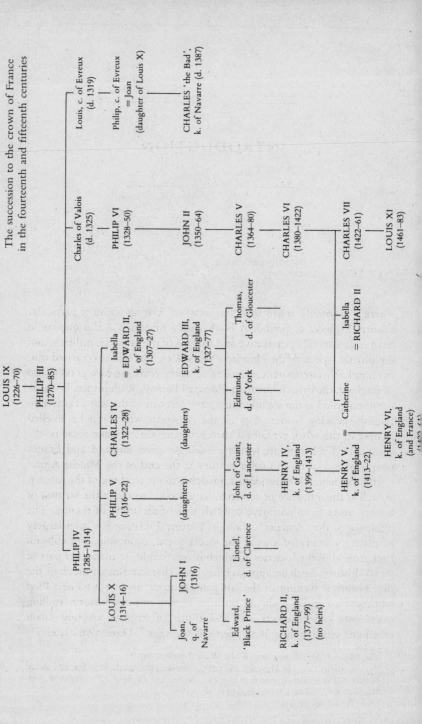

The succession to the crown of France in the fourteenth and fifteenth centuries

LOUIS IX (1226–70)

PHILIP III (1270–85)

PHILIP IV (1285–1314)

Charles of Valois (d. 1325)

Louis, c. of Evreux (d. 1319)

LOUIS X (1314–16)

PHILIP V (1316–22)

CHARLES IV (1322–28)

Isabella = EDWARD II, k. of England (1307–27)

PHILIP VI (1328–50)

Philip, c. of Evreux = Joan (daughter of Louis X)

Joan, q. of Navarre

JOHN I (1316)

(daughters)

(daughters)

EDWARD III, k. of England (1327–77)

JOHN II (1350–64)

CHARLES 'the Bad', k. of Navarre (d. 1387)

Edward, 'Black Prince'

Lionel, d. of Clarence

John of Gaunt, d. of Lancaster

Edmund, d. of York

Thomas, d. of Gloucester

CHARLES V (1364–80)

RICHARD II, k. of England (1377–99) (no heirs)

HENRY IV, k. of England (1399–1413)

Isabella = RICHARD II

CHARLES VI (1380–1422)

HENRY V, k. of England (1413–22)

Catherine

CHARLES VII (1422–61)

HENRY VI, k. of England (and France) (1422–61)

LOUIS XI (1461–83)

INTRODUCTION

There is normally more than one way of writing about a particular historical subject or period. A book with a title such as this one could have concentrated on narrative and analysis of the political, military, and diplomatic aspects of the Hundred Years War. The task was carried out, in remarkable circumstances, more than forty years ago by a good friend of England, the French historian, Edouard Perroy. With justice, his book is still regarded as the soundest narrative account of the war available to English-speaking readers. For all the criticisms which can be levelled against it, the work remains a successful attempt to make sense of the complicated relationship which existed between England and France over a period of more than a century at the end of the Middle Ages.[1]

But the demands of modern approaches to the teaching of the subject, as well as the influence of research, have tended to move the writing of history away from narrative towards that of the study of themes. The influence of the 'Annales' school of historical writing has been largely to place the study of war in the wider social, economic, and cultural background of the societies in which it was fought, to make war part of 'total' history. Such an approach has been characteristic of much of the best historical writing of the last generation or so. In 1962 Piero Pieri addressed a Parisian audience on how he saw military history 'spilling over' into other aspects and specialisms of history, creating chain reactions which would bind them all together.[2] Three years later Dr

---

[1] *The Hundred Years War*, trans. W. H. Wells (London, 1951).
[2] 'Sur les dimensions de l'histoire militaire', *Annales*, 18 (1963), 625. See also K. A. Fowler, 'War and change in late medieval France and England', *The Hundred Years War*, ed. K. A. Fowler (London, 1971), pp. 1–27.

H. J. Hewitt published his influential book, *The organization of war under Edward III, 1338–62*, in which, rather than describe activity of a narrow, military kind, he wrote about the relatively unglamorous background and preparation needed for war at that time and, indeed, ever since.[3] Others have now followed in placing war in its widest context, not only social and economic, but political, administrative, and legal. Philippe Contamine's long study, *Guerre, état et société à la fin du moyen age. Etudes sur les armées des rois de France, 1337–1494*, includes all these elements – and many more.[4] As a book on the history of men who went to war, it takes up Pieri's challenge, and meets it handsomely. One day, perhaps, somebody will attempt to do for English armies what Contamine has done for French ones.

In writing this book, it has been my intention to try to see how war, over a period of 150 years or so, affected developments and changes in two of Europe's leading societies, those of France and England. The purpose of a book of this kind is to distil the essential from modern specialised scholarship and to present the whole in some recognisable form. In this case, much of that scholarship has come out of France. Inevitably, therefore, the English-speaking reader will find that in some sections of the book the emphasis is on France and on how that country, in particular, reacted to the war. In other places, the stress is more upon England. In general, however, I have had it in mind to try (but not slavishly) to compare and contrast the effects of war upon England and France, in the belief that this approach can provide a thought-provoking approach to the subject.

This book begins with a narrative account of the main events and developments of the war. Even so apparently straightforward a task is not carried out without difficulty. The historian may relate what happened; but when it comes to explaining why events occurred as they did, and why decisions were taken as they were, he cannot always fulfil his role as he would wish. He must be ready to speculate, for the sources (in this case the chronicles and records of government which provide him with much of his material) do not always come up to expectation. By comparison with what is available to the student of more modern times, the medievalist's sources are often of very thin quality.

There are, happily, notable exceptions to this generalisation. Financial records, for instance, when they survive at all, often do so in large quantities. This is the case for the English king's financial archives which provide us with much information on the sums collected, how they were spent, and the organisation which lay behind that expenditure. In a word, even from accounts we learn how administration functioned. If

[3] Manchester, 1966.   [4] Paris: The Hague, 1972.

France's surviving financial records are not as good as English ones, her legal archives, particularly those of that great central institution, the Parlement of Paris, have left us with a remarkable human record of the effects of war upon society in France in the fourteenth and fifteenth centuries. By using such evidence the historian can come to terms with some of the everyday reality of the war, and how it touched the lives and outlook of men and women, famous and not so famous, rich and poor, whose experiences are described in the proceedings of civil and criminal cases which have come down to us in some number. The pleadings of advocates contain much valuable information of an economic and social nature; we can learn much, too, about human motivation which made men go to war. Legal records are unique in giving us an inkling of how people of the age saw the world about them.[5]

Important, too, although not always easy to evaluate, is the evidence which we may call literary, not merely the chronicles, but rather the tracts, pamphlets, newsletters and even poetry through which people expressed their ideas and views, as well as their emotions, on contemporary issues and problems, which might be the need for government to be better managed, hope of peace, or the criteria according to which society's military leaders should be chosen. Some of these texts are the work of writers whose literary fame and ability have merited the close attention of scholars of literature. Christine de Pisan and Alain Chartier are two such who also attract the attention of historians for a different reason, namely that they were observers and critics of the world of early fifteenth-century France, both of them having things to say which, they hoped, would turn it into a better world. It is in their observations and criticisms that the historian has an interest, for they enable him to judge what was important at the time, and how intelligent contemporaries reacted to the difficulties and dilemmas which faced men and women of the age.

What the historian is trying to do is not merely to record the events and happenings of war, but to study them against the background of the world in which the long Anglo-French conflict was fought. We need to know why there was a war, and what factors in the early fourteenth century were influential in encouraging it. Something, then, must be said of how men of that time regarded war, and how commonly-held attitudes may have encouraged them to take an active part in it. The conflict under way, the significant questions are those which concern its

---

[5] See the collections of texts from these records edited by P. Timbal, *La guerre de cent ans vue à travers les registres du Parlement (1337–1369)* (Paris, 1961), and by C. T. Allmand and C. A. J. Armstrong, *English suits before the Parlement of Paris, 1420–1436* (Camden fourth series, 26, London, 1982).

conduct. Far from being unimportant, the study of administration and institutions has much to tell us about the increasing effectiveness of the state and central government in an aspect of government growing more important with every passing year.

Not all will necessarily agree with the suggestion that those who fight in wars are historically more important than the wars themselves. War should be studied through those who take part in it, so that the attitudes and human reactions of those involved may be appreciated, and the phenomenon of war may thus come to be better understood. Much recent research has centred on these broader aspects of war. Few who have read Professor J. F. Verbruggen's *The art of warfare in western Europe during the Middle Ages from the eighth century to 1340* will forget this vivid approach to the subject including, for example, his description of the very human fear experienced by men about to face battle,[6] an emotion also vividly described in the more popular, but no less serious work of John Keegan, *The face of battle*.[7] In these, and other works, the soldier as an individual occupies the centre of the stage.

Since wars involve others than those who face battle, that overwhelming majority who may prefer to have nothing at all to do with war, they cannot, and should not, be omitted from any modern consideration of the subject. For the non-combatant was not to be merely the quiet underwriter of his country's military undertakings. He had an active part to play, too, behind the scenes and, particularly in France, he was to be one of the main targets of the enemy's attacks. Increasingly, historians have come to appreciate his role, and have sought in sources, often of a literary character, to understand how he faced war and reacted to the situations which it created.[8]

Finally, war served to bring all members of a society, soldier and civilian, under the umbrella of national consciousness. How that consciousness should be studied, what forms it took, how it expressed itself, are questions which those who study the subject, at whatever period, must be ready to answer. In the late Middle Ages, symbolism was widely used to express a feeling of belonging to a people; likewise institutions, such as monarchy, played an important part in creating a sense of national identity; while the writing of history was deliberately fostered to encourage a feeling which the single word 'roots' will convey to a twentieth-century reader. Since the quarrel which put the

[6] Trans. from the Dutch by S. Willard and S. C. M. Southern (Amsterdam: New York: London, 1977), pp. 50–2.

[7] Harmondsworth edn, 1978, pp. 70–2.

[8] C. T. Allmand, 'The war and the non-combatant', *The Hundred Years War*, ed. Fowler, pp. 163–83.

kingdoms of France and England at odds with each other was based upon historical differences, it was only reasonable that history should also have been used both to emphasise the differences between them, and to allow each to show itself how its own history and its own characteristics had developed.

By treating his subject as widely as possible, by seeing it in terms of the history of war, rather than as the more narrowly defined military history, the modern student will come to understand it in its many facets and complexities. In so doing he may come as near as he can ever hope to an understanding of war as people of the late Middle Ages knew it, no easy task even in the most favourable conditions, but one which cannot be attempted with any hope of success without a proper appreciation of the many threads which make up history. Not the least is the role which individuals played in war. Without them, there can be no history.

I

THE CAUSES AND PROGRESS
OF THE HUNDRED YEARS WAR

Generally speaking, the Middle Ages accepted war with fatalism. It was part of the divine plan, linked with famine, flood, and plague as a manifestation of God's punishment for sins committed. A nation which experienced years of defeat and disaster (as France did in the mid-fourteenth century) beat its breast in self-reproach and accepted war's afflictions. Since few questioned such a view, those of pacific leanings met with little sympathy. While war's excesses were often condemned, war itself was taken for granted. In a society whose social and economic system had originally been, and to a certain degree still was, organised to provide for such eventualities, this was scarcely surprising. A world geared to war was unlikely to question why it should break out. It formed part of the accustomed and natural order.

In more questioning times, with the historian seeking to exercise his right to examine the past, people have tried to explain why wars occur. Attempts to do this are far from new. Long ago, Thucydides distinguished between causes and occasions of war. In modern times, people have looked to many different aspects of human activity as sources of conflict, not all of which may be seen as appropriate to medieval societies. But some are. The Crusades may be regarded as wars fought in the name of ideology and religion. The Italian city states, and others, were for centuries in conflict in the Mediterranean over sources of, and outlets for, trade.[1] The movement of peoples, associated with the great increase in population of the thirteenth century, led to wars which, for

---

[1] W. H. McNeill, *The pursuit of power* (Oxford, 1983), ch. 3.

example, in Spain were associated with the Christian reconquest of the Iberian peninsula from Moorish control, but which were also waged to satisfy the urge to find new lands, as was to happen in northern and eastern Germany under the rule of the Teutonic Knights.

In France and England it was the breakdown of the historic feudal order, no longer able to meet the demands of changing times, and its gradual replacement by an order of nations increasingly aware of their growing national characteristics, which was the fundamental cause of the long conflict which forms the subject of this book. In all these cases, war was the result of major changes in the development of societies. In some, the need for land was important, if not paramount; in others it was the search for markets. In the case of the Hundred Years War, the causes of the conflict were to be found both in the long historic links between England and France, links which were gradually becoming weaker, and in the need to express in new terms the relationship between the two countries (arguably the two most powerful in western society in the late Middle Ages) taking into account elements such as national consciousness and diverging methods of government (to name but two) which historians recognise as being characteristic of late medieval European society as a whole.

THE CAUSES OF THE WAR

Where have historians sought the causes of the so-called Hundred Years War? Traditionally, the answer has been found in the study of the two main factors which were at issue in the years leading up to what is regarded as the moment of outbreak of war, the confiscation of the duchy of Aquitaine by King Philip VI of France in May 1337. This act brought to a head problems of long standing whose roots were to be found in two factors.[2] The first was that, since the eleventh century, the kings of England had been lords of much of north-western France, an area extending from Normandy (in the time of William the Conqueror) through Maine, Anjou, Touraine, and Poitou to the duchy of Aquitaine which, a century later, Henry II had come to control through his marriage to the duchess, Eleanor, previously the wife of Louis VII of France. There thus stretched from the Channel to the Pyrenees an 'empire' (termed Angevin), ruled by one man who was also king of England. At the same time there had grown up, mainly during the twelfth century, the extension of the authority of the royal house of France, the dynasty of Capet, through the insistence that the homage

---

[2] The reader will find much of value for this chapter in J. Le Patourel, 'The origins of the war', *The Hundred Years War*, ed. Fowler, pp. 28–50.

due from the great feudatories to their king should be 'liege'. Then, when King John took over the French lands which he had inherited in 1200, he was allowed to do so only on condition that he should recognise them as being fiefs held of the king of France. The power of that king, Philip-Augustus, over his vassal was further increased when, in 1203 and 1204, he conquered Anjou and Normandy which John, in spite of an attempt to do so in 1214, never recovered. Nor was his heir, Henry III, any more successful, although he took part in an enterprise in western France in 1230. In October 1259 Henry sealed a peace treaty with Louis IX (St Louis) of France whereby, in spite of his son's objections, he renounced his claim to Normandy, Maine, Anjou, Touraine and Poitou, while the French king, recognising Henry as his vassal in Aquitaine and other territories in the south-west, created him a peer of France. The terms might appear generous to the English. In reality, since they established a new feudal relationship between the kings of France and England, they sowed the seeds for much future trouble.

The sources of that trouble were twofold. The first was the liege homage owed by Henry III (and, in future, whenever there might be a change of king in either England or France) to the kings of France, a kind of 'priority' homage which could involve the giving of military aid against any enemy of the French crown whenever it was demanded. Equally, the giver of homage could not act in concert with, or give help to, any of his lord's enemies. By creating a peerage for Henry III, Louis IX was only emphasising further the closeness of the allegiance which bound the two men.

Secondly, and in this case a matter of particular importance, was the fact that the duchy of Aquitaine was held by a king who, for purposes of this treaty, had become a vassal of another king. Such a situation was likely to make for untold complications. Thus, for instance, there were places within the lands held by the king–duke which were subject to a hierarchy of courts ultimately controlled by the Parlement, the supreme court of France which sat in Paris. The sovereign legal rights of the French crown could, if and when required, be put to good political use in undermining the authority and prestige of the king–duke within his duchy. Appeals could be heard and judicial enquiries set in motion by bodies outside the duchy. And all the while such actions lessened the actual legal powers and authority of the king–duke, serving to encourage factional dissension within Aquitaine and, in particular, within its capital, Bordeaux.[3]

It was soon recognised that unity of interest between lord and vassal

[3] J. A. Kicklighter, 'English Bordeaux in conflict: the execution of Pierre Vigier de la Rousselle and its aftermath, 1312–24', *J. Med. H.*, 9 (1983), 1–14.

did not exist. In Flanders, an area in which French and English interests clashed over issues which were strategic, economic and legal, Edward I intervened in 1294 as king of England in defence of the count, Guy, then in dispute with Philip IV of France. But this intervention was more than a defence of English interests in north-eastern France. In the previous year Philip IV had summoned Edward I, as duke of Aquitaine, to answer for an allegedly illegal act at sea off the coast of the duchy, and for the capture of La Rochelle by men from Bayonne. Attempts to find a solution having failed, Philip announced the confiscation of the duchy of Aquitaine in May 1294. In the following month, Edward broke his feudal links with the French crown, and the two countries soon drifted into war. Although the fighting effectively ceased in 1297, peace was not established until 1303, when the duchy was returned and the *status quo* of 1294 was restored, Edward agreeing to marry his heir, the Edward II to be, to Isabella, daughter of the French king.

If, at least for some years afterwards, there was no real war, there was none the less plenty of tension in south-western France. The war just ended had shown up the divisions between the pro-French and the pro-English factions within Bordeaux. In the summer of 1306 there took place at Montreuil the first of a series of meetings ('processes') between French and English representatives to try to work out the legal position of the lands held by the English in Aquitaine. The meeting was a failure, and was followed in 1307 by civil disturbances in Bordeaux and an appeal to Paris regarding the English appointment to the mayoralty of the ducal capital. In 1311, further discussions were held at Périgueux: but, like its predecessor, this 'process' also failed to resolve fundamental differences between the two sides.

The only way now open to the English, in these years deeply involved in war against the Scots and in a domestic situation turning more and more violent, was retaliation. When Vigier de la Rousselle dared to advocate the continuation of appeals to Paris in 1312, the whole matter was taken up in a very 'political' way by the authorities in Bordeaux, who accused Vigier of contempt of ducal authority and had him executed on a charge which was, in effect, that of treason. Likewise when, in 1323, King Charles IV ordered a new fortified town, or *bastide*, to be built at Saint-Sardos, this was ineptly taken as a physical and legal attack upon the authority of the English who, probably without the knowledge of Edward II, attacked and burned the town in November 1323. In its turn, such an act provoked French retaliation: the duchy of Aquitaine was again declared confiscate to the French crown, and an army was sent to take possession. Within a short time a truce had been arranged, and in September 1325 Prince Edward, soon to become

Edward III, did homage, paid a relief (or fine), and thereby secured the return of much of the land which the French had overrun. But not all. The Agenais and other territories were not restored immediately; it needed a further war in 1326 and an agreement, concluded in March 1327, to secure the restoration of those lands. At this stage, it is unlikely that the French were anxious to carry out a conquest of Aquitaine. All that they wanted was the full recognition of their king's sovereign rights in the duchy, a moderate enough approach in which they had the support of the papacy, now becoming increasingly aware of its obligation to help in the diplomatic negotiations between the two countries.

So far the issues had been largely feudal. By 1327, however, a second matter was poised to sour relations between England and France. In January 1327 Edward II was deposed and succeeded by his son, Edward III. Little more than a year later Charles IV, uncle (through his sister Isabella) of Edward III, also died, leaving no direct heir as king of France. As nephew of the late king, Edward appeared to have a good claim, indeed perhaps the best claim, to succeed him. His right, however, had been transmitted to him through his mother, and it was this transmission through the female, later explained as the inability of a woman to pass on a claim which, as a woman, she could not herself exercise, which worked against Edward's ambition. When the French nobility, in whose hands the resolution of such a crisis lay, made its choice, that choice was to make one of their number, Philip, count of Valois, king. The grounds were essentially those of suitability: Philip was French; he was eighteen years older than his English rival (then aged only fifteen); and he had always lived in France. Although not, as Edward III was, a direct descendant of Philip IV, he was at least his nephew through his father, Charles of Valois. In the circumstances the degree of kinship was sufficiently close to secure him the support he required.

Yet, in the context of the long-standing dispute of Aquitaine, Edward III's claim was strong enough to persuade him that he ought to pursue it, if only as an alternative means of achieving sovereign rule in Aquitaine. Certainly, the claim was there to be used to Edward's advantage. None the less in 1329 he did simple homage (all that was asked of him for the moment) at Amiens, following this up with liege homage in 1331. In this mood of optimism negotiators met for another 'process', this time at Agen, in 1332 and 1333. In their discussions the fundamental differences between the two sides slowly emerged: the legal position of the king-duke and the lands held by him; and, secondly, the problem of which lands the French were to control. At the same time a polarisation of opinion in Aquitaine was gradually taking place, largely in favour of English rule, and by 1337 tension had reached a high level. On 24 May

Philip IV declared the duchy confiscate to the French crown because of Edward's many acts of disobedience and rebellion. It is this decision which is taken to mark the beginning of the Hundred Years War.

The medium and short-term causes of the outbreak of the war were, as we have seen, the problem of the feudal relationship of the king of France with his most important vassal, the duke of Aquitaine, otherwise the king of England, and that of the disputed succession to the crown of France. By changing the historian's focus, these problems can be put into another perspective. Traditionally the period of the Hundred Years War has been regarded as the time when the crown of France made great steps forward towards the achievement of a policy of centralisation begun under the Capetians some two centuries earlier. While the differences between the crown of France and its vassals were expressed in a language which was essentially feudal (a new political vocabulary more suited to developments had not yet evolved), what was really happening was something remarkably 'modern', the laying of the foundations of a national state under one monarch whose territorial authority could only be effectively exercised through annexation or conquest. Such a view tends to place less emphasis on the war between two countries and more on the internal conflict between the king of France and the duke of Aquitaine, a struggle between two blocks of territory and two rather different legal traditions: the 'Angevin empire', once ruled by the English, representing the area of customary law and local independence, the other part of France the more centralising tradition based on Roman law.

The alternative and, in the last resort, not so very different view is that which sees the Hundred Years War as a wider civil war in which a policy of royal centralisation, based on Paris, was opposed not only by the dukes of Aquitaine and Normandy (in both cases king of England), but by those of Brittany, and (late in the fourteenth and fifteenth centuries), Burgundy. On the one hand was the development of the French state, its administration, its budget, its army, together with its emphasis upon the attributes of monarchy. Pitted against it were the great princes, some with ambition to achieve political and legal independence of the crown. To a slightly later age, the idea of France as a geographical unity, with Paris as its capital, seemed self-evident. But men of the late Middle Ages did not always see things that way: for reasons of history, language, sentiment, as well as political expediency, their own independence and, consequently, the continued fragmentation of France, ought to be maintained.

Yet another view would see the war in terms of the relative geographical positions of France and England, and of the influence of these upon economic interests. On the one hand, France needed to bring her 'natural' maritime provinces (which included Aquitaine, Normandy, Brittany and Flanders) under royal control in order that the ports might be used for both commercial and military purposes. On the other, England's best interest lay in denying the French king the use of ports and access to other coastal activities such as fishing, so that English trade, whether with Flanders or Aquitaine, might be conveyed in greater safety. Aquitaine, with her valuable wine trade, was a major trading partner. Flanders, at the beginning of the war, was still the principal manufacturer of cloth made from English wool, although from the mid-fourteenth century more and more cloth was to be made in England. The loss of trade in either case (and there was the matter of England's wider markets to be considered, too) would mean a grave financial loss to the country, not to forget the crown which, since the reign of Edward I, had been taxing certain commodities, such as wool and cloth, as they left and arrived in the country. The ability to do this must be defended, by war if need be.

1337–1360

Was a long war inevitable in 1337? The hostilities which had followed upon the previous confiscations of 1294 and 1324 had not been long-lasting. Now, however, matters were more complicated. For giving moral support to Robert of Artois, who had been condemned by the French as a traitor and a declared enemy of the king of France, Edward III could be regarded as having acted against his oath of fealty through such a serious act of defiance. But the French were capable of playing a similar game. In July 1333 the Scots had been defeated at Halidon Hill, near Berwick, and Edward Balliol had done homage to Edward III for Scotland, while King David II retired to France, there to seek the support of Philip VI against England. Almost immediately Philip, realising what an opportunity such an appeal for help gave him, declared that he would make no lasting settlement with England unless the Scots were included in it. Edward had met this challenge by invading Scotland, but he was unable to bring the enemy to battle. Nor could he get the Scots and their French allies to the negotiating table; the French publicly declared for the Scots, and promised them military help if they needed it. As 'man-in-the-middle' Edward III was in a delicate and unenviable position.

His opportunity to counter the French threat came in the Low Countries, an area which had witnessed English intervention against France almost half a century earlier. None the less, Edward's task was difficult. Louis, count of Flanders, was pro-French; his subjects, however, dominated by the great cloth-weaving towns of Bruges, Ghent, and

Ypres were more likely to turn to England, the source of the wool upon which their industry and wealth depended. In Hainault the count, William, was father-in-law to Edward III and brother-in-law to Philip VI; he might support either in his quarrel with the other. It was upon such insecure foundations that the king had to build. In May 1337 a splendid embassy left for the Low Countries; by a mixture of economic bribery (in the form of direct subsidies, the promise of wool, or important trading concessions) it won Edward some allies. In September 1338, the emperor, Lewis IV, was prevailed upon – at a price – to appoint Edward imperial vicar in Germany and France, giving him rights to demand military service against France from subjects of the empire. Could Edward make proper use of such advantages? Even more important, could he afford the debts which he had contracted?

The fact was that Edward could not. Nor did the Flemings feel that he was really supporting them; he had appeared to be using them for his own ends. Thus the military activity which began in Flanders in 1339 had little effect. In January 1340 Edward formally assumed the title of king of France (to which he had already laid claim in 1337), perhaps to make his Flemish allies feel that they were legally entitled to help him oppose their traditional lord, the king of France. On 24 June Edward won the first notable victory of the war in the naval battle fought off Sluys (*Fr.* L'Ecluse) at the mouth of the river Zwyn, at which a larger French fleet was decimated by superior English tactics and the better use of prevailing conditions. Yet, although it broke the threat of a possible French invasion of England, the victory in itself brought little immediate advantage to the English. Nor did the war on land make any progress, while those who earlier had been promised English largesse demanded what was due to them. When Edward failed to pay, they abandoned him, forcing him to seal a truce with the French at Espléchin, near Tournai, on 25 September 1340.

Although the victor of a battle at sea, Edward returned home a bitterly disappointed man. In 1338 he had issued the so-called 'Walton Ordinances' to help make the raising of supplies more efficient. Once home, he sought scapegoats for his evident failure by dismissing his treasurer and chancellor, who had not, he argued, provided the backing he needed and deserved, and by turning on John Stafford, archbishop of Canterbury, whom he suspected of having been responsible for the lack of success. At an early stage Edward III had come to realise that war was expensive and that his policy of subsidising princes to act in his interest against the French was not the way forward. Other methods had to be found.

This process of discovery did not take long. The dependence on allies was soon dropped. In 1341 England and France found both a cause and a theatre of war in which they might meddle further. In April, John III, duke of Brittany, died, leaving two possible heirs, his half-brother, John de Montfort, and Charles de Blois, whose claim was through Jeanne, a niece of the last duke. Each party sought assistance of one of the rival kings. Montfort was promised the earldom of Richmond and sought active English intervention in Brittany on his behalf, while Blois obtained the support of Philip VI. The war between them was to drag on until 1364, a period of some twenty years. If its details are largely peripheral to the main story which we are tracing, its significance was considerable. Here, less than a year after the ending of the 'phoney war' in the north-east, was a proper *casus belli* which was important to each side in the wider conflict. For the French king, the opportunity of exercising a greater measure of control over Brittany, with its maritime outlets, was not to be missed. For Edward III, the possibility of establishing a 'client' ruler in a strategically placed duchy (off whose shores all English military and commercial traffic bound to and from Aquitaine and western France had to pass) was also a highly desirable political end. Furthermore, it gave the English a door into France: soldiers might land on the Breton peninsula on their way into the interior of France, and the possibility of a more co-ordinated attack from different directions came a step nearer. Both France and England had positive reasons for intervening in Brittany. In the autumn of 1342 Edward III himself did so, winning over parts of the duchy and leaving Englishmen in many of the castles and garrisons, including Brest, the port destined to remain in friendly hands for much of the next half century or so.

The war was slowly escalating. To counter this development, Pope Clement VI called the main parties to a conference at Avignon in October 1344. But it soon became apparent that the divisions between the French and English ran very deep. To the English, no settlement could be envisaged without consideration of their king's claim to the crown of France, a claim which might be compensated for by the grant of other territories in France, to be held in full sovereignty. The French, on the other hand, would only see developments which took account of the most recent feudal settlement of 1327.[4] If they gave up territories in exchange for the surrender of Aquitaine, these would have to be held feudally in dependence of the crown of France. Not surprisingly, the talks broke down. No wonder that the winning of the French crown became so important a part of Edward III's war policy.

---

[4] See the essay by J. J. N. Palmer, 'The war aims of the protagonists and the negotiations for peace', *The Hundred Years War*, ed. Fowler, pp. 51–74, which is particularly valuable for the fourteenth century.

Before long the king was back again in France. In July 1346 he landed in Normandy with an army of perhaps some 15,000 men. In this enterprise he had the support of one of the leading Norman 'dissidents', Geoffroi d'Harcourt, who represented the dissatisfaction of the duchy at the way it was being ruled by the Valois king. On this expedition Edward met little opposition. The most notable capture was that of Caen which fell at the end of July, and which, according to the chronicler Froissart, was the source of much material gain which was taken down the river Orne to the coast for shipment back to England. Continuing his march eastwards, Edward came to within not many miles of Paris before swinging northwards in the direction of the Channel. It was while he was on his way that he was overtaken by the French army at Crécy-en-Ponthieu where, on 26 August 1346, the first of the major land battles of the war was fought.

Had Edward in fact planned to meet the French army? It is possible, although we cannot be sure of it. There can be little doubt that his tactics constituted an invitation to the French to catch and challenge him. Yet in 1340 Philip VI was already showing himself to be master of the tactic which the French were to employ in the years to come, that of avoiding direct contact with the enemy. The question was, for how long could such a policy of inactivity be allowed to continue? The English manner of waging war, that of the *chevauchée*, the raid carried out largely by mounted soldiers (who were thus fully mobile) through the enemy's countryside, with the intention of pillaging enemy property, destroying crops, and thereby creating an air of insecurity, could not be allowed to continue too long unchallenged, since such an exercise undermined (as it was intended to do) the authority of the king of France, who was responsible for the defence of his people. How long could the French king continue to ignore the thief in his back garden? Thus it was that Philip VI, who was not without military skill and experience, felt obliged to seek out and, if possible, defeat the English king and his Norman supporters. The attempt was to prove disastrous. Although tired and running out of provisions, the English had several advantages: a good defensive position; a united command; and the use of an army which had already proved highly successful against the Scots, a combination of archers and dismounted men-at-arms for which, in the conditions prevailing on the day, the French cavalry and the crossbowmen of their Genoese allies proved no match.

In the event, Philip VI fled the battlefield, with both his personal and his royal reputation tarnished. The same day, however, was to make the reputation of another man, Edward, eldest son of the king of England, known since Tudor times as the Black Prince, whose courage and chivalric conduct won him general admiration. Nor was Crécy the end of the campaign. The English, fresh from their victory, went on to Calais, at that time still French. The place was besieged, and over a period of months, including a winter, the English grip tightened. French attempts to relieve the pressure failed, and on 4 August 1347, after almost a year of blockade by both land and sea, Calais fell to Edward III. This was the first of many long sieges which were to be characteristic of the war. As a result, England now had its own foothold upon France's northern coast through which trade and armies might enter; or, as the emperor-elect, Sigismund, was to express it in the next century, a second eye to match the other, Dover, in guarding the straits.

While the siege of Calais was in progress, in answer to a call from the French, the Scots attacked the north of England. In October 1346, at Neville's Cross, near Durham, they were met and defeated by the defensive forces of the region, the king of the Scots, David II, being taken prisoner. Further, in June 1347 Charles de Blois, the French candidate to the duchy of Brittany, was taken in battle by Sir Thomas Dagworth; like David II he, too, was sent to the Tower of London as a prisoner. The fighting season 1346–7 was one for the English to remember. It proved a fitting finale to what had been the first period of sustained fighting in the war.

A factor which could be regarded as an act of God now intervened. In 1348 the bubonic plague, known as the Black Death, struck Europe for the first time and, in conditions of poor sanitation, famine and undernourishment, made rapid progress. Spreading through France, it made a dramatic impact upon England and Wales in the following year, and reached Scotland in 1350. Then, for a decade or so, its effects diminished considerably. None the less these had been sufficient to bring the war almost to a stop. When it is recognised that England may have lost about one-third of her population in these critical years, the lull in military activity becomes understandable. Nor was there much inclination in France to pursue an active military policy. In the midst of this, in August 1350, Philip VI died. If, at first, his rule had appeared to be to the benefit of France, in the last years it had suffered considerable setbacks. Could his son, John, who had so far had no success against the English in the south-west of France, do any better?

It seemed not. When, in 1353 and 1354, the negotiators got down to their work again, this time in Guines, near Calais, the English made demands which the French at first seemed willing to concede: Aquitaine, Maine, Anjou, Touraine, as well as other lands would be ruled by the English in full sovereignty. At the last minute, however, when the terms were being finalised at the papal court, the French withdrew: the

making of such concessions, which involved so much principle as well
as territory, could not be countenanced. The French, however, were on
the defensive. In Normandy opposition to the crown (already seen in the
help given by Geoffroi d'Harcourt to Edward III in 1346) was increasing.
The trouble was being fanned by Charles, king of Navarre, count of
Evreux, son-in-law of King John II, who, like Edward III, had a claim
to the crown of France through being a descendant of the house of Capet
through the female line. King John was now faced by two rivals who,
for the next few years, acted together with the possibility of partitioning
the French kingdom between them. In the autumn of 1355 the Black
Prince led an expedition from Bordeaux towards France's Mediterranean
coast. This *chevauchée* was an outstanding success: the loot taken was
considerable, and the king of France was again challenged on his own
ground.

In the following April John II, fearing that the dauphin, Charles, who
was duke of Normandy, was plotting against him with members of the
Navarrese party and others, went secretly to Rouen and, as the dauphin
was entertaining his guests to dinner, arrested some and had them led
away to immediate execution. The political tension, both between the
king and heir and between the political groupings, rose rapidly. In the
summer of the same year (1356) the English planned a threefold attack
on France. The Black Prince was to march from Bordeaux into the
north-central areas of the country; Henry, duke of Lancaster, planned to
attack from Normandy; while Edward III himself was also to come from
the north. Such a multiple attack had been a possibility for some time.
In the event it failed, leaving the Black Prince alone, at the head of
an army heavily laden with booty, in central France.

For the second time the French set out to catch the English. This they
did near Poitiers in mid-September, and for two days papal representatives went to and fro between the forces in the hope of securing an
arrangement. But their efforts were unsuccessful, and on 19 September
the two armies met. By the evening the French, who lacked archers, had
been defeated by an army which, although numerically inferior, had
once again (as at Crécy) enjoyed a sound defensive position and what
seemed like an unbeatable combination of longbowmen and dismounted
men-at-arms. To this the French contributed their own mistakes which
soon lost them any advantage they may have enjoyed. To crown it all
their king, John, was captured in battle. A second king now took up
residence in the Tower of London. No wonder the people of the capital
cheered.

In France, the authority and prestige of the crown were in crisis. Two
major defeats in ten years, followed now by the capture of the king, led

to rebellion in Normandy and civil troubles in Paris which were to end
in violence. The royal authority was being challenged not only by
princes but by a growing menace of another kind, the increasing
number of freelance soldiers, or *routiers*, who were gradually becoming
a characteristic force in French society, reflecting the faltering grip of
lawfully-established authority. Although the dauphin, Charles, who
assumed power in his father's place, showed himself to be a fine leader
and a man of courage, he appeared in the circumstances to have little
choice but to negotiate without giving away too much. What terms
would the English try to impose, and what could the French hope to get
away with?

Negotiations were protracted, lasting, on and off, from 1358 to 1360.
In May 1358 the French agreed to cede Aquitaine with other territories
amounting to about a third of the kingdom, in full sovereignty, and to
pay, in addition, 4,000,000 crowns (£666,666) for the ransom of their
king. A year later, having received only part of the sum owed to him,
Edward III demanded and got more: all that he had been ceded in 1358,
to which were added Normandy, Maine, Anjou, and Touraine, also in
full sovereignty. The implementation of these concessions, made by the
captive King John in London, was refused by the council in France, and
late in 1359 Edward set out with a large army for France to see how
persuasive a strong show of force could be. The expedition was a military
failure, but it led to the treaty of Brétigny of May 1360, which gave
Edward the lands ceded to him in 1358 with a ransom reduced to
3,000,000 gold crowns. Two other clauses were to have a vital significance. Edward agreed to renounce his claim to the French crown,
while John was to abandon his demand for sovereignty over the lands
ceded to the English. Later, at a meeting held at Calais in October, the
two clauses were removed to form a separate treaty whose implementation was to depend upon the clauses concerning the cession of land
having been properly carried out. Only then were the Calais clauses to
have their full effect.

With justice the treaty of Brétigny is often regarded as the moment
at which, for the first time, both sides decided to call a halt and have
their willingness to do so formally recognised in a treaty, one of the most
important of the whole war. In terms of the concessions made by the
French, the treaty can be interpreted as a success for the English, although
historians have not always agreed about this. True, Edward's failure on
the expedition of 1359–60 (when he had not been able to capture either
Reims, where kings of France were crowned, or Paris, the capital) meant
that he had to forego the important territorial concessions made to him
in 1359, including Normandy and the Angevin lands in central-western

France. On the other hand he would have a much enlarged Aquitaine, to be held in sovereignty, the 'perpetual liberty' which he had instructed the Black Prince to demand of his royal prisoner in 1357, and which would remove at a stroke the threat of confiscation.

The fact that he had agreed to surrender his right to the greater claim – that of the crown of France – in return for concession on the sovereignty issue shows where, in 1360, Edward III's priorities lay. In the event, however, the renunciations removed from the body of the treaty's main text were never made. As a result it would be possible for the French at some future date to renew their claim to sovereignty over Aquitaine, and for the English to do the same in respect of the crown of France. The significance of this could not be ignored.

What had been some of the main characteristics and development of this, the first period of the war? Not unnaturally, it has always been traditional to see the years to 1360 as constituting a period unfavourable to France: the initiative lay largely with the English, and it was mainly the French who were on the defensive. So it was that Edward III was able to extend the areas directly involved in war and to benefit from this by using landing points on different parts of the French coast. The theatre of war slowly became enlarged, a fact which, paradoxically, was to prove something of an advantage to the kings of France as they tried, if not always with success, to unite their entire population in a common war effort against the English. For as the war spread, so the fiscal demands of the French crown to meet it could be extended with justification. By the second half of the fourteenth century, few in France could claim not to be involved in it in one way or another.

The effects on domestic politics were considerably and predictably different. In England, the needs of war (in terms of money and provisions) provoked a considerable crisis in the years 1338–41. Thereafter Edward III, having learned some valuable political lessons, was able to develop a far greater degree of co-operation with his people, in particular with the fighting nobility, a spirit fostered by the two outstanding victories won at Crécy and Poitiers. In France, by contrast, in spite of what seemed like early successes, the personal fortunes of both Philip VI and John II sank very low. Both met defeat and one suffered capture, thus becoming, in a very real sense, a national liability. The lack of strong leadership served to exacerbate these disasters, and the nobility of France was obliged to endure strong criticism for its failure to protect the kingdom and its people in their hour of need. The crisis in the royal authority was underlined by the activities of Charles of Navarre in Normandy. As much as Edward III, he was a challenge to the civil and military authority of successive French kings, whose power, for the moment, was too weak to do much about him. The existence of the *routiers* was a further aspect of the same problem. The kingdom of France was becoming the playground of Europe's footloose soldiers.

1360–1396

Yet there was no good reason why it should not recover. The treaty of Brétigny brought a measure of peace to both England and France. Open hostilities, at least, were at an end. But there were problems to be resolved. One was that, arising from the transfer of lands from one allegiance to the other, many found themselves under a new lord; and some did not like it. A more serious problem was what to do with the soldiers who, now accustomed to fighting and to war's many attractions, were finding themselves without an occupation. The 1350s had seen relatively little fighting at an 'official' level, but the decade had witnessed the growth, in both numbers and size, of bodies of soldiers who, although sometimes finding local employment, more often than not roamed the countryside in search of adventure and the easy pickings of war. Peace made it more likely that their number would increase. Certainly, returning soldiers gave the authorities in England many a headache, the country's justices being ordered in 1360 to see that the peace was not broken. Many Englishmen remained in France and joined the bands of soldiers who made their services available to whoever would lead or employ them. The significance of the danger which they constituted soon became apparent. On 6 April 1362 these *routiers* met and defeated a royal army at Brignais, in the Rhône valley. Some, too, entered the services of Charles of Navarre and helped to spread disorder in Normandy and the surrounding areas. On 16 May 1364, however, another army under Bertrand du Guesclin, a Breton who had himself led such troops before entering the king's service, defeated the Navarrese army, helped by some English, at Cocherel, in south-eastern Normandy. The event was significant, for it followed hard upon the death in April of King John II in England, where he was still a prisoner. Cocherel witnessed an important blow struck for royal authority by an army under a commander of undoubted skill and experience. With the defeat at Brignais avenged, Charles V, who had just succeeded his father as king, could go to his coronation a satisfied man.

Cocherel was a move in the right direction. But it was soon partly cancelled by the victory of the English-backed Montfortists at the battle of Auray, in southern Brittany, on 29 September 1364, at which Charles de Blois was killed and du Guesclin, not for the last time, was taken prisoner. This event led to a formal settlement of the Breton succession after more than twenty years of intermittent war. It also released more soldiers who were free to seek a living by fighting elsewhere. However, some sort of a solution to what was becoming an endemic problem was soon found. At the request of Henry of Trastamara, then seeking to wrest the succession of the kingdom of Castile from his half-brother, Peter, known as 'the Cruel', French troops, under du Guesclin, recently ransomed, crossed over into Spain to help bring about the defeat of Peter. Feeling himself threatened, Peter appealed for help to Edward III who authorised the Black Prince, since 1362 prince (and effective ruler) of Aquitaine, to intervene. The threat of alliance between the king of France and an unfriendly ruler of northern Spain was one which must have worried the English in Bordeaux. There was, in addition, an important prize at stake, the use of the Castilian galley fleet, perhaps the finest in Europe, with which the French, in particular, could give a much-needed boost to their war efforts at sea. This was something which the English would do their utmost to prevent happening. Responding to the call, the Black Prince raised a force, and, in the early spring of 1367, crossed into northern Spain through Navarre, whose king, Charles, had only recently received English help in Normandy. On 3 April his army, linked to that of King Peter, met the French and Henry of Trastamara's force at Nájera (*Fr*. Navarrette). For a second time du Guesclin found himself a prisoner of the English, who routed his army. The Black Prince had just achieved the third, and final, great victory of his career.

Contrary to what some historians have thought, the campaign in Spain was not a mere side issue.[5] It reflected the growing problem of how to deal with surplus manpower once peace had been made in a major theatre of war. It also served to show that the Hundred Years War was no longer simply a conflict between England and France: others were being caught up in it, too. But although it brought victory to the Black Prince, the battle of Nájera was to be the cause of the renewal of the war which had been halted in 1360. The English had agreed to fight in Spain if paid to do so. Yet the money had never come. Nor did Peter regain effective control of his kingdom as Henry, although defeated at Nájera, staged a political comeback. In March 1369, the armies of the two men met at Montiel, where that of Peter was defeated and the king himself was murdered by his half-brother and rival.

By this time, however, the Black Prince was in difficulties. Heavily in

---

[5] Perroy (*The Hundred Years War*, p. 157) called it 'the Castilian comedy', scarcely doing justice to its importance. Its proper significance was developed by P. Russell, *The English intervention in Spain and Portugal in the time of Edward III and Richard II* (Oxford, 1955).

debt to certain members of his nobility and to *routier* captains, and let
down by his Castilian ally, he had had to seek the financial resources
with which to pay for his Spanish expedition. His requests for money in
Aquitaine met with resistance, for in a real sense the expedition had
brought little or no advantage to the duchy. Jean d'Armagnac, following
on the reluctance of the estates, meeting at Angoulême, to contribute
their share of a tax, refused to allow it to be collected in his lands,
pleading ancient privileges which had always been enjoyed locally.
When the Black Prince announced measures against him, Armagnac
first appealed to Edward III; on receiving an unfavourable response, he
took the matter further and appealed to the king of France, Charles V.
In this he was joined by his nephew, the lord of Albret, who lodged a
similar grievance against the Black Prince.

Charles V could scarcely avoid having to respond to the appeals
lodged by Albret and Armagnac. In legal terms it seemed that he was
free to intervene; his claim to exercise sovereignty in Aquitaine had not
been renounced in 1360. Anxious to do things properly, however,
Charles sought the best specialist advice which he could get; he found
it by consulting eminent jurists of the legal centres of Bologna, Montpellier, Orléans, and Toulouse. Their opinion was that Charles was
entitled to receive the appeals made to him. In December 1368 he
announced that he would do this. In June 1369, in retaliation, Edward
III resumed the use of the title 'king of France'. Towards the end of the
year, in November, the French king confiscated Aquitaine. The two
kingdoms were once more at war.

The nature of the conflict fought in the 1370s was to be very different
from that of earlier decades, and its effects more dramatic. The French
were not unprepared, and almost immediately took the offensive. A
glance at the map on p. xii will show that the enlarged Aquitaine which
the English had to defend had very long frontiers, vulnerable to small
mobile forces which the French now used to excellent effect. In 1371 the
Black Prince, a sick man, retired from the thankless task of ruling
Aquitaine, and the English command now became fragmented. Nor did
English forces, when sent to France, properly encounter the enemy. The
use of Fabian tactics by the French frustrated the English who spent large
sums on the war, but to little purpose. The 1370s saw England neglect
the serious implications of this essentially defensive war, so that the
chevauchées led by Sir Robert Knolles in 1370 and John of Gaunt, Edward
III's third surviving son, in 1373 achieved little military advantage. The
days of Crécy and Poitiers were over.

Little by little, the French initiative paid off, as their armies 're-
occupied' first those parts ceded by treaty and then much of the duchy

of Aquitaine itself. In 1371, Charles V and Charle[s]
terms. In Brittany, in spite of the English succes[s]
drove out Duke John IV from his duchy. At s[ ]
alliance, which had sprung from the events in [ ]
1369, began to have effect. In the summer o[f]
defeated by Castilian galleys off the port of L[a]
Englishmen were taken as prisoners to Spain. For so[me]
brought much nearer home when the French (with their Cast[ilian]
began once again to attack and plunder towns and villages on the so[uth]
coast of England, the legitimate activities of English fishermen being
among those which suffered from such raids. Not surprisingly, this lack
of success provoked an outcry in England, accustomed more to victory
than defeat. Protests in 1371 were followed by further outbursts in 1376
in the so-called 'Good Parliament', whose members suspected that the
search for personal profit had, in some cases, taken precedence over the
pursuit of the national advantage. In the midst of these events, in June
1376, the Black Prince died. A year later his father followed him to the
grave.

As contemporary writing testifies, it was the sad end of a glorious
period in English history. In view of the lack of English success in the
past years, the war was now being discussed in terms which suited the
French, the emphasis being on the feudal interpretation of the treaty of
Brétigny. Once again, papal envoys took a leading part in the proceedings and, on this occasion, a possible way out was found. John of Gaunt,
it was proposed, would become a French prince and, through him, the
link with England and its royal family would be maintained while at the
same time the fundamental English objection that their king should not
be a vassal of the king of France would be met. If the plan failed, it was
because of Gaunt's personal ambitions in Spain, rather than because of
any objection of principle to the scheme. For the while the war went
on.[6]

Other issues and events now came to complicate events. In England
the death of Edward III placed his grandson, Richard II, the surviving
son of the Black Prince, upon the throne. Richard was to prove one of
the most enigmatic of kings. Two factors about him concern this story.
He was young, only ten years old, when he came to the throne. Further,
as a result of his youth, he had not known the great days of English
victories in France, although these had been concerned with the activities
of his father, and he himself had been born in Bordeaux not long before
his father had crossed to Spain to win his final victory. The effect was

[6] Palmer, 'War aims', p. 63.

...e Richard more inclined to peace than to war: war, he was to tell ...ament in 1397, caused great harm and unnecessary destruction to ...th kingdoms,[7] a view almost certainly shared by his near contemporary, Charles VI, who had succeeded his father in 1380, a year which also witnessed the death of du Guesclin. Both kings came to be surrounded by uncles who sought to further war for their own ends. Each, in his own way, reacted against avuncular pressure. Both came to favour peace.

It is evident that many had come to feel like them. Late in the 1370s and early in the 1380s the world order, already upset by long war, seemed set to suffer yet further disruption. In 1378 a schism, occasioned by a double election to the papacy, split the western Church. There were now not only two popes but two centres of papal authority, Rome and Avignon. What was worse, England and France supported opposing sides on this issue, so that the Schism, one of the most important factors dividing western Christianity in the years 1378–1417, also accentuated the existing political divisions between the two countries. It is open to debate whether the Hundred Years War helped to prolong the Schism within the Church, but that the Schism hardened the attitudes of the French and English nations to each other is undoubted. The church councils which were called in the first three decades of the fifteenth century gave each side reason and opportunity to seek support for its own attitude to the war before the remainder of Christendom. The Schism, we may say, tragically helped to polarise increasingly strong nationalist attitudes towards the war.

Domestic troubles also occurred. The summer of 1381 saw the outbreak of the Peasants' Revolt in England, an uprising against the government of the day, to whose causes the financial demands of war and the inability (or unwillingness?) of the royal administration to defend adequately the coast of southern England against French and Castilian incursions of increasing frequency and intensity certainly contributed. In June 1382 troubles in Rouen, caused partly by a reaction to the French crown's fiscal demands, were suppressed with some vigour; the events may have lost Charles VI friends and supporters in Normandy, still an area to be tended with attention by the royal authority in Paris. In 1380 it had been the turn of Thomas, earl of Buckingham, uncle of Richard II, to lead what would prove to be the last English expedition to France in the fourteenth century, while in 1383 the religious divisions of Europe were underlined by the sending of a force led by Henry Despenser,

[7] M. McKisack, *The fourteenth century, 1307–1399* (Oxford, 1959), p. 475, n. 3, citing *Rotuli parliamentorum*, III, 338.

bishop of Norwich, into Flanders under the guise of a crusade.[8] Neither produced any effects. In 1386 England was fortunate not to experience invasion from France, planned by the king's uncle, Philip, duke of Burgundy, with support not only from Brittany and Flanders but from much of the kingdom of France itself.

Yet, in spite of the aggressive spirit found among many of the nobility on both sides of the Channel, and of Richard II's personal participation in an expedition in 1385 against the Scots, at that moment in receipt of French assistance, the idea of peace was now increasingly in the air. In England the criticism of continued military activity by John Wyclif, the opposition to war expressed by men of Lollard sympathies such as William Swynderby, the lassitude provoked by so many years of conflict, mirrored in some of the works of Geoffrey Chaucer and John Gower,[9] are indicative both of people's reflection regarding the morality of war and the ways in which it was being fought, and of the apparent futility of allowing it to continue along its present drift, no real advantage accruing to either side in spite of the great cost, both human and financial, to all. This kind of sentiment was reflected in France, where the influential courtier, Philippe de Mézières, in works of a semi-polemical nature (one of them an open letter on peace addressed to Richard II) asked whether the long war should continue.

Other factors seemed to encourage a movement towards peace with which both kings appeared to sympathise. For all its successes, the French military effort of the 1370s and 1380s had failed to dislodge the English hold in France, particularly in the south-west. True, by the time that Edward III's long reign ended, only Bordeaux, Bayonne, and a coastal strip in that region could be controlled effectively by the English administration. None the less the fact was that the English had hung on, and there seemed little chance that they would be dislodged.

So peace was formally sought. The possible way forward, 'the separation of England and Aquitaine and the creation of a separate English dynasty in the duchy', had already been proposed in 1377. In 1383, the proposal got as far as a draft. Seven years later, in 1390, Richard created his uncle, John of Gaunt, duke of Aquitaine for life, an act of good intent, and a step in the right direction. Then, in 1393, a provisional agreement was reached giving the English Calais (which they already held) and that part of Aquitaine south of the river Charente (much of south-west

[8] N. Housley, 'The bishop of Norwich's crusade, May 1383', H.T., 33 (May, 1983), 15–20.
[9] V. J. Scattergood, 'Chaucer and the French war: Sir Thopas and Melibee', Court and poet, ed. G. S. Burgess (Liverpool, 1981), pp. 287–96.

France which was largely out of their hands at this time), all this to be alienated to Gaunt in the near future. Yet whatever the hopes of kings and their legal advisers, they were not shared by the people themselves. In April 1394 the population of much of the area rose in support of its attachment to the crown of England. In spite of all efforts, the well-intentioned plan of the negotiators was spoiled by the people themselves.[10]

The agreement had involved some radical thinking regarding the historic and legal legacy of Aquitaine. A way of circumventing various objections had been found without offending too many interests. Peace was clearly desired, and if it could not be arranged on these agreed terms, it must be found by other means. Between 1394 and 1396 negotiations continued, and in March 1396 the two sides agreed to a truce of twenty-eight years and the marriage of Richard II to one of Charles VI's daughters, Isabella, who was to bring with her a large dowry. Once again, even if the main points at issue had been side-stepped, the two countries were at peace, and had agreed to be so for a whole generation.

1396–1422

The problem of making a lasting peace had been postponed. In the light of the experience of thirty years earlier, what were the chances for the temporary agreement? Some may well have had their fears. In France the rule of the dukes who sought to govern in the place of Charles VI who, since 1393, had suffered from the intermittent attacks of a mental illness which was to remain with him until his death in 1422, appealed to a rising sense of nationalism which tended to favour a vigorous defence of French interests. Then, when the truce had run for little more than three years, Richard II was deposed and murdered, his place as king of England being taken by Henry IV, the son of John of Gaunt. Richard's young wife, Isabella, no longer wanted at the English court, was despatched – without her dowry – back to France, where feeling turned sharply against Henry for his deposition of the French king's son-in-law.

In such circumstances it is not surprising that the truce of 1396 was never properly observed. The French gave support to the Scots who, from very early on in the new reign, caused trouble in the north; while to the west, in Wales, where Owain Glyn Dŵr was to rise against English rule in 1400, French troops landed and at one time might have been seen in the Herefordshire countryside. This was a game which two could

---

[10] Palmer, 'War aims', pp. 64–5.

play, and the English were to raid the coast of Normandy several times between 1400 and 1410. During these years, too, piracy in the Channel was rife, probably encouraged by both sides as a matter of policy.[11] Yet neither side, partly because of the very existence of the truce, partly because of its own domestic divisions (which were becoming more serious in France as the first decade of the new century progressed) wished to raise fundamental issues. Henry IV appears to have had no burning ambition to secure the French crown, and during his reign Aquitaine suffered from relative neglect. The war had moved, well and truly, towards more northern parts of France.

Or almost so. In 1411, at the request of John, duke of Burgundy, a small English force took part in what was rapidly becoming a situation of civil war in France. In May 1412 a treaty (that of Bourges) was sealed between Henry IV and the dukes of Berry, Bourbon, and Orléans which gave the English king much of what his predecessors had spent years fighting for: a recognition that Aquitaine was rightfully English, and an undertaking to help the king defend it; the cession of twenty important towns and castles; and agreement that certain lands, notably Poitou, were to be held by them of the English crown, and would revert to it when the present holders died.[12]

Such concessions appeared momentous; yet they were made largely to secure English military help for one faction against another in a situation of civil war, and were unlikely to command lasting support, above all since the king, Charles VI, had had no part in this dismemberment of his kingdom. When the French dukes made peace among themselves at Auxerre three months later, the only losers were to be the English. When Thomas, duke of Clarence, second son of Henry IV, brought a force into France in August 1412 to fulfil the terms of the agreement made in May, he was met by a united opposition. Unable to impose himself, Clarence allowed himself to be bought off before returning home through Bordeaux, plundering on the way. Yet the text of the treaty of Bourges had made concessions which could be regarded as at least impolitic, at worst treasonable, to the French crown. Henry V was to remind the world of what had been conceded when, in his turn, he became king of England in 1413.

Once king, Henry soon set about making heavy demands of the French. In the following year these became even tougher: he demanded

[11] C. J. Ford, 'Piracy or policy: the crisis in the Channel, 1400–1403', *T.R. Hist. S.*, fifth series, 29 (1979), 63–78.
[12] J. H. Wylie, *History of England under Henry the Fourth* (4 vols., London, 1884–98), IV, 68–9; R. Vaughan, *John the Fearless. The growth of Burgundian power* (London, 1966), pp. 94–5.

the crown of France; then he reduced this to the territories of Angevin days, Normandy, Maine, Anjou, Touraine, Aquitaine (to include Poitou, part of the concession made by the princes at Bourges in 1412), together with the substantial arrears still due for the ransom of John II and, following the now well-established pattern, the hand of a daughter of the French king, this time Catherine, sister to Isabella whom Richard II had married in 1396, together with a dowry. By 1415 he showed himself willing to accept a good deal less: he would settle for the legal and territorial terms agreed at Brétigny, now more than half a century earlier, and a smaller dowry. That, for the moment, was as far as he would go. When the French refused his conditions, Henry decided on the war which his diplomacy had given him time to prepare. He would fight the enemy in a good cause: denial of justice.

In August 1415 an English army landed in Normandy and at once began the siege of Harfleur, at the mouth of the river Seine. Six weeks later the town, which had suffered heavily from the bombardment of English cannon, capitulated. The problem now was what to do next. Probably against the advice of his commanders Henry decided to lead what remained of his army, decimated by illness contracted at the siege, to Calais, thought to be about a week's march away. In fact the English were almost outmanoeuvred by the French army. Yet, on 25 October 1415, although outnumbered, Henry and his force, relying on the traditional weapon of archers and men-at-arms, met and defeated the French at Agincourt. The French, probably over-confident of victory, allowed themselves to be drawn into a cavalry advance, carried out under a hail of arrows, across recently ploughed ground made softer yet by the rain which had fallen the previous night. The chronicles record the large number of French who, at the day's end, lay dead on the field, while, by contrast, very few Englishmen lost their lives. Among the many notable prisoners taken was Charles, duke of Orléans, who was to spend the next quarter of a century an honourable captive in England, developing a considerable talent as a poet in both French and English. In the meanwhile, England and her king were to live for many years on the reputation won on that autumn day. Only too evidently had God given his judgement in favour of the English claim for justice.

In 1416 the French made a serious attempt to regain Harfleur, which they blockaded by land and sea. The garrison suffered considerably, but on 15 August 1416 John, duke of Bedford, defeated the enemy fleet in the estuary in what has come to be known as the battle of the Seine. The threat to Harfleur was now eased, and the value of being able to defeat the enemy at sea was once again proved.

In the following year, 1417, Henry returned to Normandy. Harfleur had taught him a lesson: he must be properly prepared for siege warfare, all the more so since he now planned a conquest which could only be achieved through sieges and the show of effective military might. By the summer of 1419 all Normandy was his: the major walled towns of the duchy, Caen, Falaise, Cherbourg, and Rouen had all fallen to the English besiegers. This marked an important change in English policy towards France. The day of the *chevauchée*, or prolonged raid, was now almost over. Henry wanted nothing less than military conquest. With it went the need to govern and administer lands thus acquired, and the demand that the inhabitants of those lands should recognise the legitimacy of English rule by taking an oath of allegiance to Henry. He went farther still. Those who refused him their recognition were deprived of their lands and forced into a form of internal exile within France, into that area which the Valois ruled. Lands thus confiscated were Henry's to do what he liked with. Many, ranging from large estates to small-holdings in towns, were given by him to his French supporters and to those English whom he could tempt over to settle in northern France. In this way, through a deliberate policy of conquest and settlement, Henry V extended the sharing of the profits of war (in this case largely immoveable property) to many of his compatriots, both soldiers and civilians. By so doing he changed the very character of the conflict, for through the creation of a wider involvement in its success he tried to ensure that he, and his successors, would have broad support for the continued involvement of England and Englishmen in France. The presence of those Englishmen was the most convincing proof available that, in Normandy at least, war had secured justice.

Normandy won, where would Henry turn to next? The divisions among the French, so much at odds with one another, helped him militarily. Yet when it came to negotiation, who would speak to him in the name of France? Faced by an enemy triumphant on their own territory, the French parties tried to make common cause. At Montereau, south-east of Paris, the dauphin Charles met his great political rival, John, duke of Burgundy, on 10 September 1419. At this meeting the dauphin may have implied that the duke, whose reluctance to adopt a strongly anti-English stance was generally recognised, had been guilty of treason to the French crown. An altercation blew up, and in the ensuing scene Duke John was felled by a blow from a member of the dauphin's entourage.

This political murder only aggravated the political divisions within France. It also gave Henry V the chance he needed. The brutal death of Duke John inevitably pushed Philip, his son and successor, onto the side of the one man who could help him. Henry grasped the opportunity;

it could lead to Paris (which the Burgundian party at that moment controlled) and to much else, besides. It may well have been at this moment, in the autumn of 1419, that Henry V decided that the crown of France, which none of his predecessors had achieved, might be his.[13] During the course of the coming months, the terms of what Henry could obtain in concessions from the French (or at least from that branch of the body politic which was, at that moment, dominant) were worked out. The result was the treaty of Troyes of May 1420.

This was the most important treaty of the Hundred Years War.[14] It overtook in significance and ended the sixty-year domination of the treaty of Brétigny. The reason is simple enough. The treaty arranged between Edward III and John II had adopted a mainly feudal approach to the dispute which separated the two kings and their people; it had decided who held what, and how. That arranged between Henry V and Duke Philip of Burgundy, imposed upon the sick king, Charles VI, and then formally registered (or approved) by France's highest judicial body, the Parlement, did not carve up the kingdom, at least not on paper. Its aim was to preserve the unity of France, to arrange matters in such a way that, in due course (and, in view of the king's health, not before too long) a new dynasty might assume the crown of France. That dynasty was to be the royal house of England.

The treaty of Troyes made Henry V heir to the crown of France. Charles VI, now only occasionally lucid, was to remain king until his death, but in the meantime Henry would act as regent (in effect, in control of the government) succeeding to the crown when Charles died, a fact which was soon to be interpreted to imply English recognition of the legitimacy of Charles VI's rule as king of France. To give the settlement greater weight it was also agreed that Henry should take to wife Catherine, Charles's daughter, whose hand he had sought in negotiation some years earlier. The couple were married in the cathedral at Troyes on 2 June 1420.

What the treaty did not do was to make the two kingdoms of France and England one; they were to remain separate, each with its own legal and administrative identity. The unifying factor between them was to be dynastic and personal. How effectively the king of England could direct the government of France was the most important of a number of unresolved questions left by the treaty. Translating a paper agreement into reality was likely to prove difficult; several major problems would need to be overcome. The greatest was that the dauphin, Charles (he

[13] Palmer, 'War aims', p. 69.
[14] See the assessment of M. Keen, 'Diplomacy', *Henry V. The practice of kingship*, ed. G. L. Harriss (Oxford, 1985), pp. 181–99.

was, in fact, the third dauphin, two elder brothers having died pre-
maturely) had been deprived of his legitimate right to succeed his father
as king. Much play was made of the fact that, since he had been present
at the murder of John, duke of Burgundy, at Montereau he could not
properly and worthily inherit the throne, from which he was now
excluded. Yet, it was asked, was it possible to exclude him by treaty, so
manifestly an arrangement between the king of England and the
Burgundians (the dauphin's political rivals), and then imposed upon a
sick king who was in no position to resist? To many, loyal to the idea
of direct succession within the royal family, this seemed wrong. To such,
the dauphin became the living symbol of resistance to English rule in the
years to come.

A further complication was the undertaking given by Henry V that
he would use every means at his disposal to bring under his control those
extensive areas of France not yet according him their allegiance, an
ambitious military plan which, it could be argued, was beyond his
financial and military capabilities. For not the least of Henry's problems
was how to raise the money required for the accomplishment of such an
undertaking. Would his new French subjects pay to continue a civil war
against their compatriots? Alternatively, would Englishmen be willing
to subscribe towards the accomplishment of this great task? Henry must
very soon have begun to have doubts on both scores.

The treaty of Brétigny had been termed the 'Great Peace'; that of
Troyes came to be known, at least in English circles, as the 'Final Peace'.
One can see why; but was it really to be so? Born out of a particular set
of circumstances, the treaty did little to unite France, but served rather
to underline the divisions which had existed for two decades or more.
The English had come to France encouraged to make the most of a lack
of united opposition to them. This they succeeded in doing. But it
cannot be claimed that the unity implied in the term 'Final Peace' was
achieved, either then or later. France remained a divided country. This
can best be seen in the demand made by princes who had subscribed to
the treaty that those who lived in their lands should do the same. Many
refused; even the town of Dijon, capital of the duchy of Burgundy, only
did so when ordered to do so by its duke. Classified as 'rebels', those
who would not recognise the new political order which the treaty
represented suffered the confiscation of their property and were forced
to move to the rival obedience where, over the coming years, some
helped to foster opposition to English rule in northern France.

Henry, on his part, turned seriously towards the fulfilment of his new
obligations. It was while he was away in England, crowning his wife as
queen and seeking further material support for the war, that his brother,

Thomas, duke of Clarence, was defeated and killed at Baugé, in Anjou, by a Franco-Scottish force on 22 March 1421. Had the French taken proper advantage of their unexpected victory, it is possible that they could have reversed the way the war seemed to be going. But they failed to do so, and when Henry returned to France he was able to clear the enemy from strongholds which they still held near Paris, including the formidable town and fortress of Meaux, before which he spent some seven months in 1421–2. It was while he was besieging that town that the king contracted a fatal illness. On 31 August 1422, he died at Vincennes, just outside Paris. His successor as king of England, Henry VI, was not yet a year old.

Henry V had given the war with France a new twist.[15] He had come to France (in which he spent more than half his life as king of England) and had, as contemporaries recognised, achieved considerable conquests, something which his predecessors had never done on that scale or within so short a period of time. He had done better than they had in the sense that he had claimed the crown of France and, by treaty, had come close to exercising its authority. He had done more, too, that would be of significance in the future. In Normandy, that part of France which he had made peculiarly his, he had taken over everyday government, now exercised in his name by men appointed by him. Furthermore, in an attempt to reward men for military service and to encourage others to serve in France, Henry had pursued a policy of granting lands and titles which had come into his hands, thereby creating an important interest, other than his own, in the extension and maintenance of the conquest. Englishmen were given lands to exploit, but also to defend. A number of them settled in France, took up what were essentially non-military occupations, and sometimes married French wives. Before long they had become settlers; their children knew no other life. If there were to be a failure in maintaining this conquest, the 'livelihood' of these people would be at stake. Every effort must be made to keep them there.

1422–1453

It was precisely this that John, duke of Bedford, the elder of Henry V's surviving brothers, tried to do when he became regent of France on the death of the king. Within less than two months, the ailing Charles VI followed his son-in-law to the grave, giving effect to the succession

---

[15] For much of this and what follows, see C. T. Allmand, *Lancastrian Normandy, 1415–1450. The history of a medieval occupation* (Oxford, 1983), and R. Massey, 'The land settlement in Lancastrian Normandy', *Property and politics: essays in later medieval English history*, ed. A. J. Pollard (Gloucester: New York, 1984), pp. 76–96.

clause of the treaty of Troyes. Henry VI, still less than a year old, already king of England, now assumed the crown of France, a position which his father had never quite achieved.

In France Bedford, acting for his nephew, strove to reduce the area of the country still faithful to the Valois 'claimant', the dauphin, Charles, now regarded by many as Charles VII although, like his young English nephew, still uncrowned. On 31 July 1423 an army representing the combined power of England and Burgundy defeated a Franco-Scottish army at Cravant, while a year later, on 17 August 1424, at Verneuil another army, led by Bedford himself, encountered and, after heavy fighting, convincingly defeated another such enemy army, this time reinforced by Genoese crossbowmen. The outcome had considerable significance. It marked the second French defeat in a year; it fully restored to the English their military reputation which was no longer seen to depend on one man, Henry V; and, most important of all, it opened the way southwards for further advance into central France. In Normandy, the settlers could sleep more soundly as the theatre of active war moved south. The future held considerable possibility.

For the French, on the other hand, the dark years of the war, not unlike the 1340s and 1350s, appeared to have returned. By 1427, much of Maine and Anjou, names whose familiarity stems from their frequent appearance on the list of English diplomatic demands, were in the hands of the English, now advancing southwards. It was the line of the river Loire which was to save the French. The English could not cross it leaving behind them unconquered French outposts, of which Orléans was one. In the autumn of 1428 the English, under one of their most notable commanders, Thomas, earl of Salisbury, besieged the town. In November, Salisbury, a chivalric figure, was killed, the victim of a cannonball. But still the English persisted, while all France looked to the siege. In May 1429 the struggle was resolved. An unknown peasant girl from Lorraine, Joan of Arc, persuaded the dauphin that she had been sent by God to raise the siege. In spite of scepticism and outright hostility to her at the court (how could she achieve what professional commanders had failed to do?) Joan received permission and active encouragement to attempt what she claimed she had been sent to carry out. In the event, she succeeded. On 8 May 1429 the English abandoned the siege; France, through Joan, had won a great moral victory. As Christine de Pisan put it, 'the sun began to shine once more'.

It was a victory which could, and did, lead to greater things. Within a month or so the French, having won important skirmishes at Jargeau and Patay, could turn towards achieving the next logical step of their success story, the coronation of the dauphin as king of France. On

17 July 1429, less than ten weeks after relieving Orléans, and having in the meanwhile brought back to French rule a number of towns, including Troyes where the fateful treaty had been sealed in 1420, Joan stood in the cathedral at Reims watching the dauphin as he underwent the rite of coronation, the rite by which his predecessors had become full kings of France. A fundamental challenge had been levelled at the settlement made at Troyes which had altered the line of succession to the crown of France. Could the challenge be maintained?

The English saw the coronation of Charles VII at Reims as a considerable threat to their authority. In December 1431 Henry VI, now ten years old, was brought to Paris and crowned in Notre-Dame by an English bishop; the fact that the ceremony had not taken place at Reims did not escape the notice of contemporaries. Yet in spite of the need to bring strong and immediate pressure to bear upon the English, the French were not able to follow up their successes of 1429. In the following year, indeed, Joan of Arc was captured at Compiègne and in May 1431, after what was a political trial carried out under ecclesiastical rules, she was condemned and burned at Rouen. The war was going the way of neither side. The English defences held. There was deadlock.

In the circumstances men turned to negotiation. In the summer months of 1435 there took place at Arras, in north-eastern France, a great congress attended by the representatives of a number of European states and the Church.[16] After weeks of discussion, the sides failed to agree terms, either over the crown of France or over the lands to be held by the English, and under what conditions. However the congress was the occasion of an event of some significance. Having obtained a papal dispensation, Philip, duke of Burgundy, forsook his support of the settlement made at Troyes and, hence, too, his allegiance to the English as rulers of France. From now on he either fought on the French side or acted as a neutral between the parties. If, in the years to follow, he did relatively little to help the Valois war effort, his defection greatly angered the English who reacted in strongly emotional terms to what they regarded as an act of betrayal and treason against the English crown.

In 1439 a further attempt was made to secure a diplomatic settlement when the French, the English, and the Burgundians (but not the representatives of the Church, excluded by the English for their alleged partiality at Arras) met near Calais in the summer of that year. The territorial offers were never really more than variations on others made earlier in the war. Although the French offer of a 'half-peace' (a truce for a set period of between fifteen and thirty years, in exchange for an

[16] See J. G. Dickinson, *The congress of Arras, 1435* (Oxford, 1955).

English undertaking not to use the French royal title during that period) was taken seriously at first, it was turned down when the English demanded a perpetual peace together with the grant of Normandy and an enlarged Aquitaine (as in 1360) in full sovereignty.

More significant, however, was the influence which the English settlement in Normandy came to exercise upon the proceedings. When asked to restore those Frenchmen who had lost their lands for refusing to recognise the legitimacy of English rule in the duchy, the English negotiators refused point blank. They could not give the impression that they doubted the validity of their king's claim to the crown of France, for by so doing they would have thrown doubt upon the symbolic and legal importance of Henry VI's French coronation, rendering illegal the very authority (the royal one) upon which the validity of the grants made to Englishmen (and others) in Normandy depended. Further, to have made the concession over restoration of lands would have meant depriving their own people of their French interests, something which, for both moral and financial reasons, they were not prepared to do.

If diplomacy was bringing a settlement no nearer, military events would do so only very slowly. It is true that in the late 1430s the English suffered some reverses and territorial losses. In 1435 both Dieppe and Harfleur were taken by the French and in the next year Paris went the same way. The loss of the two ports was serious, as the English now had only limited access to Normandy and to the capital, Rouen, which had come to replace Paris. Yet they fought on, trying to defend the long line which was the border of their dominion in northern France, much as their predecessors had done in Aquitaine in the 1370s. In such a situation the initiative lay with the attacker. The English must have echoed the rejoicings of the people of Rouen when it was announced, in the early summer of 1444, that a truce had been agreed between England and France, and that Henry VI was to marry Margaret of Anjou, a niece by marriage of Charles VII. Once again it was hoped to postpone a settlement and place faith upon a personal union between the royal families of the two countries to resolve the outcome of the old dispute between them.

The truce of Tours marked the beginning of another brief phase of diplomacy. At the negotiations, the English made an important concession in saying that the claim to the French crown might be traded for a sovereign Normandy. Then, in December 1445, Henry VI secretly undertook the surrender of the county of Maine, in so doing appearing to renounce sovereignty over it and implying, too, that the English might yield to further pressure, military or diplomatic.

If Henry had hoped for peace, he was to be sadly disillusioned. From

1446 to 1448 the French spared no effort to bring about the surrender of Maine which those Englishmen holding Le Mans, its capital, refused to carry out until, in March 1448, they finally gave way. Fifteen months later, under the pretext that the English had broken the truce, the French invaded Normandy from several directions. The well-planned attack led to a campaign of less than a year. By the early summer of 1450 the English, driven out of their lands and defeated in battle at Formigny in early April, had lost their hold on northern France. Only Calais remained to them. The issue had been settled by force of arms.

The final act was soon to follow. Aquitaine, still English, had not attracted much attention from either side since 1413, the military emphasis since then having been on northern France. Neither Henry V nor his son had placed the solution to the problem of Aquitaine (the old feudal problem) high in his list of priorities. Yet the duchy was not entirely forgotten. When Philip of Burgundy abandoned the English alliance and returned to that of France in 1435, he released French troops from eastern France whose services Charles VII could now employ in the south-west. In 1442 both the king and the dauphin, Louis, went on an expedition into Aquitaine which greatly troubled the government in London. Soon afterwards, the truce of Tours intervened. None the less, once war had been renewed in 1449 and Normandy had been recovered, it was time to turn again towards Aquitaine where the English must have felt isolated and apprehensive. In 1451 the French invaded, overran most of the duchy, and took Bordeaux. In the following year, however, a plot was hatched by the English and their supporters, which regained for them control of the city. The pro-English party must have realised, however, that neither they nor their masters in London were in a position to hold out for long. Nor did they. In 1453 the French returned in force and at Castillon, on 17 July, they defeated the English whose commander, John Talbot, earl of Shrewsbury, a man of long experience, was killed by the murderous fire of French cannon.

Although men of the day may not have known it, the Hundred Years War was effectively over.

2

APPROACHES TO WAR

What purpose did men think war should serve? Many would have claimed that it served none, that it was but the result of the Fall and of sin, and that it brought only harm and hurt to the world. This opinion, which had a long Christian ancestry, was still widely held and propagated in the fourteenth century. It did not, however, go unchallenged. As far back as the late fourth century two men had expressed the view that war should be fought in order to bring about peace and order. One was Augustine, whose ideas were to be fundamental in forming medieval Europe's views on the subject. The other was Vegetius, also a Christian, who likewise regarded war as a means of bringing about peace. His work on war, the *De re militari*, grew to become the main expression of the ideas of late antiquity on the aims of war and how it should best be fought. Cited in the writings of the Carolingian age, the *De re militari* began to enjoy a particular vogue during the renaissance of the twelfth century, being referred to as an authority on military matters by writers who had no first-hand knowledge of war. By the late thirteenth century, when the first translations into the vernacular were commissioned (often at the behest of men of a military cast of mind, such as Edward I, who had one made in Anglo-Norman) Vegetius was beginning to enjoy a popularity which was to last until early modern times. His view that war could be justified by the need to find peace, a view which won support from later philosophers, theologians and lawyers, was to be an influential one.

Implied in this idea was the notion that war was not, as some would have argued, the main cause of social disharmony, but rather the chief

means of attaining the restoration of an order which had been broken by
other causes. The influence of this view is clearly reflected in the works
of the two thirteenth-century Dominican friars, Raymond of Peñafort
and Thomas Aquinas, who, over a period of half a century, set out what
was to become the orthodox justification of certain wars, the 'just' wars,
as we term them. War, argued Aquinas, was the defence of peace which,
in practice, might involve the forcible protection of rights, lands, or
honours under threat or attack. This was its justification: 'All who make
war seek through war to arrive at a peace more perfect than existed
before war.'

Such a view took account of the fact that war was likely to hurt some;
for that reason every effort must be made to restrict it. But this did not
prevent the Dominicans from setting out that war could be justified as
a means of restoring order in situations of political or social disharmony,
for instance between territories (here we see the beginnings of the idea
of the territorial unit and the defence of its justifiable rights) or between
sovereign rulers and their vassals (if the vassal chose to rebel against his
lord and thus fell into a state of disobedience). Thus Aquinas, who stood
in a long tradition which came to him through the teachings of the early
canonists summed up in Gratian's *Decretum* (1140), was clear that every
state had both the right and the duty to defend itself, its legitimate
existence, and its rights when these could be legally proved ('It is
legitimate to oppose force with force', as Justinian's *Digest* put it). In this
way of thinking war was seen as an attempt to pursue a 'reasonable'
claim which was being forcibly threatened or attacked, which implied
not merely the use of force but the means of persuasion (propaganda)
and discussion (negotiation) as well. As Sir John Fortescue was to write
in the second half of the fifteenth century, 'a King's war is a legal trial
by battle [when] he seeks the right he cannot obtain by peaceful means'.
War was a means of restoring justice to society.

Legitimate war, however, was concerned not only with the defence
of sovereign or historical rights to territory. The stability of feudal
society had always depended upon a relationship of trust between lords
and vassals. In a society in which the king was regarded as God's regent,
rebellion was seen as rising against an authority divinely appointed. The
rebel or traitor was a destabilising influence, whose bad example might
tempt others to emulate him. In such circumstances, war was a necessary
and final punishment imposed upon a recalcitrant vassal who had
ignored all calls to obey his feudal lord. It is for this reason that in so
much of the literature and documentation dealing with the justification
of a war emphasis was placed upon the enemy as a rebel who must be
punished for his acts of infidelity or treason.

The French justified the war against the English in two main ways. It was an act of punishment, or vindictive justice, against an arch-rebel, the king of England as duke of Aquitaine, who had broken faith. It was also seen as a war of national self-defence against those who had invaded French territory and had incited loyal subjects into rebellion.[1] For the English kings, on the other hand, war was an attempt to assert historic and feudal rights to Aquitaine, Normandy, and other parts of France, as well as their legal claim to the French crown, which had been unjustly denied them by successive French kings. The attentive listener present at the English coronation of Henry VI in 1429 would have heard the young king being exhorted to avenge injustices ('ulciscaris iniusta') and to be 'the powerful defender of his country...triumphant over the enemy' ('sit fortissimus protector patrie...triumphator hostium'). The traditional way of doing this was through war.

The need for war, then, was fairly generally accepted, although it was widely recognized that it brought destruction and death. Although the innocent might suffer, such tragedies were often accepted philosophically as part of the divine will or punishment. In such a way of thinking, war was regarded as an invitation for divine intervention, carried out through the divine instrument, the soldier. Yet it was not merely an appeal to the strength of God that was being made. God was Goodness: He was Justice: Christ had shown himself humble even unto death. God would reward good; his judgements in battle would be just; he would favour the humble who honoured him and recognised his strength by bringing down the proud. Human power was as nothing compared with the strength of God.

Numbers on the field of battle counted for little. When Archbishop Bradwardine preached before Edward III after English victories at Crécy and Neville's Cross in 1346 he claimed that God granted victory to whomever he willed, and he had willed to grant it to the virtuous. Experience clearly showed, Bradwardine declared, that virtue, not numbers, triumphed over the iniquity of the enemy. Similarly Henry V was seen as the Judas Maccabeus of his day who, faced by great odds at Agincourt, worried little about his lack of forces but trusted in the rightness of his cause, the piety of his people at home praying for him and for his army, and in divine strength. The result of the battle showed how just was the cause of England's king. In effect, God had declared himself for the English and against the French. Had the French not been so proud, the anonymous chaplain of Henry V's household asserted,

[1] See J. T. Johnson, *Ideology, reason, and the limitation of war. Religious and secular concepts, 1200–1740* (Princeton, 1975); C. T. Allmand, *Society at war. The experience of England and France during the Hundred Years War* (Edinburgh, 1973), p. 21.

they would have recognised that earlier defeats which they had experienced (he was referring to the battles fought at Sluys in 1340 and at Poitiers in 1356), constituted a clear sign of divine arbitrament, and much bloodshed would have been avoided. But what else could be expected from such a stiff-necked people?[2]

How did defeat, even the possibility of defeat, fit into this pattern of thought? Since it was to act against hope, it was wrong to assume that defeat was an explicit sign of divine condemnation of a cause from which there could be no recovery. To think that way made it almost impossible to understand a pattern of battle results other than that which pointed consistently in one direction. How, then, to explain defeat in a war which was regarded as just? The answer lay in seeing such defeats as signs of God's temporary displeasure with a people, not with their cause, a displeasure which resulted from their sinfulness which was now being punished. On more than one occasion French writers explained the defeats and set-backs suffered by their kings and military leaders by emphasising that these were divine punishments for civil disorder and pride. Once the people had been chastised by God's flail ('flagellum Dei'), with the English acting as the instruments of his punishment, then the days of victory would return. Events were to justify such a view of things, and God was duly thanked, by the royal order that masses should be said to commemorate the defeat of the English at Formigny in April 1450, for the way he had turned his gaze towards the French cause which, for so long, had appeared to be lacking his support.[3]

If Frenchmen had doubts, Englishmen had them, too. What if the arguments conjured up to justify a war were false, or a king's motives reflected factors (naked ambition, for instance) less worthy than a seeking after justice? The lingering doubts were probably always there, even if a war received the approval of the Church that it was being fought for a good cause. For men were worried not only by the fact that the cause for which they fought might not be morally sound. A more important matter concerned them: the fate of their souls in eternity if they were to die fighting for an unjust cause. Would men, misled into fighting for a cause which, in spite of claims made on its behalf, was a war fought for the wrong motives, be eternally damned if they met their death suddenly in battle, even if they were fighting out of loyalty to their king? In such a case it was argued, following St Augustine, that since the soldier was in the service of his lord, it was the lord who must accept responsibility.

[2] *Gesta Henrici Quinti. The deeds of Henry the Fifth*, trans. and ed. F. Taylor and J. S. Roskell (Oxford, 1975), pp. 123, 125.
[3] Allmand, *Lancastrian Normandy*, pp. 305–6.

A different answer, however, might be given to a soldier who followed a leader of his own choosing – for pay; he could not plead obedience if his conscience left him uneasy. St Antonino of Florence felt that the professional soldier could not fight in a war the justice of which was not above doubt, nor could he be given absolution as long as he continued to fight in that cause.[4] The whole problem was one which drew some fine theatre from Shakespeare in *Henry V*.[5] The playwright was only reflecting, dramatically, upon one aspect of the problem of death, and its consequences, which soldiers of the later Middle Ages had constantly before them.

To the knighthood, or chivalry, of the Middle Ages war had long given a sense of purpose. For the Christian, as we have seen, wars were acts of pacification since they were fought to secure peace which depended upon justice. Had not St Augustine written: 'There are two friends, justice and peace'? The Crusades, in one view, had been an attempt to restore Christ's inheritance (into which he had entered in triumph) both to him and to his heirs, the Christian community. Seen in feudal terms, the Crusades were a defence of the Lord's rights to which, in all loyalty, all Christians should contribute, either personally or in other ways. Or, again, the Crusades might be seen, as they were in much propaganda, as wars fought to defend fellow Christians suffering physically at the hands of the Muslim world – those who took part being 'fired by the ardour of charity' towards their brothers.[6]

Such ideas might be translated into a more secular context nearer home. As Bishop Thomas Brinton of Rochester said when preaching at the time of the Black Prince's death in the summer of 1376, it was part of a knight's duty to help his king in time of war; failure to do so meant loss of the right to be called a knight, which was both a sign of honour and a mark of responsibility which had to be lived up to. The knight must be ready to fight hard when his prince required it of him; he must never desert; nor must he refuse to fight for the common good; and, above all, he must fight fearlessly. Particularly influential were the ideas of serving the feudal overlord, of fulfilling the obligation inherent in fidelity, and of helping to restore justice when the lord or his ally was deprived of what was justly his. As Bishop Brinton said, it had been to restore a rightful heir to his kingdom and to defeat tyranny that the campaign in northern Spain had been fought in 1367. Without justice there could be no peace; a knight was in honour bound to strive for justice, and at the ceremony of his dubbing his sword had been blessed

[4] See B. Jarrett, *Social theories of the Middle Ages, 1200–1500* (London, 1926), ch. 7.
[5] *Henry the Fifth*, IV, i.
[6] J. Riley-Smith, 'Crusading as an act of love', *History*, 65 (1980), 177–92.

so that, with the approval of the Church thus clearly implied, it might become a sword for justice.[7]

War gave to the chivalry of medieval Europe a sense of purpose and of justification for their existence and privileged state. It gave, too, a chance of winning merit. Essential to the ethos of chivalry was the earning of fame, which enabled the knight to hold his head high in the world, and was complementary to lordship, inheritance, or manor house as signs of his position in society. Honour, the esteem of both peer group and others, was something to be won in war. To be the first over the wall of a castle or town which was being stormed; to be encamped close to the wall of a besieged city and thus within range of missiles fired from its walls, these were acts which merited honour and respect. Martial acts might also be more dramatic or better recorded for wider public esteem. The account given by Froissart of the manner in which the Black Prince won his spurs at Crécy in 1346 shows this clearly. The young man (he was but sixteen years old at the time) was fighting for justice, for the claim of his father, Edward III, to the throne of France. By the end of the day he had not only helped to further that cause; by showing outstanding courage and skill in arms in the thick of the fighting he had shown how the knight could use situations of war to win personal renown for himself.

The importance of this was considerable. When members of the French royal order of chivalry, that of the Star, met for their annual feast, a special table was reserved for those princes, bannerets, and knights, three from each group, who were judged to have performed the most valiant deeds of war during the past year.[8] In some orders, special books of adventure were kept so as 'to give valour its due'. The words used by Froissart to express his aim in writing his great chronicle, 'that the honourable enterprises, noble adventures and deeds of arms which took place during the wars waged by France and England should be fittingly related and preserved for posterity', fit admirably into the pattern of thought and practice which regarded war as a noble way of life. 'Qui plus fait, mie[u]x vault' ('Who does most is worth most'), the refrain in the *Livre de chevalerie* written in the middle of the fourteenth century by Geoffroi de Charny, the standard-bearer of King John II of France at the battle of Poitiers, who preferred to stand and die rather

[7] *The sermons of Thomas Brinton, bishop of Rochester (1373–1389)*, ed. M. A. Devlin (Camden third series, 85, 86, London, 1954), sermon 78. On the other hand, Jean de Cardaillac could write his *Liber regalis* in 1367 in support of Henry of Trastamara's right to defend his throne through war (*Histoire littéraire de la France*, 40, Paris, 1974, pp. 203–6).

[8] M. Keen, *Chivalry* (New Haven: London, 1984), p. 192.

than run away in the moment of defeat, aptly sums up the chivalrous attitude to war.[9]

War was also a means of finding and experiencing companionship among like-minded persons. Tournaments provided opportunities for practising some of the arts and skills of war in common. It is clear that such occasions brought together, often from many countries, knights who were brought up and trained in the same martial traditions. Knights also went to war in company; a number, sometimes from the same lordship, would serve in the retinue of a great lord. It is not fanciful (we have the evidence of the fifteenth-century French lord, Jean de Bueil, to show it) to see them discussing war, its dangers, its 'occasions' rather as men today recall political or sporting occasions over a drink. The physical thrill of war and its perils, and of the intense satisfaction of a deed nobly done, is what emerges from Bueil's work.[10]

Essentially based on war, too, were the martial associations, the orders of chivalry, election to which was itself an honour and a sign of good military reputation, whose members vied with one another in the stakes for further recognition born out of daring and courage shown in war. Associated with the orders were the colour and the pageantry of war: the richness of the apparels; the emphasis on the outward trappings (say of the heralds); the sense that going to war was an occasion, just as tournaments or jousts were occasions. Some descriptions of armies on the move, left to us by writers of the chivalric tradition, notably Froissart, glow with light and colour. War was never intended to be a drab affair. Prestige, if nothing else, demanded that it be entered into with due pomp and circumstance.

Writing soon after the expulsion of the English from France in the mid-fifteenth century, the author of *Le débat des hérauts d'armes* could underline the importance of the nobility, in particular the great nobility, in French society. Their role as supporters ('pilliers') of the monarchy he regarded as specially significant. Had it always been so in the period of the conflict with England? The answer to this must be negative. On a number of occasions during the war, the role of the nobility had come under attack, in particular at moments of severe crisis. In 1357 the clerical author of the short *De miserabili statu regni Francie*, reflecting upon the disaster of Poitiers, praised the courage of the king, John II, who had fought bravely up to the very moment of his capture, but condemned in strong terms the failure and lack of heart of the nobility, the 'duces

[9] See the text in *Oeuvres de Froissart*, ed. K. de Lettenhove, I, *Chroniques* (Brussels, 1873), pp. 463–533.   [10] See Allmand, *Society at war*, pp. 27–9.

belli' who had failed in their obligation to the French state. The author's indignation was expressed ironically. Those who liked to regard themselves as heroes ('milites delicati') must show a change of heart and a will to win before any victory might be theirs.[11] Further, and more important, it was open to doubt whether the nobility was properly trained for war. Without training, all its efforts were doomed to failure.

The criticisms of the luxurious life led by the nobility (with its attendant implications of better diet and better health) were not limited to the writers of such political pamphlets. Criticisms of the same kind were also to be made by such as Philippe de Mézières, whose long reflective work on the state of French society, the *Songe du vieil pèlerin*, was written towards the end of the fourteenth century. In England, an attempt was made in 1316 to cut down the amount of luxurious food which the nobility might consume. Such may appear like attacks on the wealth and privilege of the 'haves' by the 'have nots'. In reality, it was part of a wider problem, perhaps best expressed in the *Quadrilogue invectif* of the Norman, Alain Chartier, written in 1422 when his homeland had been overrun by the English.

Chartier was reluctant to place all responsibility for this disaster upon the nobility alone. Like the clerical writer of 1357, he saw the English victory as a sign of divine displeasure and punishment for divisions within France. Where Chartier went further was in asking whether nobility was something which came to a man by virtue of his birth (and could therefore be inherited) or whether it was accorded in recognition of merit? Did nobility derive from birth, function, or attribute? The debate was an old one: 'does gentilesse proceed from birth', John Gower had asked a generation earlier in his *Confessio amantis*.[12] Its significance in 1422 lay in the way it questioned whether birth was a sufficient warrant for high military office, or whether the responsibilities of leadership in war time should only be accorded (and it was the king who accorded them) to those whose experience and reputation in military affairs merited them. Society had a right to expect the best from those with responsibilty for its defence.

War, indeed, caused questions to be asked about the nobility's role in it. Traditionally, war had given men opportunities to achieve honour through individual acts of valour and courage. Times, however, were changing. By the early fourteenth century Ramon Lull could stress the need to fight not merely for self-glorification but for the common good.

---

[11] 'Le "Tragicum argumentum de miserabili statu regni Francie" de François de Monte-Belluna (1357)', ed. A. Vernet, *Annuaire-bulletin de le société de l'histoire de France, années 1962–1963* (Paris 1964), pp. 101–63.

[12] J. Gower, *Confessio amantis*, trans. T. Tiller (Harmondsworth, 1965), p. 166.

The didactic works which the nobility used to educate their children stressed, in the words of the Burgundian, Ghillebert de Lannoy (himself a nobleman), the obligation to 'expose themselves to death for the good of the land', an ideal which many would have been able to read about in the works of classical authors such as Valerius Maximus, Livy and Caesar. Chivalry was coming to mean life in the public service under the ruler's direction. When Charles de la Trémoïlle was mortally wounded in the battle of Marignano in 1515, his death brought pride for his family since he died fighting for the public good in an engagement at which the king of France himself had been present.[13]

In a word, the nobility was being restored to its former role as the protector of society, a role which, far from contradicting the true spirit of chivalry, corresponded exactly with it. But although the spirit might be willing, there were difficulties, chiefly economic ones, to be overcome. Whether the owners of large or small estates, noblemen were members of a caste which was expected to live nobly with a certain liberality and panache ('vivre noblement') as befitted their rank. Yet to do this was proving increasingly expensive, for articles of luxury were fast rising in price. But none could deny that a fine house was a symbol of status and wealth. In border areas, dwellings which incorporated architectural features concerned with defence (the 'maison-fortes' of France) were both dwellings for a family and, in certain circumstances, they might provide some measure of protection for local people, in so doing underlining the nobleman's responsibility for the defence of the people.[14]

The expenses incurred in participating in campaigns were, by the early fourteenth century, already considerable. Furthermore, they were rising. There was the war horse to be thought of: a fine animal might be worth the value of a small lordship or, put differently, in the mid-fifteenth century a charger could cost a French man-at-arms the equivalent of anything from six months' to two years' wages. The higher a man's rank, the better the mount he was expected to have, so that the horse of a knight could cost twice that expected of an esquire, while a banneret might, in turn, pay double the price a knight-bachelor could pay for his. In addition, the cost of equipment and armour, the quality of which could vary considerably, added greatly to the expense of going to war.

[13] P. Contamine, 'L'idée de guerre à la fin du moyen âge: aspects juridiques et éthiques', *Comptes-rendus de l'académie des inscriptions et belles-lettres* (1979), pp. 82–3, and n. 45.
[14] M. G. A. Vale, 'Seigneurial fortification and private war in later medieval Gascony', *Gentry and lesser nobility in late medieval Europe*, ed. M. Jones (Gloucester: New York, 1986), pp. 133–43.

It was the matter of cost which played an important part in changing noble attitudes towards the practice of war. In the summer of 1297, the earl of Arundel may not have wished to accompany his king, Edward I, on an expedition to Flanders. But the excuse which he gave had a genuine ring about it: he could not afford to go, for none would serve in his retinue unless he rewarded them with revenues from his own lands, which would entail a loss of status ('grant abesement de mon estat') which the king would not wish. Nor could the earl find anyone who would lend him money to be secured on his landed revenue.[15]

Arundel's predicament was an early warning of difficulties to come. The economic boom of the thirteenth century, accompanied by an expansion in the population of Europe, was beginning to tail off. By the late thirteenth century, those for whom landed income was the chief source of revenue faced an uncertain future. A century later the French nobility would be among the worst affected victims of the activities of the *routiers*, often called Companies, whose particular style of war entailed the destruction of a wide variety of noble revenues. The hazard of confiscation by Frenchmen of opposing loyalties in times of political turbulence, or at the hands of the English during the occupation of much of northern France between 1417 and 1450, could also lead to greatly diminished revenues. The need to pay ransoms could be ruinous since, to raise the cash required, land often had to be sold. The trouble was that it did not necessarily sell well so that in some cases, such as that of the Burgundian lord, Guillaume de Châteauvillain, both he and his family, who acted as guarantors for the payment of 20,000 *saluts* which he had agreed to pay when captured by the French in 1430, faced financial ruin.[16] The French and English kings sometimes had to help those who had served them to regain their freedom: in 1444 Sir John Handford, who had been in France for more than twenty years, received 1,500 *livres* from Henry VI as a contribution towards the purchase of his freedom; while Jean de Rodemack got a substantial sum towards the payment of his ransom from René d'Anjou,[17] and Georges de la Trémoïlle received a *seigneurie* in Poitou from Charles VII in lieu of ransom promised but not paid. Similarly, the insistence of lords that their tenants perform their feudal duty of watch and ward (*guet et garde*), or carry out necessary repairs to castle wall or ditch, as their predecessors had customarily done, was an insistence which reflected economic necessity. It

---

[15] M. Prestwich (ed.), *Documents illustrating the crisis of 1297–98 in England* (Camden fourth series, 24, London, 1980), p. 142.

[16] A. Bossuat, 'Les prisonniers de guerre au xve siècle: la rançon de Guillaume, seigneur de Châteauvillain', *A.B.*, 23 (1951), 7–35.

[17] Allmand, *Lancastrian Normandy*, p. 77; A. Bossuat, 'Les prisonniers de guerre au xve siècle: la rançon de Jean, seigneur de Rodemack', *A. Est*, 5e sér., 3 (1951), 145–62.

was that same necessity which forced tenants to refuse their service or, as in the case between Guy le Bouteillier, as lord of La Roche-Guyon, and the people of the town, to have the dispute between them on these matters heard before the Parlement of Paris.

Few could resist pressures which were making the waging of war, never cheap, more expensive than ever before. The fourteenth century was to see a change among the natural leaders of military society from free service in the fulfilment of obligation to service in return for pay or reward. In a very real sense war was becoming an important supplementary source of livelihood, for which the nobility increasingly sold their services to the king in return for wages and promises of opportunities of obtaining what were euphemistically known as the 'advantages' of war: the profits of ransoms; booty; and grants of land seized from the conquered. As in the case of war presenting the knight with a chance of achieving reputation, so in this different context the key word was 'opportunity'.

War gave to men of initiative many such opportunities. Sir John Fastolf, involved in a long drawn-out lawsuit in Paris between 1432 and 1435, could remind the court that he had been the first to jump into the sea when Henry V had come ashore in France in 1415, and that the king had rewarded him with the grant of the first house which he had seen in France.[18] Being the first ashore was an honourable achievement which brought its own reward; respectability was what Fastolf was claiming. Some of the books which he is known to have possessed, which included Christine de Pisan's *Letter of Othea to Hector*, a didactic work for knights, reinforce this view. At the same time Fastolf's attitude to the practicalities of war reflect a hardheadedness which was essentially of this world: the plan which he drew up in 1435 favouring a 'tough' approach to the war made little concession to romantic ideas of chivalry which would influence a knight's conduct in war.[19] His long career in France which led him to hold high military and administrative posts, as well as amassing a fortune through the capture of prisoners in battle, the seizing of property and the exploitation of estates, shows him to have been a 'realistic' person in all that he did.

As often the case, Froissart had a story which illustrates this point. Describing Edward III's arrival at Calais in 1359 with a sizeable army, the chronicler recalled that a large number of men, of different backgrounds and nationalities, were there waiting in the hope of being allowed to join him, some, he added significantly, wishing to advance

---

[18] Allmand and Armstrong (eds.), *English suits*, pp. 263–4.
[19] M. G. A. Vale, 'Sir John Fastolf's "Report" of 1435: a new interpretation reconsidered', *Nottingham Medieval Studies*, 17 (1973), 78–84.

their honour, others intent upon pillaging the kingdom of France. In many cases, those who had come had spent large sums preparing themselves adequately to join the English ranks, such was their keenness to serve under a commander of high reputation.[20] Their motives, at least as described by Froissart, indicate that the profit motive was increasingly important in attracting men to war, and that mundane, as well as idealistic, motives provided a double purpose for the achievement of skill in arms.

Society was faced with two images of the soldier. On the one hand was the traditional knight of chivalry, the figure of the romances, and, more recently, of the new chivalric orders, one of whose social functions was the defence of those in physical need and danger. Not surprisingly, St George and St Michael were the patrons of new orders: both were depicted in art as the defenders of the innocent against the forces of evil. On the other hand was the image, conveyed with increasing frequency by the chroniclers, of the common soldier as a symbol of something to be feared, the perpetrator of violence and destruction, whether this took the form of attacks on property (pillage and arson) or on people (murder and rape).

The image of the drunken and ill-disciplined soldier, a figure who aroused an emotional response, more often that of fear than that of respect, was nothing new in this age. Mercenaries, like the hireling of the bible, could not be trusted: the bells which warned the inhabitants of the villages and towns of southern France of the danger of the approaching Companies reflect society's fear and mistrust of such men. If soldiers could find a defender from outside their number (as they did in the poet Thomas Hoccleve, who pleaded that greater respect be paid to their economic predicament in old age),[21] more often than not they suffered from the verbal and literary lash of preachers, moralists and other writers. The mid-fourteenth-century English Dominican, John Bromyard, launched into what he regarded as the increasingly unChristian spirit of those, both knights and common soldiers, who went to war with the vilest of intentions and 'oaths and curses in their mouths'. The views of his French contemporary, the Carmelite, Jean de Venette, corresponded almost exactly; not without reason did the poor people of France have little trust in the nobility who abused them and their property and virtually held them to ransom in the most disgraceful way. The remark of Honoré Bouvet, a Benedictine who was a contemporary of both Bromyard and Venette, that no man who did not know how to set

[20] Froissart, *Chroniques*, ed. Lettenhove, VI, 204.
[21] T. Hoccleve, *Works, III: The regement of princes*, ed. F. J. Furnivall (E.E.T.S., London, 1897), pp. 32–4: Allmand, *Society at war*, pp. 179–81.

places on fire was worthy of the name of soldier, might be cynical, but it was not entirely unmerited.[22]

The gamekeeper, it would seem, had turned poacher, leaving much of society undefended. If war was a means of achieving peace, or social and political harmony and order, how compatible were the activities of many soldiers with that aim? Were not soldiers, and their activities, the enemies of peace? It was for reasons such as this that every attempt was made to bring a measure of order to war. Although it was difficult, in practice, to stop war from breaking out, serious attempts were made to control it by emphasising that only a war duly and properly declared by a soverign authority could be regarded as just. The causes lying behind such a declaration had to be serious (the denial of rights, the breaking of the feudal bond), and every attempt to resolve a possible conflict by negotiation had to be made. War was only to be a last resort.

There was, too, the matter of the methods used by the soldier in war. They had to be reasonable (no sledge-hammer to crack a nut), controlled, and moral. Were all weapons moral? The Church certainly had doubts about the crossbow, with its deadly bolt or quarrel, a reaction which was about to be extended among certain circles to the use of cannon in its early days. Should all members of the enemy's population be equally at risk in time of war? An unarmed cleric must not be harmed; but no more should women, children or old men, and even students travelling to their place of study should not be molested or put to ransom. But what of the farmer who grew crops to feed the enemy's army, or who paid taxes to the enemy king (and more and more people were now doing this, in one form or another), or whose farmyard provided feathers for enemy arrows? The maker of weapons, the fletcher or the bowyer, might not so easily claim immunity from war. The problem was to know where to stop. And who would say that enough was enough, and would take on the task of punishing those who transgressed the rules of the game?

At this stage, the need to control war to prevent it becoming a tragic and self-defeating activity demanded strong action. War had its rules and conventions, the so-called laws of war ('jus in bello'), which, internationally understood, bound military society together by providing a common code of practice and a moderating influence upon its conduct.[23] There were ways of treating prisoners properly, and of recognising that they had certain claims upon their captors; there were

[22] *The Tree of Battles of Honoré Bonet*, trans. G. W. Coopland (Liverpool, 1949), p. 189.

[23] M. H. Keen, *The laws of war in the late Middle Ages* (London: Toronto, 1965); N. A. R. Wright, 'The *Tree of Battles* of Honoré Bouvet and the laws of war', *War, literature and politics in the late Middle Ages*, ed. C. T. Allmand (Liverpool, 1976), pp. 12–31.

also rules about the taking, sharing, and disposing of booty and pillage; there were signs of formal war, such as the unfurling of banners or the setting off of a cannon at the start of a siege, which informed all those present that a certain legal situation now existed, hostilities having been formally declared. Indeed, as the study of the law emerging from the application of these laws makes clear, it was the formalisation of war, bringing a set of rules to apply to its conduct, which men were trying to achieve. The parallel with the tournament or the joust, where the constraints imposed by space and regulations applied, cannot be ignored. The free-for-all of war had to be curtailed.

The formulation of rules, however, was not sufficient. There must be people officially appointed to apply them. Heralds were an essential aspect of the waging of war, just as they were of chivalry. Their task was not limited to the granting of coats of arms; they had to be experts in recognising such armorials to identify both the dead and those who performed noble (and base) deeds in war. It was in their power to make and break military reputations; men gave of their best in front of them. Equally, however, the constable and marshal of the army had authority delegated to them to try in their courts (in which the military law was applied) men such as deserters and those who broke the rules of discipline.[24] Unlike the herald who sought to observe and note the outstanding (the chroniclers, notably Froissart, made good use of the reports of battle given to them by heralds), the constable and marshal were more concerned with maintaining order. They shared a common aim, however, for each was trying to keep the standard of soldierly behaviour up to at least that of an acceptable minimum.

The heralds and the disciplinary officers could achieve much; but it is clear that no factor could ensure a greater respect for the rules of war and for the interests and property of the non-combatant than could firm leadership. To the outstanding leaders, the chroniclers and others gave unstinted praise. One can readily understand why. The ability to lead was a characteristic once associated with nobility, an attribute of social rank. As the period wore on, leadership became increasingly associated with personal qualities and skills which earned nobility, thus bringing renown to the man blessed with them. The application of such skills led to the greater control of an army and, as a consequence, to its more effective use as a military arm. At the same time it assured that those who, under weaker leadership, might have suffered at the hands of

[24] G. D. Squibb, *The high court of chivalry* (Oxford, 1959), ch. 1: M. Keen, 'The jurisdiction and origins of the constable's court', *War and government in the Middle Ages*, ed. J. Gillingham and J. C. Holt (Woodbridge, 1984), pp. 159–69.

armies, could live in greater security. From this stems the historical importance of the ordinances of war issued by kings on campaign: by Richard II during the Scottish war of 1385; by Henry V in France in 1419; and by his brother John, duke of Bedford, in Normandy in 1428, all three attempts to control the illegal or 'un-peaceful' activities of soldiers, in particular in their relationships with non-combatants. That relationship, an uneasy one in all societies, was best served by personality. The praise lavished upon Henry V by his contemporaries, by no means all English, is indicative of the admiration accorded to one whose hold upon his men was such that, for a while, those parts of France under English control were freed of the worst excesses committed by soldiers. To the anonymous writer of the *Parisian Journal* the Armagnacs ('faulx Armignaz') were like Saracens, as they hanged, burned, ransomed and raped at will. He might have reservations about the English but, generally speaking, under their rule both military and civilian knew where they stood. That was something to be thankful for.

It was not so much the existence of war as the manner of fighting it which aroused the criticism of an increasingly outspoken body of persons who reflected the views of society in the growing vernacular literature and poetry of the time. Honoré Bouvet, whose *Tree of Battles*, composed in the late fourteenth century, was soon to become a kind of handbook on the conventions of war, was deeply influenced by the many human tragedies caused by war. As a result, he was inclined to take a view which favoured the rights of the non-combatants against those of the soldier. The least that can be said for him was that he convinced many that the non-combatants' interests were worthy of consideration. Bouvet's writings reflected the opinions of many chroniclers of the period who wrote as vociferous critics of the excesses of the soldiery. When Jean de Venette, whose native village of that name had been destroyed by English troops, described the activities of armies, both regular and irregular, he condemned their excesses and bestowed his sympathy upon the victims. Similarly, if in a much more restrained manner, the Englishman, John Page, himself a soldier in Henry V's army, described in detail and in passages of considerable emotion the sufferings of the helpless civilians during the six-month-long siege of Rouen which ended in January 1419. If Venette attacked the soldiers, Page did not, perhaps because the man in charge of the operation was his own king who put the blame for the fate of the civilians firmly upon the shoulders of the French. Yet the sensitivities of both for the sufferings of men, women, and children drawn unwillingly into the war reflect something of the way in which thinking men asked themselves whether war was, in fact, not so much a way to peace as the prolongation of bitter conflict.[25]

Like all ages, the late Middle Ages had its critics who took swipes at the activities of soldiers. We should not leave this brief consideration of how war was regarded by people of the time with the impression that greed and anarchy prevailed. What emerges from recent study of this important period is that war was increasingly coming to be seen as an instrument of state, to be organised by the king for the common good of his people and country. Gradually the idea of serving the king in his wars was being replaced by the need to serve the *res publica*, a less particular and more all-embracing higher good. We shall see later how, in the fourteenth century, taxation came to be voted in ever larger sums for the purpose of war; this was, indirectly, the contribution of communities towards their self-defence.

Out of the monies voted from this public purse wages were to be paid to soldiers to carry out that work of defence. The soldier, of whatever rank, thus became a public servant whose task it was, under the command of the king, to defend the community's interests through war. To do this successfully, the soldier had to be ready: he had to train in military skills which he might be called upon to use. This no longer applied only to the knight who took part in tournaments. In England, the obligation to own arms and to train in the use of them was shared by all male adults, as the Assize of Arms of 1181 and the Statute of Winchester of 1285 made clear. The fourteenth century saw the matter being taken further. In 1363 Edward III ordered that regular training at the butts should take the place of football; a century later, in 1456, the difficulties experienced in Scotland in summoning and arming a proper fighting force were recognised in the proscription of football and golf in favour of archery practice.

Training in arms on an increasingly wide scale was a characteristic of the period. The philosophical message of Vegetius's *De re militari* centred upon the need to defend the common good, and for that need to be met not by the employment of mercenaries but by members of the community adequately prepared to fight. The matter of leadership, and who should be entrusted with it, was much discussed. These were far from sterile debates. Fundamentally, what was at issue was whether the army, now ideally composed of men with at least a modicum of training and military skill, should be led by men who merited their responsibilities,

---

[25] *The chronicle of Jean de Venette*, trans. and ed. J. Birdsall and R. A. Newhall (New York, 1953): 'John Page's poem on the siege of Rouen', *The historical collections of a citizen of London in the fifteenth century*, ed. J. Gairdner (Camden Society, London, 1876), pp. 1–46: *The Brut*, ed. F. W. D. Brie (E.E.T.S., London, 1908), II, 404–22.

awarded to them on behalf of the community by the king who paid them from public funds ('la peccune publique'). If, as Honoré Bouvet wrote, the soldier who acted *qua* soldier did so as the king's deputy, all the more so did war's new leaders act in his name. These leaders were now slowly becoming officers. Before long, in the sixteenth century, the age of the military academy, where soldiers (and above all officers) were to be trained, would arise. A new attitude to war was being developed.[26]

The academy was for the future. Yet at the time of the Hundred Years War, with the concept of the nation state, and of the need for its interests to be defended, taking root, the *raison d'être* of war was slowly changing. It certainly continued to give opportunity for glory, for self-advancement, and for material gain; in that respect it has not changed much to this day. None the less war was coming increasingly to be regarded as a form of activity to be carried out by the whole community, which would endeavour in common, under the leadership of the king, to defend its honour and safety. If men had accepted the likelihood of death in war as a means of achieving honour, war fought in defence of a greater good, that of the community, was becoming just as honourable, if not more so. 'Pugna pro patria', 'Fight for your country', was a call which Bishop Brinton could make from the pulpit in the 1370s. By the middle years of the fifteenth century litigants in civil suits before the Parlement of Paris could send word that they would not appear in person because they were engaged in war for the public good ('in expedicione causa rei publice') or were being detained as prisoners by the enemy. Both excuses were practical ones; it is evident that they were honourable excuses, too. 'Pro patria mori', 'Die for your country', would be the next step.[27] Death on the battlefield, fighting for a just cause and, preferably in the presence of the king who led and represented the community, was, for the fighting man like Charles de la Trémoïlle, the supreme accolade. A new view of war, albeit one which had close links with past ideas, was gradually emerging.

[26] On this development, see J. R. Hale, *Renaissance war studies* (London, 1983), chs. 8–10.
[27] E. Kantorowicz, '*Pro patria mori* in medieval political thought', *A.H.R.*, 56 (1951), 472–92: reprinted in the author's *Selected studies* (New York, 1965), pp. 308–24.

3

THE CONDUCT OF WAR

What were the main military objectives of the participants of the war and, in particular, what were those of the English, the aggressors? The names of the battles are known, some better than others; for most these are the moments in the war which stand out. A rather closer look at the diary of military events easily conveys the impression of times of intense activity, followed by periods when little or nothing seemed to occur. If military methods were as aimless as they may appear, should we not concentrate on those moments, perhaps the decisive moments, of violent action when the armies of the two sides clashed in battles which have become part of national myth?

It takes little knowledge of history to appreciate that relatively few of the battles recorded in history have had a decisive effect upon the future of those involved. This is certainly true of the Hundred Years War, and it is as well to remember that at Crécy, Poitiers, and Agincourt, although the English emerged as victors, on each occasion they were not entering the French kingdom to attempt its conquest, but were actually leaving it, heading for the coast in search of transport to take them back to England, the main aim of the expedition already fulfilled. If each success brought reputation (as it did) to the victors, and loss of men and morale to the vanquished, none brought immediate territorial advantage.

Was an army's main aim, then, not to draw the enemy to battle? The *chevauchée* may have been seen as a challenge to the enemy's pride and ability to defend his territory, but it is doubtful whether the leader of a *chevauchée*, often at the head of but a few thousand men, and needing to make the expedition profitable through the taking of booty and prisoners, was seeking battle. In fact, the opposite was nearer the case. Vegetius's teaching on war was not likely to have been interpreted in terms of trying to draw the enemy onto the field so that he might be met and defeated. Furthermore, a battle was regarded by many as an invitation to God to intervene in human affairs, and God had the disconcerting habit of bringing defeat upon those who faced the prospect of victory with overconfidence. In a word, rather than seek battle, it was better to avoid it. Such a doctrine would be formally expressed late in the fifteenth century by Philippe de Commynes who displayed an unheroic attitude to war and a marked preference for diplomacy. In the meanwhile, we may perhaps see here a reflection of a decline of noble and, possibly, of literary influence on the place accorded to the battle in war, in which it was no longer regarded as the great opportunity for individual acts of courage, but more as the culmination of a military process whose aim was the achievement of a particular political goal.

If battles, in themselves, did not usually lead to the achievements of such goals, what would? What were the enemy's weaknesses (not necessarily military ones) which could be attacked? In the middle years of the fourteenth century French kings had such weaknesses. For instance, how widely were they accepted as the legitimate kings of France? Propaganda could be used to undermine their subjects' faith in their legitimacy, while a war of successful raids (or *chevauchées*) might shake that confidence yet further by showing that, as kings, they lacked the power to fulfil one of their prime roles, the defence of their people against the English. In this way their credibility would be undermined and their power weakened. The *chevauchée*, then, had as its prime aim the undermining of the enemy king's authority by challenging his military effectiveness. The campaigns of the Black Prince in 1355 and 1356, the defeats of French armies at Crécy and Poitiers (not to mention that at Brignais in 1362) served to underline that lack of effectiveness and to increase the fears of the doubters.

French weakness could be emphasised still further by taking the war to the non-combatant population. The civilian became the soldiers' main target. Eventually, it was hoped, this would lead to a demand for peace which could not be ignored, at which moment the stronger party would be able to dictate the terms it wished. Secondly, wars which involved civilian targets were less dangerous and cheaper to organise, but very costly for the defender. Not only was there an imperative to respond to threatened attacks by diverting much time, energy, and, above all, money into defence, principally into the building of urban fortifications and castles; when the raids occurred the defenders' means of production (crops, fishponds, mills, barns) were among the prime targets for destruction, so that their economic capability was seriously undermined. With their material resources diminished, and fears for their physical safety dampening such vital initiatives as rebuilding and continued cultivation (for who would carry out such tasks when the risks of further loss and destruction were high?), civilians became a political, and even a financial liability to their king. What was more they could not, or claimed they could not, pay taxes, direct or indirect, so that the king of France soon came to feel the impact on his fiscal policy of English raids into certain parts of his kingdom. That was what the *chevauchée* was intended to achieve.

What of the French response? Failure to react would allow the English to think that they could do as they wished. Inaction would likewise be taken as a sign of weakness by the French people themselves. At a time when neither the French army nor fiscal arrangements to meet its needs had been sufficiently developed to respond to a new military situation, the only possible response was none the less to call traditional forces together to form an army with which to intercept and, it was hoped, to defeat the English. By 1356 such a way of approaching the problem had clearly failed. Less than twenty years later, however, things had changed. The French army had become relatively small and manageable; it was now comprised of picked men; its leaders, too, were the best available; and its task was the specific one of taking the initiative and winning back the areas of land ceded by the terms agreed at Brétigny – and more, if possible. Instead of trying to confront the English in pitched engagements, the French tried the tactic of clearing towns and castles of their garrisons, employing units of mounted – hence mobile – troops to do this. The system worked well. In the 1370s the English, lacking good leadership and the necessary commitment of men and money to defend a long frontier (available money might have been better spent on defence than on more popular campaigns through France), soon lost the ground which they had gained by treaty.

Treaty. The word serves to remind us of the importance of that element so far not introduced into the discussion: diplomacy. Its role could have been vital, for in theory skilful negotiators might have made the most of military situations which, at a given moment, greatly favoured one side rather than the other. In 1360 French weakness (and in particular the capture of King John) gave the negotiators reason to make some fairly radical alterations to the map of France. In 1420, French weakness and Anglo-Burgundian strength were to settle the question of the succession in favour of the English king. At no other time, however, did the current military situation make its impression deeply felt upon diplomatic bargaining. Yet even in 1360 the French royal council did not feel weak enough to be obliged to accept the terms ceded by the captive king in London. The use of the 'half-peace' (with each side making a major concession which left neither side fully satisfied)[1] and of the truce were proof of the failure of military pressure to force a final settlement of the war, one way or the other, through diplomatic negotiation.

Such, briefly, was Henry V's inheritance from the fourteenth century. How did he change it? Of Henry, as of Edward III, we must admit that we do not know what his precise political ambitions in France were. Yet no doubt exists about the different approach of the two kings to the conflict with France. From the first, Henry V set out to conquer, and then to maintain, that conquest. Harfleur was taken by siege and, in the year which followed, everything was done to ensure that it should not be lost. In 1417, Henry began the more systematic conquest of Normandy. Places which felt they could resist did so, were besieged, and were taken. Henry's new subjects were asked for their loyalty on oath; those who refused were expelled, and their properties confiscated. An administration to rule in his name was also set up. Garrisons were established to police the conquered area and to act as islands of English authority, attempts being made to keep the soldiery under some discipline. Castles also acted as bases for field armies which were used to extend and defend the frontier with Valois France. In every way, Henry V acted as if all that he did was to be lasting in its effects. It was from this position of moral and physical strength that he negotiated the treaty of Troyes, whose terms suggest that he wanted to change as little as possible. Only the dynasty would be new. Normal life would go on as usual if people accepted him as heir to the French crown. He was using the treaty not so much to conquer as to acquire legitimately what he regarded as his own by right.

Once again, we ask what was the French response? We need scarcely remind ourselves that the 1420s marked the nadir of French fortunes. A flash of hope after the unexpected success at Baugé in 1421; but Cravant and, in particular, Verneuil put paid to hopes of a quick revival. As the English moved southwards into Maine and Anjou, so French prospects grew bleaker. Reconquest would take time, in particular if diplomacy did not come to their help. In the end, it was geography (in the form of the river Loire) and Joan of Arc that saved them. Charles VII's rule was legitimised by his coronation. Valois morale slowly began to rise,

---

[1] On this concept, see Palmer, 'War aims', p. 53.

while English morale, in particular after the loss of the Burgundian alliance, declined.

The French were to win the final set by a combination of factors. They appealed increasingly to popular opinion: Charles VII was now the true king who should be supported by all loyal Frenchmen. Then his military successes, modest at first, increased in number. The career of John Talbot, earl of Shrewsbury, shows that in the late 1430s and 1440s the English were waging an increasingly defensive war: now a stronghold here, now a castle there was coming under attack and being lost.[2] Over a decade (so reminiscent of the 1370s in the south-west) English military power, together with its dependent legal and administrative authority, was eroded away. English morale sank further, and both its political and military commitment to the war declined. It is notable that, on the final French campaign of 1449–50, carefully and confidently organised by the king, and carried out by a much-reformed army, the majority of fortified places did not resist, preferring to open their gates to the side which not only controlled more firepower but claimed with greater vigour to represent legitimate and effective rule. In Aquitaine, between 1451 and 1453, French armies did indeed meet with resistance: but the fact remains that the battles of Formigny (1450) and Castillon (1453) only finished off in dramatic fashion processes which were all but complete when the opposing armies met. It had been shown that the essentially non-dramatic tactic, slow as it might be, was in the last resort the one which brought results. And results were what war was increasingly about.

LAND FORCES

A late-medieval army was, essentially, composed of two groups, those who fought on horseback and those who fought on foot. In itself, the horse was both an arm and a sign of social distinction, as well as a means of transport. In the English civil wars of the mid-thirteenth century the cavalry had been in command; but fifty years later, things were beginning to change. If the cavalry were still, in every sense, the army's natural leaders, the victories of the Flemish burgher forces and militia over French knights at Courtrai in July 1302, and that of the mountaineers of Schwyz and Uri over the formidable feudal array of knights and footmen belonging to Leopold of Austria at Morgarten in November 1315 had shown what could be done in conditions and terrain unsuited to the effective use of cavalry. Not surprisingly, some saw these victories as signs that the days of the mounted knight as the dominant military arm were coming to an end.

[2] A. J. Pollard, *John Talbot and the war in France, 1427–1453* (London, 1983).

Yet care must be taken not to dismiss too readily the value of cavalry as an arm – or worse, as a relic – of the past. The mounted soldier still had a long way to go and his influence was very considerable in the whole period covered by this book.[3] None the less, as has been argued, the Hundred Years War would never be settled by a major engagement in which the cavalry alone played the decisive role. It is important to recognise this, for an acceptance of this fundamental point leads more easily to an understanding of the reasons which caused an increase in the military significance of those who did not fight on horseback.

For what sort of wars are we concerned with? Those of the first two Edwards were fought against enemies whose common aim was to rid their countries of the English aggressor, but whose methods of doing so differed. In both cases the leaders did their best to avoid full-scale confrontation. In Wales (under Edward I), in Scotland (under the first three Edwards) and in France (from Edward I to Henry VI) England fought a succession of wars in which she was, in fact, the aggressor. In spite of this, how far did the initiative really lie with England, and to what extent was she able to dictate the kind of war which she wanted to fight? In all cases English kings had to come to terms with the conditions which they found in these three different countries; and in all cases they had to show an ability to adapt themselves and their armies to new conditions, military, social and economic, as well as to new thinking in the ways that armies were formed and war was fought.

The English were faced by the different physical conditions and social organisation of the countries which they invaded. The army which Edward I led against Llewelyn ap Gruffydd in north Wales in 1277 consisted of less than 1,000 feudal cavalry and some 15,000 foot soldiers; in 1282 the king had only some 750 cavalry as against 8,000 or 9,000 foot soldiers, including archers and crossbowmen, most of them paid troops. In Wales the nature of the war was largely dominated by physical factors: in mountainous territory foot soldiers were of greater use than heavy cavalry would ever be. Ideally, a way should be found to employ both arms together. At Maes Moydog, near Montgomery, in March 1295 that way was found. The cavalry, combined with archers and crossbowmen, played havoc among the Welsh. A new weapon had been discovered.

That weapon may have been used to good effect against the Scots who were defeated at Falkirk in July 1298. Here, in a major battle, two factors were emphasised. One was the effectiveness of the longbow in the hands of the Welsh archers of whom Edward I had over 10,000, all of them paid, on campaign that summer. The other factor was the

[3] M. G. A. Vale, *War and chivalry. Warfare and aristocratic culture in England, France and Burgundy at the end of the Middle Ages* (London, 1981), ch. 4 (I).

importance of the formations which allowed the archers to act in liaison with the cavalry, of whom some 2,500 served that year. Here were the two developments, the use of the longbow and the adaptation of the traditional use of cavalry, which were to bring victories to the English in a number of foreign fields in the coming century or so.

It was the willingness to adapt which was important. The process begun under Edward I was continued in July 1333 when, at Halidon Hill, outside Berwick, the English showed that they had learned to co-ordinate the use of 'traditional' cavalry with the 'new' archer force, the combination on this occasion being that of archers and dismounted men-at-arms drawn up in a defensive position which showed what successes a measure of flexibility could bring to an army led by men willing to experiment.

Yet, in the immediate future, the success of English arms would be limited. The Scottish leaders, notably Robert Bruce, understood well the need to approach the enemy with care. Bruce, therefore, became a kind of guerilla leader whose main means of harming the English was to harass them rather than seek a formal confrontation with them. Using highly mobile soldiers to avoid battle, Bruce used the physical geography of Scotland to make conditions as difficult as he could for the English who, risking starvation and ambush, had to be very careful not to overstretch themselves and to keep open their lines of communication as best they could through the control of castles, in particular the vital one at Stirling, which dominated the lowest point at which the river Forth could be crossed by bridge.

It was with this kind of experience of rapidly changing war behind them that the English began their long conflict against France. There they were to face yet another situation, a large country whose main physical characteristic was open countryside ('plat pays') broken up by rivers, with the social and economic characteristic of castles and towns (some already fortified) which helped society to defend itself against enemies from both within and without. In practice the countryside was easy to conquer; but it could only be controlled properly if the fortified places upon which it depended for its economic well-being and defence were also in friendly hands. Control of the towns and castles of France, therefore, was the first objective which the English needed to achieve. As regards the French, their aim must be to harass the English as best they could, to make their task of governing those parts of France which they controlled, and of conquering those not yet in their hands, as difficult and as expensive as possible. In this process, battles did little to help either side achieve its military aim, and were not to be an important part of the strategies pursued by the two main protagonists in the Hundred Years War.

If battles were to assume a role of secondary significance, then the cavalry, who might play a vital part on such occasions, were likely to become less important. A further – and connected – factor contributed to this change: the expense which the individual cavalryman had to incur in order to fulfil his proper role in war. There can be little doubt that this fact proved influential in reducing the strength of the cavalry (a strength which, as we have seen, was contracting because of the new requirements of war) and of turning many who might have fought on horseback into men-at-arms who rode into battle, dismounted, and then fought on foot. In such circumstances, the armour needed by each individual provided less cover and was less cumbersome and cheaper than that required by the mounted knight. In these conditions, too, the mount required either to give a force mobility or to approach a battle-field could be of inferior breed, and consequently cheaper, than a cavalry horse capable of carrying a fully armoured knight, in addition to its own armour.

Thus the hobelar, a form of light horseman, came to provide the mobile and versatile force which was to be characteristic of so much war on the Anglo-Scottish border in the early fourteenth century. For a few decades, too, the English also used hobelars with success along the borders which separated them from the enemy in France, and in particular at the siege of Calais in 1346–7, where they had some 600 or so to help them keep the French at a distance. Nor was the lesson lost upon the French whose army, which harassed the English borders in south-western France in the 1370s, contained a preponderance of mounted soldiers.

The weapon of the day was to be the bow. The crossbow, most useful in defence when the crossbowman, who needed protection for the time required to wind up his weapon, could hide himself behind a wall, was an elitist weapon, most effective in the hands of Gascons, who fought in Wales for Edward I, and of Genoese, a large contingent of whom fought on the French side at Crécy. But it was the longbow, with its range of up to 200 metres, its power of penetration which was to compel the development of more effective plate armour in the first half of the fourteenth century, its rate of fire which was easily twice that of the crossbow, and which, held vertically, (earlier bows and crossbows were held horizontally) could be aimed more accurately along the line of the bow, which was to give the archer, above all those serving in English armies, so important a role to play in every form of war at this time. The bow's greatest asset was its versatility. It could be used in sieges; it was valuable when used in the open by a lightly armed foot solder; likewise, a mounted archer, who did not need a first-class horse to ride, could prove to be a very mobile and effective combatant. In the early thirteenth century Gerald of Wales had advocated the combined use of archers and knights; it was precisely this combination which, as shown above, was to be employed to such good effect in defensive positions against the Scots in the first half of the fourteenth century, before being used, in broadly similar conditions, against the French at Crécy, Poitiers and, later, at Agincourt.

What essential changes did this new combination of archers and men-at-arms, some mounted, others on foot, bring about? In attack, the archers could break up either those massed in defensive position or, as at Agincourt, they could disperse cavalry which had begun to charge, leaving the frightened and wounded horses to turn upon their own side. In such conditions, concentrated fire from the archers on the wings wrought such havoc that the French could provide but little resistance to those English who set upon them. In defence, the dismounted men-at-arms and archers (the archers being either in 'wedges' or set out before the men-at-arms) provided density of resistance, giving each other support, the men-at-arms being all the better protected, since the archers were able to fire their weapons a considerable distance against an advancing enemy, thus disrupting them before they reached the defending men-at-arms who, with their own cavalry, could then mount a counter-attack. The ability of each group to fight alongside the other (something which depended upon a very disciplined approach) was undoubtedly one of the main tactical developments of the fourteenth century, and was to play an important part in helping bring about a succession of English victories in battle.

The other important development was that of the use of the mounted archer, who, paid twice the wage of the foot archer, was first found in English armies in 1334. By the time of the war in Brittany in 1342 there were already more than 1,700 of them in service. Not all may agree with one critic who termed these 'the finest fighting men of the Middle Ages'.[4] None the less, their ability to achieve rapid movements not only in battle but, more important, before it, and to act in unison with the men-at-arms (who were also mounted) made them into 'by far the most important element in the armies which fought in France'.[5] By the time

---

[4] J. E. Morris, 'Mounted infantry in mediaeval warfare', *T. R. Hist. S.*, third series, 8 (1914), 78.

[5] M. Prestwich, 'English armies in the early stages of the Hundred Years War: a scheme of 1341', *B.I.H.R*, 56 (1983), 110.

of the Crécy campaign in 1346 men-at-arms and mounted archers, who would fight on foot in positions chosen, as far as possible, for their defensive possibilities, were being recruited in broadly the same numbers. In both England and France the need to make armies mobile was perhaps one of the major developments of the period, and shows how important versatility was coming to be regarded by the leaders of the day.

It was this factor which contributed heavily to the successes achieved by the French army in the 1370s. Yet we should not forget another: the significance of the noble contribution to the relatively small army of some 3,000 or so men (increased by half for part of the year), drawn largely from local men, all of them volunteers, all regularly paid and reviewed. These were factors of telling importance as the army sought to fight a war which would rely on its mobility to achieve success, a war in which confrontation on a large scale would be avoided. Well organised and well led, the small French army fulfilled these important, if un-dramatic, military objectives with complete success.

For the French the peace of the last years of the fourteenth century led to little more than the need to garrison their frontiers. But then the civil war of the first years of the new century caused what was virtually the collapse of the French army, a collapse confirmed by the defeat at Agincourt at the hands of English men-at-arms and archers. For much of the next generation there could scarcely be said to be such a thing as a French army, for a sizeable proportion of Charles VII's soldiers came from Scotland. On the English side, what was needed was an army to fulfil two essential functions: conquest and maintenance of that conquest, requirements which demanded both field armies and garrisons. Partly because those who served in garrisons had to be ready to serve in the field when required (for a castle acted as a base where soldiers could remain when not in the field, and from which they could control the countryside around by mounted raids within a radius of, say, a dozen miles), partly because of an increasing difficulty in securing active support from the nobility and gentry for the war in France, English armies at the end of the war sometimes included a greater ratio of archers to men-at-arms than ever before, sometimes 7:1 or even 10:1, rather than the more usual 3:1 under Henry V and the parity of archers to men-at-arms normally found in the second half of the fourteenth century. We should also recall that the nature of the war, sieges pursued by both sides and the defence of a long frontier stretching from Le Crotoy in the east to Mont-Saint-Michel in the west, dictated a kind of war in which heavy cavalry played relatively little part other than in defence. An important change was coming about.

As already suggested, it was paid participation in war which saved a large number of the nobility and, in certain cases, helped them improve their social status. Fewer of the French nobility were drawn to looking after their estates. Rather they preferred to farm them out at a fixed rent, at leases which, in the fourteenth century, became progressively longer, and to enjoy the freedom to take up offices or to serve in the army. To a certain extent, it could be argued, taxes paid on their lands and its products could be recouped from the crown by entering royal service. Thus, instead of raiding the countryside under cover of defending it, or stealing money to pay for horses and their harnesses, the nobility entered the royal service in large numbers in both England and France so that, ironically, 'the budget of the State was to some extent a budget of noble assistance';[6] used by kings on both sides of the Channel to pay the nobility, among others, for their services in war. In France many noblemen, especially those of middling to lower rank, were so impoverished that they needed the king's wages, which provided them with a better and surer income than did their lands. In the period of the reforms carried out under Charles V, much of the French army was composed of members of the lower-ranking nobility. Being a soldier, they found, could be profitable.

In the England of Edward I, if the great feudatories had refused payment for fear of losing caste, by the reign of Edward III all were 'now prepared to accept wages for military service'. The king himself was not paid (although Edward Balliol, 'king' of Scots, drew payment both in times of war and peace) but dukes received 13s. 4d; earls 6s. 8d; knights-baneret 4s; knights-bachelor 2s; and esquires 1s; these last sums corresponding proportionately to the amount each might expect to spend on a horse (as outlined above) whose value was agreed in advance, so that compensation for its loss could be paid by the crown.

Both the great nobility and the armigerous gentry, whose influence was more local, played a significant role in the organisation of military service, the gentry acting as sub-contractors in the work of raising forces. Together they acted as recruiters responsible for bringing together the large numbers of men who constituted the armies of the day. In this role the importance of the nobility in enlisting not only their feudal tenants but, in some cases, members of their households or those bound to them by indenture for service in war and peace, is considerable. As captains, they served sometimes as leaders of small expeditions, sometimes under the personal leadership of the king; as lieutenants, they exercised authority in castles and garrisons; while others still served as men-at-arms in the armies of both sides.

[6] P. Contamine, 'The French nobility and the War', *The Hundred Years War*, ed. Fowler, p. 151.

However, not all chose the way of active service in war, for other outlets, appropriate to their ranks and talents, could be found. War policy was settled in the councils of kings; many members of the nobility made the giving of counsel their contribution to war. Not far distanced from the council, in England at any rate, was Parliament, dominated for much of the fourteenth century by the peerage; and in that body, too, matters of policy and national finance were frequently discussed, for it was there that kings liked to benefit from the practical experience of men who had taken an active part in war. For others still, the administration which war inevitably brought in its wake provided further opportunities to serve their country's cause.

Did the nobility, however, keep up with the changes in war taking place in this period? There has been (and there may still be) a tendency to run down the role of the European nobility in the wars so characteristic of the late Middle Ages. To many, the world in which they appear to have lived seems to have been distanced from reality. Changes in social status; changes in the technology of war; changes in the geographical and temporal scale on which it was fought are seen as having led to a decline in noble influence upon its conduct.

Some of these observations are well founded. The long occupation of northern France by the Lancastrian kings could never have been carried out without the active participation of men, many of them not yet noble, performing the tasks of their captains who, as noblemen with lands in England, had to return every so often to their estates to see to their upkeep. In this case it was the prolongation of war which gave an opportunity to men lacking landed ties in England to show how important their presence in France could be. For if the majority of the great nobility joined Henry V on his first expedition to France in 1415, such support could not long be maintained. By the end of the reign it was already falling off, and while Henry VI had much noble support for his coronation expedition in 1430–1, those who continued to serve him in the French war in the years to come constituted a relatively small group of men. In allotting commands, both English and French kings had to recognise that the extension of war was making considerable demands upon the nobility, and that changes were being forced upon them.

It is sometimes argued, too, that developments of a technological nature eventually forced the decline of the nobility as a fighting force. The successes of the English archers at the great battles of the Hundred Years War appear to point to that conclusion. Froissart's account of the way in which many of the leading French nobility, by going forward at the battle of Crécy, in effect chose the likelihood of death to a dishonourable flight, suggests to the modern reader a group more intent upon self-immolation than upon the serious business of achieving victory through order and discipline. But the protective armour upon which a mounted knight and his horse, both very vulnerable in battle, depended did not remain undeveloped. The middle years of the fourteenth century saw the change from mail armour to plate, while the coming century or so witnessed many improvements in design, so that arrows, bolts, and pikes were met with glancing surfaces which, like the changes in architecture intended to counter the effect of the cannon ball, caused the deflection of the missile away from its target. Such developments, to which can be added improvements in the quality of steel used in the making of armour; the ability, as a consequence, to abandon the use of the shield, thereby freeing the left arm; and the development of special rests which permitted the use of a much heavier lance, meant that the cavalryman, far from being an outmoded liability on the field, remained an indispensable element of the army, one whose value was, as we have seen, enhanced by training and by association with men using other weapons. The long-lasting value of cavalry as a 'follow-up' force after a battle was shown on several occasions: at Verneuil in 1424 and, half a century later, in the battles involving the French, the Swiss and Charles the Bold, duke of Burgundy.

It is arguable that a decline in the traditional role of the military nobility in war was presaged by the ever-greater use made of artillery, that most 'un-noble' and indiscriminate causer of death, which claimed among its victims several great noblemen, among them the Bastard of Bourbon, killed at Soisson in 1414; Thomas, earl of Salisbury ('a worthi werrioure amonge all Cristen men...slayne at the sege of Orliaunce with a Gonné', as the author of the *Brut* reported the event);[7] John Talbot, earl of Shrewsbury, killed at Castillon in July 1453; and Jacques de Lalaing, 'le bon chevalier', killed in the very same month at the siege of Poeke, near Ghent. It is undeniable that artillery was making progress, and that its development was one of the major changes associated with the conduct of war at this time. But a sense of proportion must be maintained, and to regard artillery as an alternative to cavalry would be a mistake. The vision of Talbot and his mounted companions being mown down by an enfilade of artillery (as they were) was not typical of the time. The action smacked too much of the grandiose, if futile, gesture of the French nobility at Crécy just over a century earlier.

By and large, the occasions when the nobility might exploit a situation as cavalry and those when artillery could be used to best effect were not the same. One arm was valuable in certain circumstances, the other in

---

[7] *The Brut*, II, 454.

different ones. It would be more profitable to relate the temporary decline in the use of cavalry to other factors. The wars of this period presented little opportunity to shock troops fighting on horseback. In the fourteenth century the Fabian tactics of the *chevauchée* found greater favour on both sides, although there were notable exceptions when the heavy cavalry did play a major role. Above all, it must be recalled that, at least in the fifteenth century, military objectives could best be achieved through siege warfare, which gave the cavalry less opportunity than it had enjoyed before. It is to these factors, rather than to artillery itself, that we should turn if we wish to see which arms were proving to be of the greatest significance in the war.

But one thing is clear. Knightly warfare, if it no longer enjoyed the supremacy of past centuries, was far from dead. It was still there, and would be used to good effect in the relatively near future when the pitched battle returned as the more usual way of deciding the outcome of wars. In 1494, it is as well to remember, at least one half of the army which Charles VIII led into Italy was composed of heavy cavalry.

LEADERSHIP

It is evident that the success achieved by any army depends very much upon the quality of its leadership, a subject much discussed by writers of the day. There were two closely related matters which concerned men of the late Middle Ages. One was the recognition that leadership was of prime importance if discipline was to be maintained and armies kept together as teams rather than as collections of individuals. The other was to ask who were to be the leaders of armies, and by what criteria they might claim to lead.

On the first of these the influence of the ancient world was to be considerable. Ever since the twelfth century a particular form of didactic literature, an instruction manual written for princes giving them both moral and practical advice on how best to rule those under their care, had been developing. Reasonably enough, princes required to be taught how to make war, and since many of the authors of these works were clerics, they turned to what were the standard handbooks on war to find the information they needed. Broadly, such advice came in two forms. One was the collection of anecdotes, culled from Greek and Roman history, which made points of military importance: armies should avoid having their backs to a river when confronting the enemy in battle (Bertrand du Guesclin ignored this advice, with fatal results, at Nájera in April 1367); or, attempts should be made to manoeuvre armies so that the sun shone in the enemy's eyes. These maxims, many of them reflecting nothing more than common sense, and taken from the recorded experience of the past, were to be found mainly in two works: the *Facta et dicta memorabilia* of Valerius Maximus, written in the first century AD, and the *Stratagemata* of Frontinus, composed in the same century by a man who had been for a short while Roman governor of Britain. Both works were to be translated from Latin into the vernacular languages in the course of the fourteenth and fifteenth centuries; both were known in military circles; and both may have had some influence on the formation of changing attitudes to leadership.

More important, however, was the most read handbook on the military art, the *De re militari* of Vegetius, compiled in the late fourth century AD. It was to this work that most writers of manuals on the exercise of princely authority turned if they wanted to learn how war should be fought. Vegetius was important less for his technical advice than for the general philosophical message on the conduct of war which his work contained. For, like Frontinus, he set great store by leadership, the moral qualities required of those who aspired to it, and the experience of war which they required to achieve it. In brief, the good leader, the man who could inspire his army, not merely he who could avoid the obvious pitfalls of generalship which Frontinus had pointed out, might be born with certain inherent qualities, but these had to be developed in the only way that could lead to success, through practice and experience.

There was implied, in what Vegetius wrote, a most important message: leaders did not choose themselves, but had to be chosen. Put into the social context of the late Middle Ages this meant that the class which had traditionally provided the leadership of armies was having its position, founded largely on social factors, questioned if not undermined. For the drift of the argument was essentially that men did not assume leadership, but that it was granted to them according to criteria which took merit and experience, as well as birth and social standing, into consideration. We may see this idea reflected in a number of ways. When John Barbour, archdeacon of Aberdeen, wrote his long verse account of the career of Robert Bruce, king of Scots, about 1380, he emphasised that his hero's successes against the English stemmed from his military qualities, his understanding of his men, his appreciation of the tactics required for victory, in a word his 'professionalism' as a man in arms. Likewise, the lives of other soldier-heroes of the period, the Black Prince, du Guesclin, even that of Henry V, although written in the chivalric vein, stress that these men were successful largely because their inherent qualities of leadership had benefited from training and experience. Similarly we may note that the feeling which was so openly exhibited against the French nobility after the battle of Poitiers reflected something of a growing opinion that, in spite of tradition, the nobility had no absolute right to assume positions of responsibility within the army. If they exercised them, it should be because they had earned them.

The historian is entitled to regard the matter of leadership as an 'issue' in the minds of the men of this time. We cannot ignore the fact that long-held attitudes were in the process of change. War was too important to be left to those who, by tradition, had been charged with supervising it. This discussion – if we may call it that – was part of a wider, on-going debate of what constituted true nobility. Was it birth and lineage, or could a man acquire nobility, and if so, how? Was it something which could be conferred, by means of an act of dubbing, or by the issue of a patent? And, if so, did the assumption of nobility mean that a man must act nobly to merit his new position? Such problems received considerable attention at this time; it is clear that nothing was being taken for granted.

How far was reality influenced by such ideas? Certainly, the decline of the feudal force did not lead to the demise of the traditional leadership in war. In both England and France, at the beginning of the Hundred Years War, the command structures were broadly similar. At the head of each were the kings, advised by men of martial experience who might be their kin or, at least, members of the nobility who frequented the courts. Beneath them, in France, there existed an ordered and fairly hierarchical structure which saw to the day-to-day defence of the country, from those with wide territorial jurisdictions to those who might be sent to a particular area, town or castle to organise its defence in time of crisis. By and large, the more important a command (importance being judged by the size of territorial authority, or, more appropriately in time of peace, by the numbers of men involved) the more likely it was to be given to a man who had achieved it as a result of attendance at court. For it was at court, as the more astute realised, that positions of power and wealth were to be found.

In time of war the presence of a king on campaign was an asset to be exploited. Not only did it give prestige and add a sense of urgency to an undertaking, it also exerted the pressure of old feudal practice upon vassals to join their lord in person. Expeditions led by a king were regarded as being of greater importance and were invariably larger than those led by others, however exalted in rank a royal lieutenant might be. There are numerous examples of kings themselves leading in battle. Philip VI did so at Crécy in 1346; John II was captured at the battle of Poitiers in 1356; Charles VII personally led the assault on Pontoise in

1441; while on the English side Edward III and Henry V provide us with excellent examples of the martial qualities demonstrated by certain kings.

The command structure, then, began at court and centred around the king. This fact, and the importance of royal patronage in the granting of military authority, gave a considerable advantage to those whose birth gave them natural access to kings.[8] In France the brothers of Charles V, Louis, duke of Anjou, John, duke of Berry, and Philip, duke of Burgundy, all gained military advantage for themselves, their clients and dependants from their close relationship with successive kings. In England, Edward III was to make the fullest use of the military capabilities of his sons, in particular of Edward, Black Prince, whose employment in the war stressed the importance to the family of their father's claim to the French throne. Such a policy of employing royal sons or brothers continued under the Lancastrians, as all four of Henry IV's sons fought in France, and three were to die in that country.

Beneath the very greatest in the land, others were ready to act in positions of command when circumstances, such as war on a number of fronts, demanded it. In France whose who held high command, sometimes as *lieutenants du roi*, were usually princes or men who had achieved the rank of banneret, those senior knights whose swallow-tailed pennons had been cut to the square banners of their new rank. In England, too, the members of the highest nobility, from dukes to earls, gave service and exercised commands throughout the war. Edward III always recognised the importance of noble support in his wars, and, both in his reign and in that of his grandson, Richard II who succeeded him in 1377, the nobility led from the front.

We should be careful, however, to emphasise that the nobility (or *noblesse*, as we would term it in a French context) also had its high, middling and lower ranks. The highest nobility were only very few in numbers, so that when we speak of their hold upon military commands we must, consciously or not, include those who had inherited relatively low noble rank or who had only risen that far through their own efforts. These men were, largely, in a class apart, for even the English knight could be a man of importance in the county society in which he mixed. As war developed and the need for multiple commands increased, it was to such men that the monarchies of both England and France turned. They proved to have a vital, if at times unspectacular, role to play in the organisation of war. If the great aristocracy was responsible for providing large contingents for the war (and, in England, at least, it was

---

[8] See J. B. Henneman, 'The military class and the French monarchy in the late Middle Ages', *A.H.R.*, 83 (1978), 946–65.

they who, after the king, provided the largest) the work of raising these soldiers was often done by men of local knowledge and influence who subcontracted with the royal captains to raise the troops required. For the raising of armies depended upon networks of connection, based upon bonds of vassalage, regional influence, family and office. In this matter the lower nobility had a crucial role to play.

It went further than that. Because of its sometimes precarious economic position, no rank would refuse to accept the king's wage. Many turned to war as a serious, full-time occupation, while others, constituting a large proportion of the lower nobility, saw military service at some time or other. As a result of this, their professional commitment to arms grew: in France, in the second half of the fourteenth century, some esquires (men on the very fringe of *noblesse*) were promoted over the heads of knights, whose numbers in the French army declined anyhow after about 1380, a suggestion that professionalism was coming to be well regarded. And in the persons of men such as Bertrand du Guesclin, Sir Thomas Dagworth, Sir Robert Knolles and Sir Hugh Calveley, the lower ranks of the aristocracy asserted themselves even further. For these were the real 'professionals' who, at certain times in the war, took over either as commanders appointed by the crown or as leaders of groups of freelance soldiers who could ignore royal orders and get away with it. Such men depended upon success for support: for while du Guesclin might play upon his Breton origin to gather a force (or *route*) around him, the English could not do so with the same ease, and therefore came to rely upon their reputations to draw men to their service. These were the first men of less than fully aristocratic background to gain prominence through their merit.

By the fifteenth century the higher ranks of the nobility had taken over again. In France the factionalism from which the country suffered was largely inspired by the nobility, so that command of the army, as the tragedy experienced at Agincourt in 1415 demonstrated, was chiefly in the hands of noble leaders who gave the army a character as noble as it had had in the 1330s. If the same could be said of the English army (with this difference, that the nobility was totally committed to Henry V, who had complete control over it) matters were to change under the rule of the duke of Bedford, acting in the name of the young Henry VI. First, a rift grew between the royal council in England and those whose daily task it was to face the French in France. Secondly, as the war became less lucrative (with fewer expeditions into enemy territory) and the needs of defence came to dominate military activity, so the glamour of war which had undoubtedly existed both in the previous century and under Henry V, began to diminish. Members of the high aristocracy took turns to rule Normandy, with mixed success. The number of places which needed guarding and which required the presence of a person of authority meant that, in some cases, men of military talent and experience, but not necessarily of high birth, were given positions of considerable responsibility. The exigencies of war were such that those with long years of service to their name (and there were probably more of them in the fifteenth than in the fourteenth century) almost inevitably found themselves in positions of command. And because of a decline in the number of knights in the English army by 1450, it was upon those of lower social status that many of these commands devolved.

In the mid-1440s, Charles VII organised major reforms within the French army. The aim appears to have been two-fold: to reassert the authority of the crown to appoint to military commands and, by a ruthless dismissal of the majority of commanders who had come to assume such commands, to make the army once more an efficient weapon of state in royal hands. The exercise was remarkably successful. Most of those whom the king preserved in office were men of the middle nobility, men whose experience would enable them to take effective charge of those placed under them. The king was fortunate: he had plenty from whom to choose, and he could afford to take only the best into his service.

If, then, we recall that there were degrees of nobility and aristocracy, we can admit that the leadership of French and English armies during the Hundred Years War was very largely noble. Both in the giving of counsel and in the recruitment of forces and, later, on campaign and in battle, the nobility played a dominant role as the servants of their respective kings. This was the traditional pattern which one would expect to see continued, as indeed it was, into the sixteenth century. Yet, as was suggested earlier in this section, new ideas were being bandied about. In a climate of opinion which laid greater stress upon collective success than upon the fame or reputation of any one individual, could the desire for fame, which might impair the effectiveness of the army, survive? The answer lay not in trying to play down the search for glory in war, but in channelling these energies towards the service of the king who represented the public good and honour of a nation or people. After 1400, it has been noted, lawyers in the Parlement of Paris consistently tried to show the respectability of their soldier-clients by underlining their service to the king and the public good: '...a longuement servy le roy'; '...tient frontier contre les enemis'; '...il a esté grevé car lui estant en expedicion pour la chose publique' are phrases which, when used regularly, tell us something of the values of the society in which they are uttered, and of the soldier's role in it.

The emphasis was now to be increasingly on service, given to and paid for by the state, which assumed the right to appoint its commanders (this was made easier by the fact that all accepted the state's money for service in war) and to demand that it got the best available in return for its money. The leaders of its armies, appointed by commission (as Charles VII appointed his chief lieutenants in 1445) rather than by the 'natural' right of birth, were to become its officers for whom advancement would be a recognition of merit. The logical outcome of this slow change of direction was to come later, but not much later. By the sixteenth century, no longer assuming that it had a right to positions of leadership in the armies, the aristocracy began to attend military academies where it learned the art of making war. This is what the work of Vegetius and others was destined to achieve.[9]

MERCENARIES

Into a pattern of military administration which may appear deceptively well organised there stepped a class of soldier, the mercenary, whose presence to people of the late Middle Ages meant destruction and disorder. While they made a deep impression upon French society in this age, it should not be forgotten that mercenaries constituted a phenomenon encountered elsewhere, in Spain, in Germany and, in particular, in the country dominated by merchant states, Italy. In that country they first appeared in the mid-thirteenth century, groups of men who, under the leadership of enterprising leaders, contracted (hence the name *condottiere* which they were given) with individual city states which lacked their own armies but had the funds necessary to pay them, to guard their territory and maintain a measure of order. From such relatively peaceful origins they came, by the end of the century, to undertake external war for their employers, pitting themselves against other such groups (the Companies or *routiers*), in which might be found not only Italians and Germans, but Flemings, Spaniards, Frenchmen and, at times, a few Englishmen. By 1300 such men were coming to form an essential part of the Italian military and political scene. For us, their appearance elsewhere in Europe constitutes an early example of the principle of payment for military service which, as we have seen, became an integral element of the formation of royal armies in England and France in these years.

Such mercenaries were specialist fighters, owing no firm allegiance, men who fought for pay and what they could get out of war. They were

[9] See Hale, *Renaissance war studies*, chs. 8–10.

specialists in that they were full-time soldiers; war was their life. They were specialists, too, in that they favoured one type of war, that of surprise in which the dawn raid was more effective than the siege. Since their success depended upon their mobility, they could not take cumbersome engines with them; instead, they developed military skills sometimes rather different from those employed by more conventional soldiers. Nor were these men, like their predecessors in Italy, always concerned with the niceties of loyalty. John Hawkwood, as leader of the White Company, spent years fighting against the interests of Florence before entering Florentine service: changing sides did not unduly worry him. What attracted men like him was the prospect of pay in return for war service. It was, then, peace or truce which threatened their existence, and it was because of the termination of hostilities between England and France which resulted from the treaty of Brétigny in 1360, followed as this was in 1364 by the ending of the Navarrese challenge to the royal authority in Normandy and the war of Breton succession, that France, Italy and Spain were to be hosts to the Companies in the 1360s. The problem arose again thirty years later, when their energies were channelled off on a crusade which ended in defeat at Nicopolis in 1396, and yet again in 1444–5 when, after the truce of Tours, the 'Ecorcheurs' who were, as their name implied, 'skinning' France, were led off for a while to Switzerland and the imperial lands. On all three occasions, peace had created unemployment among soldiers who were looking for adventure and pay. No ruler, possibly other than in Italy, had the means or the wish to employ large forces when there was no war.

To no other group of soldiers functioning in this period was leadership a factor of such prime importance. Freelance soldiers that they were, they depended upon their captains for recruitment, organisation, distribution of booty, and pay. The form of 'unofficial' war which they fought was more characteristic of brigandage and open robbery, but it would be wrong to assume that those who constituted the Companies were all, of necessity, men of criminal background or low degree. Indeed, the opposite was frequently nearer the truth, for their leaders were often members of the lower nobility, driven to making war in this way by economic factors and, in some cases, by being younger sons with little hope of inheritance. The members themselves are more difficult to assess and describe. But one important factor is clear: the English element was a considerable one. By the mid-fourteenth century, the predominance of those of English origin was, indeed, so marked that the term 'Inglese' and 'Les Anglais' became virtually generic names for these groups. Yet many came from elsewhere, notably from Brittany and Gascony. As Philippe de Mézières wrote in the late fourteenth century, some may well have come from those members of the lower nobility who did not normally go to war except when summoned by the king, but who, in certain cases, were now being forced to take up arms as a business. Others were men of 'petit état' who, out of daring or a wish to commit pillage, took to this way of life. Others still were from the very lowest ranks of the Church who preferred the more exciting life of the camp. One of the most notorious, Arnaud de Cervole, was not known as 'the Archpriest' for nothing.

Generally speaking the Companies had a bad name among the populations for their greed, unscrupulous attitude to the law, and apparent contempt for the forces of order. In Italy, it was said, an 'Inglese italianato è un diavolo incarnato', an Italianate Englishman is the devil in person. Their methods were often far from respecting the chivalric norms of war. Roamers of the countryside, surprise was their chief weapon, great daring being shown in what some regarded as the finest military feats of all, the capture of walled towns and castles which were then ransomed, having perhaps been used in the meanwhile as bases for military activity further afield. Yet, for all that, many of these men, either singly or as members of a larger group, entered royal service and did well in it. In the fourteenth century, for instance, Arnaud de Cervole was in and out of royal employment and was actually appointed royal chamberlain in 1363, while his son had the duke of Burgundy as his godfather. Similarly, Amiel de Baux held office under the French crown, and was serving in the royal army when it entered Aquitaine in 1371. On the English side Hugh Calveley, having at first sold his services in Spain to du Guesclin, changed sides and served the Black Prince there in 1367; later he was to join John of Gaunt, and he even worked for Richard II in France. Sir Robert Knolles, likewise, fought both for himself and for his king. In a similar way the French crown was able to make good use of the experience of such men, the Valois intervention in Castile in the mid-1360s, under the leadership of du Guesclin (who understood their mentality well), being based largely on the services of these mercenaries.

In the fifteenth century, the freelance soldiers had an important part to play in the war. Henry V and his son employed some whose names can be spotted on muster rolls, not infrequently fulfilling a specialist capacity, especially in the artillery trains. François de Surienne certainly showed himself capable of independent activity before throwing in his lot for some years with Henry VI, whom he served before being elected a Knight of the Garter.

But it was in the French army of the first half of the century that the mercenaries were most prominent. In the decade 1420–30, a sizeable proportion of Charles VII's army was composed of Scots who fought at both Cravant and Verneuil, a strong contingent of Genoese also taking part in this second battle against the English. The king also depended to a considerable degree upon individuals who, like the leaders of the companies of the previous century, served in the royal army: Poton de Xaintrailles was for a period a 'véritable routier', pillaging in different parts of France before accepting office under Charles VII; Antoine de Chabannes, a captain of *routiers*, at one time had command of 1,000 horsemen before finding employment under the crown. These, and others, like Hawkwood in Italy, fought against authority before joining it. Some of them received high command in the mid-fifteenth century, and some introduced their own characteristics to the fighting of war. Etienne de Vignolles, known by the name of La Hire which his Burgundian enemies had given him, brought off a spectacular stroke with the capture of Château-Gaillard, on the river Seine, in 1430, while in the following year Ambroise de Loré and his band travelled across much of Normandy to attack a fair near Caen, before retreating in good order with their prisoners. Such *coups* gave the perpetrators of these daring acts something of a romantic image in the popular mind. Some assumed, or were given, names other than their own: Jacques d'Espailly was known as Forte-Epice; La Hire had a cannon named after him, as did Guillaume de Flavy; while, in the eighteenth century, La Hire was to become the named knave of hearts on French playing cards. These were the fighting heroes of their day, whose exploits lived long in the popular imagination.

FORTIFICATION AND ARTILLERY

We have seen that war leaders of the late Middle Ages sought the achievement of their military aims either through the devastation of the countryside or, in certain circumstances, by seeking to gain control of the towns and castles which dominated it. Because an army's main aim may have been the devastation of land, the destruction of its produce, and the seizure of moveable property, there can be little doubt that war's chief victims were those who, if they did not live within reasonable distance of a defended town or garrisoned castle, ran great risk to their personal safety. It is true that small local fortifications, sometimes churches adapted at great expense by the addition of towers, parapets, walls and even moats, might bring some measure of safety, at least against small bands of soldiers or evil-doers.[10] Yet since these cannot

[10] N. A. R. Wright, 'French peasants in the Hundred Years War', *H.T.*, 33 (June 1983), 38–42.

have presented much of an obstacle, they were of little or no use against large and determined forces of men, against whom only walled towns and castles constituted reasonably sure places of safety.

We have also remarked how, at least in the fourteenth century, campaign leaders, often inadequately equipped as they were, commonly avoided attacking well-fortified towns and castles. In a short campaigning season curtailed by either seasonal or financial considerations, or by both, the advantage did not lie with the attacker who, if he began a siege, risked being caught between the place he was seeking to capture and (a constant fear) a force coming to relieve the besieged. Further, he would also require some very heavy and unwieldy equipment, including siege engines; even these might not bring the desired success. It might require a stroke of luck, such as a shortage of provisions or water among the besieged, or an act of treason, to deliver the well-defended place into enemy hands. In hostile territory a siege was not lightly undertaken; if certain reasonable precautions had been taken, those who sought refuge inside a town or castle could reasonably hope to survive, in particular if their refuge were a town which, with its generally greater size and more generous ameneties which favoured the defender, presented a besieger with a greater challenge than did even the best defended castle.

In France the escalation of war in the 1340s (after some four generations of relative peace) led to a number of significant developments. Before this time, as Froissart was to note and Edward III to experience, many towns had no proper defences other than what could be provided by ditches and water works, neither of which would cause a determined army much trouble. Nor was there proper central control over the building and maintenance of fortifications, many of which were sadly out-of-date or in bad need of repair by the time that the English began to invade France. But by galvanising men into action, the English invasions were to change all that. On royal orders, the towns were directed to see to their defences, and they had to do so by finding their own sources of finance through local effort. At first, much building was done on the cheap. Where possible, material which could be salvaged from old buildings or walls was recycled into the new fortifications, while in many places no indemnity was paid to those who were forced 'pro bono publico' to surrender property on which walls might be built or to provide the open ground, outside a wall, vital for effective defence. At the same time, it is evident that the bulk of the money needed to pay for urban defence had to be raised locally, although, from 1367 onwards, the king of France often allowed a quarter of the value of royal taxes raised in a town to be retained as a contribution towards it. Land was often acquired for little or nothing; in many places the citizens and those living within the jurisdiction of a town gave their services in the building of walls, the equivalent, it may be argued, of a tax intended to cover building expenses. Loans and gifts were sought as contributions. But the biggest and best-organised part of the exercise of fund-raising was undoubtedly the levy of an increasing number of local taxes on the trade of goods, including consumables, of which the most profitable were those imposed on drink, in particular on wine. Always done with royal approval, which was sought beforehand, the collection of such levies emphasised two factors: that the crown's right to tax and to organise the general defence of France was recognised; equally, that, in practice, the responsibility for carrying out defensive projects was left to local initiative and energy. The result, it now appears, was that local administrators, with important defensive budgets to collect and administer, took advantage of the experience thus gained to develop their own powers in particular when, over a period of some decades, taxes originally levied for short periods came to be collected for longer and longer periods, until they became all but permanently established as part of the regular income of a town or city.

Towns, therefore, were coming to assume greater importance as places of defence and refuge for the surrounding countryside. At Reims, for instance, the process of fortification, begun early in the fourteenth century on the orders of Philip IV, was later abandoned, only to be reactivated after the English victory at Crécy. Between 1346 and 1348, and again, after the visitation of the Black Death, between 1356 and 1358, the people of Reims completed the construction of their city's defence, with the gratifying effect that even the king of England, Edward III himself, could not force an entry in the early winter of 1359–60. Elsewhere, too, in different parts of France, this period witnessed much building of urban defences. The walls of Caen were constructed in the years following Edward III's capture of the town in 1346; those of Rouen were begun at the same time on the orders of Philip VI, making the city one of the few properly defended towns, or 'villes closes' of upper Normandy; Avignon's wall was started at the instigation of Pope Innocent VI about 1355; while the defences of Tours, in course of construction in 1356, were probably sufficiently advanced to deter the Black Prince from attacking the town on his *chevauchée* in the summer of that year.

Such building, multiplied many times over, provided France with a network of fortified towns (some of them very large by the standards of the day), impressive traces of which can still be seen today. From the middle years of the fourteenth century, such steps were sufficient to keep all but the most determined attackers at bay. Few commanders would have wished to expend the time and energy required to overcome places so heavily defended.

Change, however, was not far away. While the widespread building of town walls in the second half of the fourteenth century provided a measure of safety against marauding forces (even against the Companies), such fortifications could not be ignored by an enemy bent upon conquest. To the English, when they returned in the fifteenth century, fortified towns provided both a military threat and a challenge which they could not ignore. Paradoxically, therefore, instead of providing refuge for those fleeing from the countryside, the very existence of these fortified towns drew the attention of the invader to them. As the narratives of the siege of Rouen, pursued by Henry V between July 1418 and January 1419, underline, the results, both for the civilians who had sought safety there and for the garrison who had led the resistance, could be devastating.

The existence of walled towns and castles created two problems. Had the invader the means of taking these newly fortified places? Conversely, had the defenders the means of effective resistance? At the time when the Hundred Years war broke out, a defender had a more than even chance of beating off an attack. By the time the war ended, the reverse was probably true. This was in part due to changes and developments in weaponry. Against an immobile target, such as a wall, even the early cannon could inflict quite considerable damage. There are references to such 'gonnes' in accounts of the siege of Berwick as early as 1333, while it is likely that some form of artillery was brought across the sea by the English for the long siege of Calais of 1346–7. During the next generation both old and new siege weapons were to be used in tandem. In 1369 a trebuchet, used for slinging stones, was employed at the siege of La-Roche-sur-Yon, and in 1370 another was in evidence at the siege of Rennes; as late as 1378 another was in use before Cherbourg, having been brought there in pieces and assembled on the spot. Yet three years earlier, at the important siege of nearby Saint-Sauveur-le-Vicomte, the French had used thirty-two cannons, gunstones for them having been conveyed there in carts and by packhorse. These years clearly constituted a period of transition.

The siege of Saint-Sauveur can be regarded as something of a landmark in the development of the practical use of artillery. When Henry V landed for the first time on French soil nearly forty years later, it was soon put beyond doubt that in his artillery he possessed a potential match-winner. While the accounts of the siege of Harfleur in the late summer of 1415 refer to the time-honoured methods of mining and blockade used by the English, pride of place for effectiveness is given to their artillery, which caused both fear and destruction to the beleaguered town. The siege had shown that, with artillery, Henry V had the capability of fulfilling his military ambition. Setting out for France again two years later, the king was described by the anonymous author of the *Brut* as leaving England with 'ordynaunce gadred and welle stuffyd, as longyd to such a ryalle Kinge'.[11] Once again it was the towns and castles of Normandy which attracted Henry, bent, as he was, upon conquest. Yet again the chronicles emphasise the part played by the artillery in the capture of Caen and Falaise and, a little later, in that of Rouen. Thirty years later, the rapid reconquest of the duchy by the French owed much to the threat posed by the French king's artillery against the defences of towns which preferred to surrender than to make a fight of it. Most, it had to be recognised, would have been unable to resist a heavy and sustained bombardment.

Could nothing be done to restore the traditional balance of advantage to the defender? Was there to be no resistance to this 'new' weapon? The suddenness of the increased use of artillery in the third quarter of the fourteenth century is evidenced by the fact that when Gaston Fébus, *vicomte* of Béarn in the Pyrenees, had a network of fortifications constructed between 1365 and 1380 (a period during which many castles were built in France) he must have been building some of the last fortifications to take no account of artillery, which was very soon to compel important developments in the art of defence. For cannons could be fired not only at fortifications but from them, too. As early as 1339, the town of Cambrai had begun to introduce firepower into its defensive system, an exceptionally early example of the use of such techniques. When Henry Yevele designed the west gate at Canterbury in 1378, he included round gunports on the drum towers, gunports having been introduced into England some years earlier. In the same year the town of Southampton, not infrequently threatened by attack from the sea, appointed Thomas Tredington, said to be 'skilled with guns and artillery', to take charge of the municipal armoury.[12] Such examples are taken from the English scene: German towns could provide many more. But modern scholarship has made it clear that it was in France, more so than in England, that urban defensive requirements played a major part in securing the widespread acceptance of artillery as a means of deterring or countering a prospective enemy. All over France, from Lille and Dijon in the north and east to Bordeaux in the south-west, artillery became an essential and accepted part of the growing defensive system

---

[11] *The Brut*, II, 382.
[12] C. Platt, *Medieval Southampton. The port and trading community A.D. 1000–1600* (London: Boston, Mass., 1973), p. 130.

associated with towns. Materials were collected in advance and stored in anticipation of their use; powder slowly got cheaper in the course of the fifteenth century; while many towns employed one or more men to supervise the effective use of artillery in case of attack. As Christine de Pisan was to show in the first quarter of the century, the use of artillery for defensive purposes was now regarded as necessary and normal.

However, resistance to the increasing employment of artillery in the capture of walled towns and castles would be even more effective if it stemmed from a reassessment of architectural design. Largely in the hope of preventing or deterring attempts at scaling, walls had traditionally been built high: thickness and solidity had been sacrificed to this need, for walls could not be both high and thick. Yet, with the advent of cannon, thickness was precisely the main characteristic which the defender demanded of the wall which protected him. The onus now lay upon the architect to come up with new designs and new ideas with which to counter the rapidly growing effectiveness of artillery aided, from about 1430, by the reversion to the use of cast-iron shot which, although more expensive than stone shot, did not shatter on impact, could be made more uniformly in greater quantities (the making of stone shot was, to say the least, laborious) and in smaller calibre, thereby increasing efficiency by reducing the need for very large and unwieldy cannon.

The architectural solution was ultimately to be found and perfected in Italy in the sixteenth century, but the contributions of English and French experience to these discoveries was not negligible.[13] By lowering the height of the wall, and thereby enabling it to be built more thickly, it could be made more effective in both defence and counter-attack. To this could be added the possibility of building the towers only as high as the wall itself, thus enabling the cannon used for defence to be moved along its length (now on one level) to whichever part it was most needed. Furthermore, as Yevele had shown at Canterbury, the defensive value of the round tower was becoming better appreciated; even if it did not always deflect a cannon shot aimed at it, such a tower could withstand an impact better than could a straight-facing surface. In addition, the need to achieve both vertical and lateral defence was also dealt with. Machicolations, usually regarded as a sign of nobility, had their practical value in that they permitted vertical defence against those who might have reached the dead ground near a wall, and might be setting about digging or mining under it. At the same time the building of what were to become bastions, towers standing out from the line of the wall,

---

[13] Hale, *Renaissance war studies*, chs. 1–6; H. L. Turner, *Towns defences in England and Wales* (London, 1971); J. H. Harvey, *Henry Yevele* (London, 1944).

enabled defenders to fire all round, and in particular laterally, against approaching men or machines, as the design for Bodiam Castle in Sussex, which, like Cooling Castle in Kent, was built at the time of the French invasion scares of the 1380s, clearly shows. The building, about 1440, at the Mont-Saint-Michel, of a form of bastion not dissimilar to that to be developed in Italy, underlines how this matter of overcoming the defensive problems created by the development of artillery was being dealt with. By the sixteenth century the initiative long held by the defender, surrendered in the late fourteenth century, had been largely regained.

NAVAL OBJECTIVES

Strangely, and certainly wrongly, the history of the naval war between France and England at the end of the Middle Ages is an under-estimated subject, its contribution not yet fully studied by historians. The apparent ineffectiveness of naval forces, particularly when contrasted with the vital role which they came to play in the sixteenth century, may have turned students against the subject. Yet, the fact remains that, although we are dealing with an age when history was not decided by battles at sea, the first major battle of the Hundred Years War was fought at sea in June 1340. The subject has an importance in the history of war at this period which merits emphasis.

During the thirteenth and fourteenth centuries, France developed what was nothing less than a long-term naval strategy. In 1200 the king of France, ruling in Paris, was virtually land-locked, the county of Ponthieu, around Boulogne, being his only access to the sea. With the conquest of Normandy, however, Philip-Augustus gained control of a long stretch of coastline opposite England, from which he could also 'oversee' Brittany, while access from the mouth of the Seine gave him a means of developing trade and a wider market. It also meant that in 1213, and again in 1215–17, the French king was able to take the war to England, a thing unheard of only a generation earlier. Ten years later the French, now ruled by Louis VIII, broke out in another direction, this time in the Bay of Biscay, with the capture of La Rochelle in 1224. Twenty years later still, under Louis IX and with the needs of the crusade in mind, a port was built at Aigues-Mortes on the Mediterranean, to be used for commercial and, even more so, for military purposes. The vessels used by the French had to be brought from Marseille and Genoa. These were still days of innovation.

It is all too easy to see the development of France in terms of an inexorable and inevitable process of expansion from early beginnings in the Ile de France around Paris to the country we know today. Yet it may be argued that part of the process was a search for the open sea which France had been denied until the early years of the thirteenth century, and that the desire to win control of the peripheral duchies of Aquitaine, Brittany and Normandy was but an aspect of a wider policy which included an ambition to have access to, and control of, the ports on the Atlantic, Mediterranean and Channel coasts for military as well as for commercial reasons.

As the rivalry with England grew in the late thirteenth century, so the sea, which separated the two countries, took on added importance. By 1294 there already existed at Rouen, on the river Seine, a shipyard controlled by the king and employing specialist ship-builders brought in from Genoa. These were the signs for the future, but at the moment only signs. When Philip IV tried to attack England in 1295, he still had to seek transport ships from the Baltic ports and from those which he could seize in French harbours, together with sailors from Flanders. But, as the king found, he could not rely upon the Flemings; their links with England were too strong for them to act with determination against those who supplied them with the wool upon which their own economic prosperity depended.

The fourteenth century showed how valuable access to the sea, and in particular to northern waters, was to be for France. The sea coasts provided sailors to man the vessels used in war, a large number of which were requisitioned fishing or trading vessels, as the records make clear. The ports, such as Harfleur, at the mouth of the Seine, could develop ship-building facilities, and the control of the lower Seine effectively made Rouen into a sea port and a shipyard. It was probably the success of these steps which, in 1337, caused Philip VI to decide upon the building of a naval base at La Rochelle, a base which was to be ceded to the English by the terms of the treaty of Brétigny, thereby underlining the significance of ports as pawns in international diplomacy. In addition, we should not forget the value of the sea as a source of fish which provided an essential dietary element to people of the Middle Ages. Many French people, not merely Parisians, benefited from fish caught in the Channel or nearby waters.

At the begining of the war with England the French crown, denied the use of the ports and coastline of Brittany and Aquitaine, had to witness the English army enjoying access to both, and using them as bastions on the continental mainland from which to launch attacks into territories ruled by the king of France. In the fifteenth century the problem became more acute. Part of the strategic significance of the English occupation of Normandy, and of the alliance with the dukes of Burgundy, lay in the zone of control which was thereby created: for not only did the English rule both sides of the Channel and the Seine below Paris, but their Burgundian allies controlled the upper reaches above the capital. In terms of policy it thus became essential to try to weaken the English grip upon both the sea and the main rivers, such as the Oise, which flowed into the Seine, by seeking to detach the Burgundians from their English links. The vital role (which contemporaries fully appreciated) played by such relatively small ports as Le Crotoy, at the mouth of the river Somme, in the period 1420–50, together with the fact that the ports of Dieppe and Harfleur were among the first places to be snatched from English control in 1435 (leaving them with Cherbourg as the only port from which they could maintain regular links with England between 1435 and 1440, a vital period in the military history of the occupation), shows how important the Burgundian connection was to both main protagonists as they struggled to acquire and maintain a measure of control over the sea.

The French crown, it is rightly argued, had a definite policy with relation to the sea which it had followed since the early thirteenth century. Ports it must have, particularly in the Channel. One of the last examples for this period was the conscious creation of a further naval base at Granville, in western Normandy, called the 'clef du pays par mer et par terre' by Charles VII in the charter by which he granted privileges to those who would come to settle there to keep it for the good of France.[14] But there must also be ships, and while France could not provide a sufficient number of them for herself, she was obliged (as the English were on some occasions) to seek them elsewhere. Thus both Castile and Genoa became suppliers of galleys which often fought on the French side, notably in 1416 when the Genoese provided part of the fleet which suffered defeat at the hands of the English at the battle of the Seine, off Harfleur. If one is seeking an example of a naval battle which was to have consequences, one need look no further than this one. At stake lay more than the future of the English garrison in the town which the French were besieging and blockading by land and sea. By sinking several Genoese vessels and taking others captive, the English made sure that the port remained in English hands, that (for some while) they would control the wide estuary of the Seine, and that they might, in the phrase of the day, 'sweep' the French off its waters by patrolling the sea. This was not simply lucky, nor was it unimportant. It emphasised that there were men, in both France and England, who understood the role of the sea in war and of the part which it might play in determining the outcome of future English expeditions to France. After 1416, the English had reason to be optimistic.

[14] *Ordonnances des rois de France de la troisième race*, XIII (1782), 459–61.

Indeed, there is no doubt that control of French mainland ports was vitally important to the English, and that much diplomacy in the course of the war was concerned with securing and maintaining access to the use of their facilities. In this respect England's relations with Brittany were likely to be of great importance, not only for the positive reason that a friendly duke of Brittany would allow the use of his duchy as a stepping-off place into the mainland, but for the negative one that a hostile duke might cause untold harm to English maritime interests, both military and commercial, by failing to stop the activities of Breton pirates and privateers whose ships gave much trouble at sea, as complaints in Parliament and in some of the political literature of the time, notably *The Libelle of Englyshe Polycye*, testify.

In the case of the Low Countries, England had a similar interest which was both military and commercial. The capture of Calais by Edward III in 1347 had given England virtual control of the Straits. But it was a control which required active defence, to which the Cinque Ports contributed a good deal, particularly in the late fourteenth century. As a trade depot and naval base, Calais was to serve as an entrepôt for trade in and out of England, and as a back door, which armies might and did use, into France. But so physically restricted was the Calais area, and so often was it under French pressure, that for long years at a time all the needs of the garrison, whether in provisions or materials, had to be shipped in from England. In such conditions every effort had to be made to keep the sea passages open – and safe.

The military involvement of England in continental war meant an unusually high concern for achieving and maintaining some measure of control of the sea. Trade was vulnerable to attack, and cases of piracy were common. Fishing, too, required protection, for the activities of hostile seamen could easily lead to the loss of catches and vessels, for which there was no insurance provision. The defence of the coastline had also to be seen to, and was not infrequently found to be wanting, most particularly when small forces of enemy soldiers attacked the English shore and ravaged villages and towns which they found undefended. So important was this regarded that in the final quarter of the fourteenth century a system of coastal defence on land was developed, essentially a second line to carry the burden of defence once the enemy had managed to effect a landing on English soil.[15] Likewise, at the time when armies and their accompanying equipment were being shipped over to France, efforts were made (as they were by Henry V in 1417) to keep the sea-

---

[15] See Hewitt, *The organization of war under Edward III*, ch.1; J. R. Alban, 'English coastal defence: some fourteenth-century modifications within the system', *Patronage, the crown, and the provinces in later medieval England*, ed. R. A. Griffiths (Gloucester, 1981), pp. 57–78.

lanes clear by sending out other ships on patrol, thereby ensuring a minimum of safety for those going to fight abroad.

The appreciation of the growing role of the sea in war can be observed in the positive attitudes of some kings of France and England to this matter. Kings neglected the sea at their peril. In England, as has been shown, both Edward III and Richard II reacted to mercantile opinion expressed in Parliament by impressing large numbers of ships for purposes of defence, such fleets at times employing almost as many soldiers at sea as did field armies on land, all at great expense.[16] The development of the Clos des Galées at Rouen, under the patronage of the French crown (notably in the reign of Charles V), is matched by the steps taken by Henry V to develop a royal shipyard at Southampton, so much better positioned than the traditional one at the Tower of London, and by the appointment of royal officers to supervise its working and administration. Historians have tended to ignore these important developments, which implied the growing need for a small supply of vessels specially built for war (like heavy artillery, these could only be afforded by the crown), the facilities for their maintenance, and the growing appreciation that England's commercial interests should be defended by ships built for that purpose. Furthermore, sieges which were in effect blockades by both land and sea (Calais by the English in 1346–7; Harfleur by the French and their allies in 1416) show that an understanding of the value of the naval arm, used in conjunction with that of land forces, was developing.

The importance attached to the sea by more reflective Englishmen and Frenchmen at the end of the Hundred Years War may also be seen in two works: *The Libelle of Englyshe Polycye*, written about 1437, and *Le débat des hérauts d'armes*, composed about 1455. The first, a vigorous piece of polemic written in verse, leaves the reader in no doubt about the strongly-held views of its anonymous author on the very positive policy which the royal council was urged to adopt towards the sea which, if England were not careful, foreigners from many nations would use for purposes, both commercial and military, detrimental to English interests. Among those whom the author singled out for praise were Edward III, who recalled his victory against the French at Sluys in June 1340 by introducing a fighting ship onto the noble of England, and Henry V, who built great ships and dealt firmly with those who were causing trouble to English shipping. Action for the good of England was something which the writer admired, and he demanded it to forestall the enemy.

[16] J. W. Sherborne, 'The Hundred Years' War. The English navy: shipping and man-power, 1369–1389', *P&P.*, 37 (1967), 163–75.

The French tract, while not primarily concerned with the sea and the exercise of sea power, none the less tried to show not merely France's equality but its superiority over England in matters maritime. No longer might the English call themselves 'roys de la mer', for France had not only good rivers but good ports, too, the list given including the new port of Granville. Moreover, France had good ships in quantity and merchandise in plenty with which to trade. To the author, French superiority in this respect was only one aspect of the more general superiority of his country over the other. It was a conjunction of war and natural conditions which had brought this about. It should not escape our notice that it was not only successes on land but those associated with aspects of the war at sea which had contributed towards the satisfactory situation which he described.

NAVAL FORCES

Unlike war on land, war at sea was not an occupation for which the nobility was trained. Indeed, the author of *Le débat des hérauts d'armes* could state that the French nobility did not regard fighting at sea as being a noble activity: it is perhaps for this reason that naval warfare did not feature in the chronicles in the way that war on land did. Nor did it seem apparent to all that the war fought at sea, the damage which might be inflicted upon enemy vessels and morale, and the consequences which victory at sea could have for those who lived in areas close to coasts, were all part of a wider war which could not be restricted to the fighting on land.

So it was that when the Hundred Years War began, although both the French and the English kingdoms had particular naval objectives which they needed to further for military reasons, neither could be said to have possessed a proper navy. Up to that time the maritime needs of the two countries had not been very demanding. Philip IV was the first French king to try to pursue an active naval war against England. Before his time no king had needed many ships, least of all ships on demand; the great expense both of building and of maintaining them, procedures which required special and costly facilities, had deterred kings from ship-building on a large scale. Furthermore, the organisation associated with the wide use of a major arm was lacking. It was to the credit of Philip IV that he laid the foundations for a dockyard at Rouen, while only a few years later in England, Edward II, whose father had built some galleys, was to possess a small squadron of 'royal' ships. Looking back, we may say that the years around 1300 were to attain some significance in this domain. But to argue that such developments marked anything more than a beginning would be to over-estimate the significance of what was done.

When required for use in war, large numbers of merchant vessels were impressed *ad hoc*. The procedures were simple enough. Royal officers, under the charge of admirals, were despatched to the ports with instructions to impress or requisition vessels for the king's use, whether this was to transport men, animals, or equipment across the sea. The exercise of this right, whose origins went back many centuries, could not always be easily achieved. As in the matter of purveyance (which, in a sense, the requisitioning of ships was) protests and opposition were frequently met, for this kind of procedure disrupted trade and fishing, the two occupations which created a permanent need for ships. Payment was never made for a vessel taken from its owner for royal service; nor was compensation for loss of a ship, or even damage to its equipment, normally given. In brief, requisitioning was unpopular, not least since it was often carried out in the period between spring and autumn when trading and fishing conditions might normally be expected to be better than at other times of the year.

Nor was that all. Once requisitioned, vessels originally built for commercial purposes had to be adapted for military ones. A ship which was to be used mainly for conveying animals abroad needed work done to its hold: special hurdles, for instance, were required to accommodate horses. If a ship was intended for patrolling the sea, it had to be equipped to take part in action against the enemy: the building of castles, fore and aft, and, in the fifteenth century, the possible installation of cannon on the deck (guns were placed below decks, to fire out of 'ports', only in the very first years of the sixteenth century) had to be carried out. The frequent complaint that ships, once requisitioned, were not actually used for several months, thereby denying their owners the use of them in between times, was not always the fault of the wind or weather. Shortages of cash to pay soldiers and sailors, insufficiency of crews, and the slow assembly of retinues to be shipped across the sea often combined to delay ships assembled at ports of concentration.

The kind of ships needed on the two sides of the Channel differed a little. For the English, the main need was initially that of transporting men, horses and weapons to and from the European mainland. The vessels best equipped for this were 'cogs', ships of high sides well suited for commercial traffic from which, indeed, most of them were taken. On the French side, with its needs which did not, generally speaking, include the transportation of armies or invasion troops, a different kind of vessel was more suitable: the galley. This, a fast, flat-bottomed vessel propelled by oars or sail, or both, which could, because of its lack of keel, come very close into land, was essentially a vessel of interception, intended to catch attackers off the coast.[17] But it did serve another purpose. It could cross the open sea, and land on the enemy coast small groups of men who, in raids lasting perhaps a few hours or, at most, a day or two, could do much damage to both enemy property and morale. The inhabitants of the southern coastal counties of England suffered considerably in this respect, in particular in the late 1370s, when several places on the south coast experienced attacks and, in the case of Winchelsea in 1380, virtual destruction.

The French, therefore, set about building galleys, their principal repair yard being the Clos des Galées at Rouen, which came to be developed in the course of the fourteenth century, and which saw its heyday during the successful wars waged by Charles V in the 1370s.[18] By contrast, the English seem to have had fewer ships at this period, although Edward III had some royal ships, and vessels were built for largely defensive purposes. But for the English the system of requisitioning, together with a few ships which might be built in both inland and seaside ports, and those constructed at Bayonne, were sufficient to meet most of their needs. The list of some forty ports which provided 146 vessels, crewed by 2,350 mariners and some 294 boys, to convey Henry of Lancaster and his army from England to Bordeaux in 1347, is impressive.[19] But it does not suggest that any basic change in the traditional means of taking large numbers of soldiers to the continent was yet being considered.

The beginning of the fifteenth century, however, was to see changes in attitudes and practices. Although these had seen their origin in the reign of Henry IV, it was to be in his son's brief reign that something of a revolution (whose effects, however, were not to last) took place. Henry V needed to achieve two things. He had to take action against pirates and sailors who used the port of Harfleur as their main base, and who were encouraged by the French king to carry out raids upon English shipping in the Channel and the English coast. He also needed ships to patrol the Channel and to transport his armies to France. The first he achieved through military means: Harfleur was captured in September 1415 and later successfully defended by the naval victory won by the duke of Bedford in August 1416. The second was achieved by the creation of the first significant royal fleet, an improvement on that of Edward III, which, based in Southampton under the control of a clerk

---

[17] B. Waites, 'The fighting galley', *H.T.*, 18 (1968), 337–43.

[18] A. Merlin-Chazdas (ed.), *Documents relatifs au clos des galées de Rouen et aux armées de mer du roi de France de 1293 à 1418* (2 vols., Paris, 1977–8).

[19] Calculated from Hewitt, *Organization of war*, app. II.

of the king's ships, and enjoying easy access to the Channel, came to number thirty-five vessels, some bought, some captured, others still specially built.[20] With justice Henry V is credited not only with having understood, better than did any of his contemporaries, what were the naval problems which faced England in the early fifteenth century, but also with having done much towards the creation of a fleet of ships, some of them very large, almost 'prestige-type' vessels, which would make it possible for the English to take to sea quickly and thus try to wrest the initiative from any enemy who might be coming against them.

Unfortunately, when Henry V died in 1422, his fleet was already less useful than its royal founder had hoped. In the years which followed, some of his ships (which belonged to the king personally) were sold to repay his debts; others were left so long that they eventually rotted. Yet, writing half a century later, Sir John Fortescue recognised that Henry V had been right: 'though we have not alwey werre uppon the see, yet it shalbe nescessarie that the kynge [Edward IV] have alway some ffloute apon the see, ffor the repressynge off rovers, savynge off owre marchauntes, owre ffishers, and the dwellers uppon owre costes; and that the kynge kepe alway some grete and myghty vessels, ffor the brekynge off an armye when any shall be made ayen hym apon the see; ffor thanne it shall be to late to do make such vessailles'.[21] Fortescue saw what the problem was: the defence of English interests both on land and at sea, which needed to be acted upon with a speed which only the existence of some form of permanent naval force would allow. In so saying, Fortescue had all but admitted that Henry V had been ahead of his time.

[20] S. Rose (ed.), *The navy of the Lancastrian kings: accounts and inventories of William Soper, keeper of the king's ships, 1422–1427* (London, 1982), pp. 28–56.

[21] Sir John Fortescue, *The governance of England*, ed. C. Plummer (Oxford, 1885), p. 123. On the impact of coastal attacks upon the lives of civilian populations, see *Paston letters and papers of the fifteenth century*, ed. N. Davis, 1 (Oxford, 1971), nos. 20 and 136.

4

THE INSTITUTIONS OF WAR

CENTRAL ORGANISATION

One of the most striking developments in late medieval European society proved to be the ability, found at least among the monarchies of England, France, and Spain, to make military power more effective through proper organisation. The demands of long periods of war, while requiring some response, also provided opportunities. All over Europe, in Italy and in Iberia, in France as well as in England, armies, answering the demands made of them by increasingly powerful masters who controlled the purse strings, grew to meet the needs of the times. In Italy, Florence and Venice were, by the fourteenth century, dictating terms and conditions of service and pay to the *condottieri*, who brought their private bands to serve them. In such circumstances, continuity of organisation was essential; it had to exist in peace time as in war. It needed structures of personnel; it needed, too, continuity among decision-makers who had themselves to be servants of the state, which alone had the right to decide its military policy in the light of its wider interests. Although they did it in different ways, both Florence and Venice acted together in the essential task of making the pursuit of war a matter of state, which became, in these and in other instances, the paymaster.[1]

Among the monarchies of Europe, much the same story can be told; the differences are mainly ones of degree. In Spain, it was the crown

[1] M. E. Mallett and J. R. Hale, *The military organisation of a renaissance state. Venice, c.1400–1617* (Cambridge, 1984).

which provided the essential continuity required to pursue the long war
of reconquest against the Moors. In England and in France the Hundred
Years War soon led to the recognition that war, now of ever-increasing
complexity and expense, needed to be administered from the centre.
This could only be done effectively through the gradual development
and use of military institutions. Many of these were at hand at the
beginning of our period, but it needed long years of war to bring them
to a fruition which would be as important for the development of the
state's institutions as it was for the organisation of its military endeavour.

RECRUITMENT

The history of the recruitment of armies, from the Middle Ages to
modern times, has passed through three main phases. The first was the
fulfilment, through military service, of the feudal obligation to take part
in defence. The second was that which made military service voluntary;
men served mainly because they wished to, or because some other
obligation compelled them to. The third phase was that of conscription,
obligatory service in the name of the state. By the time that our period
begins, the first of these phases was ending. Soldiers were coming to
serve largely because they chose to do so; sailors, on the other hand,
were enlisted by conscription. The period is, therefore, one of change.

In 1327, in what may have appeared as a retrograde step given that the
trend, in England, was strongly towards a paid army, a general summons
to the feudal levy was issued. In 1334, however, the Scottish campaign
of Edward III was to be based on a paid army, no general feudal service
being demanded, although some mounted troops still gave obligatory
service until 1336. In the following year, when the theatre of war moved
to France, the largely voluntary element in the army prevailed. There
was now no general feudal summons, although certain individuals were
called upon to provide their obligatory service. Persuasion, rather than
obligation, was winning the day. At local meetings, magnates had the
king's needs explained to them; recruiting agents were sent round the
counties to raise foot soldiers through commissions of array; emphasis
was placed upon the pay and the possibility of material benefits to be
derived from war. The days of the feudal army were all but over: after
1385 it would be a thing of the past.[2]

In France the trend was much in the same direction. Yet it should be
recalled that, in broad terms, Frenchmen were being called upon to fight
a defensive war, the aim of which was to thwart English military

---

[2] For the controversy regarding this matter, see the bibliography for ch. 4, *sub* Lewis,
N. B. and Palmer, J. J. N.

ambition. The country's defensive needs meant that the more traditional, feudal form of the French king's army might have a longer life than had its English counterpart. Since the beginning of the fourteenth century, the king of France had had a relic of the feudal army available in the form of the *arrière-ban*, a call to those between the ages of eighteen and sixty to serve in times of dire necessity. This essentially defensive institution was called out on at least seven occasions between 1338 (when the war against England effectively broke out) and 1356 (the year of the defeat at Poitiers). Mainly associated with the interior regions of the country best controlled by the crown, its services could be commuted for the payment of money (as country districts often did), or, as in the case of towns, for service fulfilled by certain citizens paid for by a town. Nor was this the only form of service demanded. The nobility, sometimes called out separately, joined in when the *arrière-ban* was called; the towns provided urban militias, notably crossbowmen; while the Church, normally forbidden an active role in war, contributed carts or, sometimes, cash.

Such was the basis of France's defensive potential in the early fourteenth century. It was a system with built-in deficiencies which could not effectively live up to the rapidly developing needs of the French crown, faced with attack from different directions. The system lacked both reliability and uniformity and, in the case of the service due from feudal vassals, it was difficult to impose and organise. Most important of all, it could not be summoned quickly enough to meet emergencies which were developing as a result of the English war, so that much of the onus for local defence was left in the hands of the localities themselves, which were made responsible for the guard of castles and towns, largely through the system of watch and ward (*guet et garde*), as genuine an example of feudal defence as one could find.

In the first half of the fourteenth century both England and France were moving away from their historic reliance upon obligation towards a voluntary system to provide them with an army. But such a system had to be paid for; money had to be found. Traditionally, this had been done through scutage, a fine paid in lieu of service, and other fines. In essence, this tradition was carried on. In France much allegedly feudal service was compounded for by payment of fines, while in England ecclesiastics, such as abbots and priors, and women who held from the king, paid money in place of personal service. Such a system, however, was unreliable and the sums paid were not always realistic. The result was that it became apparent that the financing of war, both offensive and defensive, could only be properly carried out if large sums of money became available, sums which could only be found through taxation.

There was an additional factor which encouraged this general development in both countries. War was coming to be regarded as necessary for the common good, for whose defence each country needed the best available army, ready to fight for the common utility. In both countries, the levying of taxation nationwide was both a symbolic and a practical way of getting all the kings' subjects to provide for these armies.

The instrument which typified the new system was the indenture, perhaps the most important administrative development in the English army in the late Middle Ages. The earliest indenture dates from the last years of the reign of Henry III, but it was not until the fourteenth century that it assumed its normal form. The military indenture was a binding agreement, formalising conditions of service between the king (as the employer) and his captains (usually members of the nobility) and those captains and their sub-contractors of lower rank, in time of war. The terms of the agreement were set out twice on parchment, then cut along a wavy or 'indented' (i.e. tooth-like) line, each party preserving one copy. In any case of dispute, the two 'halves' had to be confronted to see if they fitted; if they did not, accusations of fraud could be brought. The terms of the English indenture normally specified the size and composition (men-at-arms, mounted archers) of the retinue to be brought; the time and place of service; wages, and any bonuses which might be paid; the division of the 'advantages' of war, including special provisions regarding prisoners; details regarding transport; and, especially in early indentures, what compensation would be paid for the loss of that most expensive animal, the war horse.

In France and England a *lettre de retenue* or indenture (the former not normally so detailed as the latter) was a contract between the king and a commander (in Italy the contract, or *condotta*, was made for a period which might be six months or a year (*ferma*) with the possibility of an extension (*de beneplacito*) between the state and the leader of the group being employed) to raise troops. The commander's first task, then, was to ensure the recruitment of sufficient soldiers of adequate standard, either from his own estates or those of others, perhaps through the dying feudal 'network'. His indenture which, more than anything else, symbolised the new, paid, and centrally organised army, also gave him rights, for his copy was an authority to raise a retinue, while the king's copy was sent to those responsible for the administration of payments for war. It is important to appreciate that the extension of war at this time also meant the development of institutions which dealt with its administration. In Venice the supervision of the rapidly developing system of recruiting, supervising and paying soldiers was in the hands of *collaterali* and *provveditori*, whose task it was to see to the day-to-day control of soldiers in the pay of the state. The proper and regular payment of soldiers was but one very important aspect of the development of a machinery for war much wider than that provided by the fighting forces alone. The indenture was to prove to be a document of vital importance in the long history of war finance which was being rapidly developed during these years. Its importance must not be underestimated.

While the manner in which armies were recruited remained reasonably static in England after the changes of the 1330s, the same was not true of France. There the *arrière-ban* proved unsatisfactory; it became unpopular and mistrusted, a political stick with which to beat the crown, and went out of use after 1356. There soon followed, under Charles V, a major restructuring of recruitment. Although the crown's vassals were called out on three occasions when English expeditions caused moments of crisis, the main objective of regaining land lost to the English was accomplished through the creation of a moderately sized army, based almost entirely upon volunteers, and bound to the king through *lettres de retenue*. The emphasis was towards an army whose recruitment was organised centrally, whose commanders were appointed by the king, and whose military and organisational structures were created to meet the prime need of the day: reconquest. Above all, the king insisted on keeping firm control both of his captains and of those who served under them. It was to be very much a royal army, properly disciplined and properly controlled.

If the reign of Charles V witnessed a conscious attempt to make the army more of an instrument of state than it had been before, the death of both the king and du Guesclin in 1380, and the growing political disorder of the following decades, led to a decline in the military effectiveness of the French army. With the return to power of the princes, the local force, carrying out its traditional role, came once again to the fore; the nobility, too, reclaimed its traditional place in the leadership; and, after 1410, the old *arrière-ban*, virtually excluded since the disaster of Poitiers, reappeared. The political divisions of the day manifested themselves very clearly in the organisation of war. The projected invasion of England of 1386 failed – and not merely because of adverse weather. In 1415 the lack of unity showed itself again; the result was defeat at Agincourt. At no time is a unified command more valuable than in a defensive situation. The fate suffered by French armies during these years underlines the truth of that observation.

An aggressor, however, above all one not concerned with total conquest, can afford to give his commanders a freer hand. The result of this was that, although well organised, the armies of Edward III and Richard II were seldom centrally commanded as were those of Charles V. By the middle of the fourteenth century, the system of recruiting a volunteer army through indentures was well established and changed but little. Captains, some of them sons of Edward III, others men of high military repute, served under the king on those occasions when he went to war in person. On other occasions they led expeditions of their own, recruiting from their estates or from among those who had served under them before. On the whole, these armies were a powerful force of destruction in those parts of France in which they moved; however, in terms of securing military advantage it is doubtful whether they constituted the threat which, in theory, it was in their power to pose.

England's changing war aims under Henry V and his son (conquest and the defence of that conquest) meant, first, that the short, sometimes relatively profitable campaigns of the previous century became a thing of the past. Now, with both field armies and garrisons being required, men not infrequently returned to France on several 'tours of duty'. By the time that the war ended, the number of Englishmen who had seen service in France could probably be calculated in tens of thousands.

It was from the hands of these men and their captains that King Charles VII had to prise control of the duchies of Normandy and Aquitaine. His reign was notable in more than one way, not least for the attempt, more than partly successful, to restore royal control over the composition and discipline of the French army. As under Charles V, it was realised how essential it was for the crown to nominate the army's leaders: the days of the princes must be ended. In 1445, having already taken practical steps to bring this about, the king issued an ordinance re-establishing royal control over the army. From now on, the crown would designate the leading captains and would provide the money from which they, and the rest of the army, would be paid. Three years later, in 1448, Charles announced the creation of a new force, the *francs-archers* who, representing every community and committed to regular training in the use of arms, would form the core of the permanent, national army which the king wished to create. The crown of France, more so than that of England, had stamped its influence upon the recruitment of the new-styled army.

SUPPLIES

The soldier of the late Middle Ages was in receipt of a wage. There was, therefore, no obligation upon his paymaster, the crown, to provide him with the food and drink which he would need on campaign. Yet, if the task of finding provisions was left to the soldiers themselves, the results could be disastrous, for the men might become more involved with that preoccupation than with their prime concern, that of making war. Discipline could suffer. Moreover, they might take it out on the population of the country through which they were advancing: Henry V had to issue orders that all food consumed by his army in Normandy should be paid for on the spot, so that the local population should not be antagonised. There was the added, and very serious, danger that food would run out; a scorched earth policy was, after all, intended to make life as difficult as possible for those who expected to be able to live off the land. Not without reason it has been claimed that 'few problems facing governments in the pre-industrial age could have been as difficult as that of providing sufficient food for an army in the field.'[3]

There was a close relationship between providing an army with its subsistence and that army's success as a military machine. Feeding an army was one way of making it efficient. Provisioning was, in itself, a test of efficiency. Castles, outlying garrisons, and ships at sea had all to be catered for. Calais, for instance, was almost totally dependent upon England for its food, its munitions, and the other materials required for its defence as a bastion of English power on the continent. In the fourteenth century its large garrison (up to 1,000 men or more in time of war) was provided with food as part payment of its wages under a system organized by the Keeper of the King's Victuals. The importance of maintaining such places with all that they required was underlined in March 1416 when the earl of Dorset, captain of Harfleur in Normandy, which was being blockaded by the French by both land and sea, had to make what turned out to be a very dangerous sortie to secure food which was fast running out.

Everything pointed to the fact that, in time of war, provisioning could not be left to hazard. In this respect the problems faced by the French and English crowns were a little different. Fighting mainly in their own country, the French were less likely to meet opposition to the collecting of victuals and other provisions than the English, the enemy fighting in a foreign country, would do. They could probably rely on greater co-operation when buying on the spot; they could more easily anticipate the needs of their armies by sending agents ahead to see to the levy of provisions in the areas through which an army might pass; and they might also, with greater ease, organise merchants (to whom safe-conducts would be given) to provide for the needs of the army at certain pre-arranged places. All this was essential if a degree of efficiency was to be established by avoiding the need for the army to live off the land and protecting the interests of the civilian population.

[3] C. S. L. Davies, 'Provision for armies, 1509–50: a study in the effectiveness of early Tudor government', *Econ. H.R.*, second series, 17 (1964–5), 234.

When they fought in France, and to a certain extent in Scotland, the English could not count upon the advantages of fighting 'at home'. Basically this involved them in a system which was an extension (at least in scale) of the way they provided for the needs of the Calais garrison, for even if an army could live off the land, it was none the less advisable for it to have easy access to the everyday provisions which it required. In a war of sieges, an army seeking to starve out a garrison had to be free of such practical problems as providing its own food, so that during the long sieges of Calais in 1346–7 and of Rouen in 1418–19, both Edward III and Henry V had supplies specially shipped to them from England.

In both England and France the systems used to provide for the country's military needs had much in common. In France the *prise* was the normal way of raising provisions, from both individuals and institutions. An official of the royal household, called the *Panetier du Roi*, had charge, designating his powers to the regions, sometimes to *baillis*, sometimes to royal captains and others. Under Philip VI those responsible were divided into three main groups: those who collected cereal products, those with responsibility for raising wine, and those who sought the large quantities of fodder required for the horses and other animals. The work of these people was, militarily, of the very greatest importance, but the system was open to abuse, with many disputes arising out of acts committed by over-zealous officials against, significantly, exemptions from the *prise*, ending up in the courts.

In England the system of purveyance, as it was called, was to become a major cause of dispute between the crown and its subjects. 'Purveyors', wrote William of Pagula, 'were sent to act in this world as the devil acts in Hell'. The financial difficulties experienced by Edward I led him to try to exploit the crown's claims to the full, but with only moderate success. The issue between king and subjects was both a financial one (was it right that those who had already paid taxes should have to contribute substantially towards the upkeep of the army by providing it with cheap food?) and a constitutional one, for the crown, by extending the idea that the king's army, in T. F. Tout's words, 'was essentially the household in arms' which the country could be called upon to provide for, was demanding help to feed that now greatly extended household of, perhaps, several thousand men. However, opposition to this had reached its limits by about the middle years of the fourteenth century, and thereafter, with royal agents acting more reasonably, purveyance became much less of an issue between crown and people.

Unpopular though it was, the system none the less helped to make England's fighting forces abroad more efficient. In its least objectionable form it enabled the sheriff to compel the purchase of provisions which he had been ordered to contribute towards a general requisition which was going on all over, or in most parts of, the country at the time. All were liable to contribute. Monasteries, with the produce of their estates stored in barns and granges, were particularly vulnerable, although some, the rich or locally influential, might purchase exemptions from the need to contribute; some counties, on the other hand, had demands made upon them more frequently than others. During the first years of the war against France the task of raising provisions for the army was handed over to merchants who, with a network of subordinate agents, combed the countryside exerting pressure on all to contribute. Obtained at rates usually below the current market price, and paid for in a way which often made it difficult for the seller to obtain the money owed him, the produce of land (essentially bread, meat, beer or wine), together with fish, but little or no fresh fruit or vegetables (a dull diet at best), and oats for horses, was taken away to sustain the army or, as on some occasions, to stores and depots.

The regular supply of arms was also becoming increasingly important at this period. It was accepted that, when leaving his county, the English soldier raised by commission of array would be adequately armed, his locality having assumed responsibility for the payment of his weapons. The cheaper and simpler weapons could be demanded from the localities: bows, arrows, not to forget the six wing feathers which, in 1417, the sheriffs were ordered to obtain from every goose in their jurisdiction at a low price, could all be demanded from the country at large. But in both France and England weapons needed to be provided by the crown, too. Bows could be lost; arrows would certainly be used up, even if they were sometimes retrieved and used again, as the evidence of manuscript illumination suggests they were. In this essential work the English king's privy wardrobe, a vital part in his household, played the leading role. Its centre was the Tower of London where, in the reign of Edward III, the Keeper of the King's Arms had his base from which he organised the work of purchasing, storing, and finally distributing arms to armies, garrisons, and ships. In 1360, the store held over 11,000 bows and some 23,600 sheaves, each holding twenty-four arrows. By 1381 there were less than 1,000 sheaves left, an indication of the need for constant replenishment of stock, above all in time of war. But it was not only bows and arrows which were kept in this, the nearest which the Middle Ages had to a national armaments depot. Other essentials had to be maintained: tents for the soldiers; saddlery; crossbows and bolts; shields; lances; heavy siege-engines; all had to be provided.

The provision of cannon was to require radical measures. In France, the cost of manufacturing artillery was borne almost entirely by the crown, and, in this way, cannon became essentially a weapon of state which now took on an increasingly important role in providing the equipment for its armies.[4] The argument can be supported by noting that in both England and France those who were made responsible for the founding of cannon, their distribution and use did so under royal auspices, holding their position by authority of the crown and being paid directly by it. Theirs was a specialist's work, which sometimes ran in families. In 1375 Milet de Lyon succeeded his father, Jean, as head of the French king's artillery, while in England, at about the same time, four men of the Byker family served Edward III and Richard II in the work of providing slings and, finally, small iron cannon.

The trend continued in the fifteenth century. The work of the Bureau brothers, whose reconstruction of Charles VII's artillery train played so considerable a part in bringing about the defeat of the English, is well known. But the French kings were not alone in developing the use of artillery. James II of Scotland, who died of injuries incurred when one of his cannon, ironically called 'Lion', exploded in 1460, had a royal gunner. Before him, Henry IV of England was said to be interested in cannon. His son, Henry V, certainly was, and used the weapon to good effect in the sieges of his campaigns in France between 1415 and 1422. Henry took the matter of the organisation of his artillery very seriously: he had no real choice, for cannon were essential to him if he was to bring his war of sieges to a successful conclusion. He kept officials busy, ordering cannon to be shipped to him from England while he was in France and arranging for gunstones, 'salt pietre, cole and brymstoon', stored at Caen 'in ye howse of oure ordennance' and at Harfleur, to be sent to the siege of Meaux in March 1422 (the Musée de l'Armée in Paris still shows pieces of artillery left by the English after their successful siege). On Henry's death, John, duke of Bedford, established an organisation under the 'maistre de l'artillerie du roy' which carried out the unspectacular but vital work of ordering the construction and repair of cannon, large and small, the purchase of the ingredients of gunpowder, the transport of weapons (since they were heavy and difficult to move, this was done as often as possible by water) from one siege to another, and the rendering of what was becoming increasingly professional advice on the problems of how to place the pieces of artillery to achieve maximum effect. The growing professionalism required to make the

---

[4] Contamine, *Guerre, état et société*, p. 299. See also his 'Les industries de guerre dans la France de la renaissance: l'exemple de l'artillerie', *R.H.*, 550 (1984), 249–80, and D. H. Caldwell, 'Royal patronage of arms and armour-making in fifteenth and sixteenth-century Scotland', *Scottish weapons and fortifications, 1100–1800*, ed. D. H. Caldwell (Edinburgh, 1981), pp. 72–93.

most of this relatively new weapon is emphasised by the fact that those
who had charge of the English artillery in France in the fifteenth century
were at the head of retinues which consisted of specialists who stayed
together in teams, sometimes for years at a time, thereby adding a strong
element of cohesion to their efforts which were often well rewarded.

What of the horses? These, as we have seen, were very expensive.
'Hors flesche', wrote William Paston from London in February 1492, 'is
of suche a price here that my purce is schante able to bye on horse.'[5] In
the war's early phases, at least, a knight who provided a horse might, if
it were injured or killed, claim compensation under the old custom of
restor (frequently invoked in French indentures). For this purpose horses
were valued by experts before a campaign, rather as today's knight of
the road values his vehicle in agreement with his insurers. In addition to
a horse, a knight would also be expected to provide himself with armour,
the nature of which was changing from mail to plate by the mid-
fourteenth century. The notion that a man, even under contract, should
provide his mount, his armour, and his weapons died hard. The high
social ranks armed themselves; in return, it should not be forgotten, they
received more pay.

There must have been a great variety in the clothing worn by, and the
arms carried by, armies of this era. Yet the achievement of a certain level
of standardisation of dress and armament was slowly being introduced.
This was to be accomplished in two ways. The first was the result of
musters, at which were noted not only the absences of individual soldiers,
but also the failure of those present to keep themselves properly in arms
and armour. The other way was the gradual introduction of the uniform.
This, in the modern meaning of the word, was yet to come, but in 1340
the town of Tournai provided Philip VI with 2,000 foot soldiers 'all
clothed identically', while, from the mid-fourteenth century onwards,
others coming from Cheshire and North Wales were often dressed in
green and white 'uniforms'.

The provision and transport of weapons were increasingly organised
centrally. Bows and arrows made in the country were sent up to London
to be stored in the Tower (in Paris weapons were kept in the Louvre and
the Bastille) from where, packed in chests together with spare bow-
strings, feathers and arrowheads specially manufactured in areas such as
the Forest of Dean (where iron was worked), they were despatched
when required to the ports, such as Sandwich or Southampton, for
forwarding to armies overseas. When all was ready, time was often
spent waiting for a favourable wind to blow, during which period

---

[5] *Paston letters and papers*, 1, no. 414.

soldiers had to be fed and their morale maintained, as those who lived near ports of embarkation realised, sometimes to their cost. One cannot but wonder that the departure of a transport fleet bearing an army and its equipment was an event which amounted to a considerable managerial achievement, reflected in certain chronicles as something of which men could be proud.

TAXATION AND FISCAL INSTITUTIONS

It was a characteristic of all governments of the Middle Ages to grow in size and scope. Since no government can exist without financial support, as personnel grew and documentation increased, so government became more and more expensive. Within those rising expenses the costs of war can be seen to have played a major part. The demands of war, now becoming more frequent and more prolonged, rose from the late thirteenth century onwards, to the point when, two centuries later, war might account for between half and two-thirds of public receipts and expenditure.

It is undeniable that not only in France and England, but in other parts of Europe such as Spain and Italy, the graph of public military expenditure rose very sharply in the closing centuries of the Middle Ages. In some respects there was nothing new in this. In England, for instance, the need to provide some paid troops had been recognised in the mid-twelfth century; more had been progressively spent on war ever since the beginning of the thirteenth century, which had witnessed fiscal innovations in the reign of King John, whose financial resources for the task of saving Normandy were already inadequate. But it was the final quarter of the thirteenth century which, in both France (involved in war in Aragon, Flanders, and Aquitaine) and in England (taken up in conflict in France, Wales, and Scotland), witnessed an increase in war taxation on an unprecedented scale. In England, this rise in expenditure was part of a wider difference between Edward I and his great nobility on the matter of their obligation to render him military service abroad; while in France, in the years 1302–4, Philip IV raised considerable taxation from his subjects in commutation for their obligation to serve him in the defence of the country. Generally speaking, the English king had an advantage over his French counterpart at this period. France had been involved in relatively few wars in the course of the thirteenth century; England, on the other hand, had been involved in both Wales and Scotland, a practical experience, both in the raising of troops and in securing material payment for them, which was to prove invaluable in the early years of the Hundred Years War.

We need to know why and how such historically significant developments took place. In France the thirteenth century had witnessed a
gradual advance in what was regarded as a vassal's obligation, from
defence of his lord (the king) to defence of the crown (the *corona*) and,
by the end of the century, defence of the kingdom (the *regnum*).[6] In the
last case the kingdom could mean both a physically delineated area of
land and a concept, the common welfare of those who inhabited it. Both
meanings were important, but, perhaps because it was a reality which
could be expressed in conceptual terms, more could be made of the
notion of the common welfare. Emphasis was placed upon the general
obligation to contribute, either directly through personal service or
indirectly, through taxation, to the defence of that welfare. In exceptional circumstances, such as in moments of attack from without, the
king, responsible for the protection of those under his charge, could
demand help which none, either privileged or exempted, could refuse.
War, or threatened invasion of territory, came to constitute an emergency, which necessitated an immediate and unsparing response. When
the king judged that a state of common peril had been reached, his
subjects, concerned for the common welfare, were expected to fulfil
their obligation, both towards it and towards their ruler, by giving
unstinted assistance in whatever form it might reasonably be sought.

The lord who issued the summons or demanded the tax was the king
acting as *curator* of the kingdom as a whole. But this did not mean that
the best interests of the kingdom might not be served at a local level. It
was the king of England who called out the local 'reservists' to counter
an attack upon the maritime lands; likewise the king of France might
authorise a local tax, as Charles VI did in April 1383 when he ordered
the people of Perigueux to tax themselves for three years at a rate of 5
per cent on goods sold within their jurisdiction, the money raised to be
employed towards the repair and improvement of the defences of the
town, at that moment in an area threatened by the English. Furthermore,
the text reveals, the raising of such a tax had been carried out locally for
some time without royal approval: in pardoning the people this technical
offence, the king made it clear that over-all direction of matters of
defence, even at a very local level, should be carried out under royal
supervision. When, in March 1440, the people of Dieppe sought permission from Charles VII to tax their commercial activities in order to
pay for their town's fortification, they emphasised to him that they
dared not do this without royal permission, and that accounts of the
sums collected would be made available to the royal captain. Local

---

[6] J. R. Strayer, 'Defense of the realm and royal power in France', *Medieval statecraft and
the perspectives of history* (Princeton, 1971), pp. 293–4.

defence was thus seen in the wider context of the defence of the country as a whole, and as a matter to be controlled by the crown. The implications of this were clear. War, even its local ramifications, was becoming a matter of state.

In France, what had happened under Philip IV to make the nation responsible for giving all assistance to the king, his lieutenants and officials in times of recognisable peril to the community came to be accepted during the first half of the fourteenth century as the norm, in spite of a short period of protest in 1314 and 1315 when the newly-evolving doctrines clashed with local interests and privileges, especially in Normandy. But one important matter was not yet clear. What would happen if there were a period of no recognisable peril, not to speak of a truce or peace? Could taxes, justified in time of war, be imposed in changed circumstances? And if imposed and collected, but not yet spent, what would happen to them if hostilities ceased? The question was first formally raised in 1298 by Pierre d'Auvergne who argued that once the cause for levying taxes had passed, then they should no longer be raised, since the cause for their being raised no longer existed or applied ('Cessanta causa, cessare debet effectus').[7] Implied here was the notion that taxes were exceptional, and were only to be raised in emergencies. What constituted an emergency was something to trouble the conscience of the king and his advisers. But one thing, already clear by the end of the thirteenth century, became even clearer by the end of the next generation: the king's subjects would pay taxes only in time of real military crisis (hence the need to declare war formally) and they came to demand refunds (which they received in 1302, 1304, 1313, and 1314) when taxes paid were not used because of an early cessation of hostilities. Not surprisingly the cynical argued that it was best not to pay until there was peace: then there would be no reason for paying at all!

Under the Capetians prolonged war was exceptional. The conflict between Valois and Plantagenet, however, changed all that. From the time in, say, 1325 when the principle of 'cessante causa' was still applied, it would be only some thirty years or so before another principle, momentous in its implications, would quietly win acceptance: the right of the ruler to raise permanent and general taxation. There can be little doubt that it was war and its needs which constituted the major cause in bringing about this change. In France the war against England led to a great and probably unforeseen extension in the financial demands made by the crown upon the country. Most influential was the need to raise

---

[7] E. A. R. Brown, 'Cessante causa and the taxes of the last Capetians: the political applications of a philosophical maxim', *Studia Gratiana*, 15 (1972), 567–87.

the ransom promised to the king of England by the terms of the treaty of Brétigny. The financial millstone which the ransom represented (some sixty years later Henry V was still demanding that it should be paid off in full) was the first and most important factor in justifying the French crown in the logical development of its fiscal policy, the making permanent over a period of years, and in peace time, of a tax raised to satisfy a major expense of war, the ransoming of the king.

To this a second factor came to make its own contribution. Although the decade 1359–69 may appear as a period of relative peace in France, it was also the period in which the Companies showed themselves most active, resulting in the urgent need to raise funds required to build defences against this new social scourge. In this case, if the authorisation to raise taxes came from the centre, the levy and expenditure was largely local. The importance of this, however, lies primarily in the fact that whole areas of France were continuously subject to demands for greater sums in taxation. It might be some consolation that monies thus raised would probably be spent locally, for this undoubtedly encouraged people in their willingness to pay, in some places considerably more than in time of open war against the English. What seems certain is that the meeting of such regular demands, together with the raising of con- tributions towards the royal ransom, gradually made people accustomed both to the idea and the practice of taxes raised for the common good.

In England the story was not radically different. As already suggested, the wars against Scotland had accustomed the population to the payment of taxes for war. It was a fact, too, that English people had for some time been used to paying direct taxation on moveable property and that from about the time the war against France began in Edward III's reign such subsidies, standardised in value in 1334, with each local community paying a sum which it divided among itself, were regularly granted by Parliament. In England, as in France, the 1360s (paradoxically the period of relatively restrained military activity) witnessed the most telling developments. In 1362 and 1365 to save the king's 'estate and honour' (in fact to help pay for the defence of Calais, Aquitaine, and the Scottish border) Parliament voted a wool subsidy, followed in 1368 by a further two-year subsidy, again on wool. In 1369, inspired by fears of possible attacks on Calais and English coastal counties, the lords and commons jointly authorised yet another, this time a three-year, levy on wool, in effect the imposition of an indirect tax to meet an alleged deficit in the royal finances. It is clear that such decisions constituted a recognition of general obligation to pay for the country's defence in peacetime. Thus both England and France were reaching a broadly similar stage in the development of their respective taxation systems at much the same time.

One great difference between the Middle Ages and later times was that the medieval state scarcely used the credit system to start wars. A ruler, wrote the English Dominican, John Bromyard, about 1360, ought not to embark upon a war unless he could reasonably expect to pay for it, a view which would have been widely accepted at the time. From the very first steps, the practical need to have cash readily available imposed itself. The custom of paying indentured soldiers a 'prest' (or *prêt* or *imprestanza*), an advance on their wages to enable them to pay for their equipment, placed a considerable burden upon the king. Such an example underlines the need to raise money quickly, and in part explains the great difficulties experienced by Edward III when his cash resources ran out in 1341. What, then, was available to a ruler bent on war? He could farm out the collection of a tax which had been authorised: this had the advantage of bringing the money in quickly, the disadvantage that the farming system was open to abuse and was consequently unpopular. The grant of a loan, in itself a form of taxation since the ruler had use of the money for what was sometimes an indefinite period, was also a common practice: for this to work, the king's credit had to be good, so that even so great a grantor of credit as Cardinal Beaufort had one of his loans to Henry V formally recorded in the Roll of Parliament to ensure repayment. The practice of 'advancing' the date by which a subsidy should be collected was also employed: Parliament had to ask Henry V not to continue doing this when, half way through his reign, his need for money suddenly grew. Finally, there was the practice of debasement carried out by princes whose prerogative it was to decide the value of currency. By 1295 Philip IV, in urgent need of cash, was using this method which he undertook to end by 1306, but only in return for the promise of a subsidy. Such manipulations of currency, which were not difficult to arrange, were particularly unpopular among the nobility and clergy whose revenues came largely in prearranged sums from landed sources; the bourgeoisie, on the other hand, especially those who derived their wealth from cash sources based on trade, were less alarmed. None the less, for all its short-term advantages to the crown, debasement was a divisive factor in society, a weapon to be used only in times of extreme crisis. As might be expected, the practice gradually disappeared as other resources of royal revenue became more widely and permanently established.

Taxation was basically of two kinds. Direct taxes were those raised on an assessment of sources of wealth, both fixed and moveable. In England, mainly since the reign of Edward I, such taxation had been granted with regularity by Parliament. In France, the practice of direct taxation did not come into being until the reign of Philip IV, Edward I's contemporary. On a number of occasions during his reign subsidies were raised in time of war or threatened war, in 1295 at the rate of 1 per cent (*centième*), in 1296 at double the rate (*cinquantième*), the levies being regarded as alternatives to military service, thereby linking taxation closely to war. A hearth tax (*fouage*), which townspeople paid at a higher rate than their country neighbours, and the rich more than the poor, was also levied; in 1355 it was decided that 100 hearths should pay for a man-at-arms and an archer. The tax, however, bore heavily on the people, and in his last years Charles V tried to grant remissions or reductions to communities known to him to have suffered particularly from the war. One of his very last acts, as he was dying, was to abolish it altogether.

In both France and England the clergy contributed to national taxation. In the last years of the thirteenth century clerical taxation had become a *cause célèbre* between Pope Boniface VIII, Philip IV, and Edward I: should the clergy contribute to royal taxation? By the early years of the fourteenth century, however, the obstacle of clerical immunity had been largely overcome and the clergy contributed substantial sums when asked to do so.

It was, however, through indirect taxation that the war, both in France and, in particular, in England, was chiefly to be funded. In France the need to raise money in 1341 led, at a time of truce when direct taxation could not be justified, to the establishment of the salt tax (*gabelle*), which was to last until the French Revolution. If everyone needed salt, other taxes on consumption, principally drink (the medieval value-added tax) were unpopular among the poor who could less well afford than could the richer classes taxes which all had to pay and which were most easily collected in towns, in which they contributed a high proportion of urban taxation, six times more in 1360 than in 1292. Loans, too, were a form of taxation which might be extracted from both individuals and institutions. In England, for instance, royal officials were on occasion expected to forego their salaries which were withheld as contributions towards seeing the government through a financial crisis. On a different scale were the loans occasionally demanded from towns and, in particular, from the city of London to help pay for the war. For if war were to lead to economic advantage, the better pleased and more enthusiastic the towns – and principally the ports – would be.

The ports, much more firmly under royal control in England than in France where, for most of the war, the king did not have regular access to his own coastline, were the collecting points of what was to prove the most lucrative of all forms of indirect taxation, customs dues. Here, the contrast between England and France was very marked. France, more self-sufficient than England, depended less than did her rival upon import trade through her ports, and it was to be only in the sixteenth century that France imposed duties on incoming goods, although exports were taxed in the fourteenth century, especially after 1360, when the need to raise money to pay for King John's ransom began to make very great demands upon the country. In England, however, the situation was different, taxes being levied on both incoming and outgoing trade. Ever since the end of the twelfth century English kings had been making sporadic, but increasing, use of wool as the basis for an export tax which was becoming more profitable and which, after 1275, came firmly under the control of the crown. By the fourteenth century, perhaps one third of the English king's revenue came from the export tax, chiefly on wool, wool hides and skins, while tunnage and poundage, the tax on wine and other merchandise raised to protect trade, was becoming increasingly regular and lucrative by the end of the century. We may feel that the French king had, to a certain extent, missed an opportunity; certainly the kings of England must have rejoiced at the contrast in practice which brought them such advantage over their French counterparts.[8] Indeed, had it not been for the large sums raised from trade, England's smaller population and more restricted resources could not have supported a foreign war for so long.

Taxes voted to the crown had to be collected and managed. New taxes would require new methods of organisation to make the most of what was coming to be increasingly regarded as public money, or 'la pecune publique'. Under the Valois, attempts were made to impose a degree of centralisation upon fiscal measures, particularly in the 1370s. New offices were created. Salt was placed in the hands of *grenetiers*, many of whom farmed their position; after 1355 *élus* were appointed to *élections*, districts in which they acted as assessors of taxes; for the settling of disputes arising out of demands for indirect taxation, a special *cour des aides* was established in 1390; while a *trésorier des guerres* oversaw the general problems of handling war finances, in particular the payment of armies.

In England the system, which had already proved itself in war, was to be less in need of radical innovation. The accounting system which has come down to us through the public records shows that while expeditions under the command of royal lieutenants were normally

---

[8] On the taxation of international trade, see B. Guenée, *States and rulers in later medieval Europe* (Oxford, 1985), p. 99.

financed through the Exchequer, those led by the king himself were
organised by a department of the royal household, the Wardrobe, whose
work was to be, in Tout's words, 'the executive agent in the field'.
Sometimes assisted by another household department, the Chamber, the
Wardrobe, with an expanded staff, ordered the levy of troops, the
purchase of horses, stores and equipment, and was, in addition, closely
involved in the diplomatic business of the king, as was appropriate for
a body so close to the royal person and members of his council staff who,
together, were responsible for decisions regarding war.

But we should not think of the English war machine, in its financial
aspects, as completely traditional and unreformed. The publication by
Edward III in July 1338 of the so-called 'Walton Ordinances' was an
attempt to make efficient the government of England, and that included
the administration of war. The emphasis was on saving, on 'value for
money', and on the use of the audit to control expenditure in both war
and diplomacy, as the appointment of a special treasurer for war was
intended to show.[9] Time would prove that the system was not always
reliable and was open to abuse. None the less, the use of essentially
household departments to finance and organise war, traditional as they
may have seemed, enabled the king and his councillors to keep in close
touch with those responsible for the huge background effort which war
required, and which is all too easily forgotten. That such a successful
soldier-king as Henry V should have used the Wardrobe as his basic
financial and administrative unit in organising and fighting war speaks
a good deal for at least the efficiency of the system, however un-
innovative it may appear.

In both England and France, we may be sure, war gave a great boost
to the development of centralised institutions and to the royal authority.
Equally, it should be emphasised that not all public expenditure related
to war was the direct result of centralised intervention or initiative.
French historians have, of late, stressed the important factor that in their
country there existed two financial systems, one national, the other local,
which worked side by side, and which were built up together. This
should cause no surprise, given the importance of the region or province
in the French political structure. Opposition to the raising of taxes which
might be spent in another part of the kingdom militated against involvement in a war being fought perhaps hundreds of miles away. Equally,
only when their region and, consequently, their common profit was
threatened, were people ready to act. Indeed, it can be argued that the

[9] T. F. Tout, *Chapters in the administrative history of medieval England*, IV (Manchester,
1928), 69–80, 143–50. C. Given–Wilson, *The royal household and the king's affinity.
Service, politics and finance in England 1360–1413* (New Haven: London, 1986), pp. 121–30.

piecemeal and local nature of war dictated by both the English (the enemy from without) and by the Companies (the enemy from within), to say nothing of the very local character of the civil war which dominated so much of Charles VI's reign, encouraged people to see war in local, rather than national, terms, and that this led naturally to the need for the reaction to come from local initiatives and to be based on local wealth.

The system which was developed in the second half of the fourteenth century fits into this pattern. In some places rudimentary local taxation already existed by 1340. What was lacking was the ability and authority to lay hands upon sufficient financial resources to build, repair, and maintain local defensive systems (principally walls) which constituted the only reasonable form of defence in the war which the enemy was waging. How were these needs to be met, and who was to pay? The answers emerged fairly quickly. Generally speaking, the regions were left to organise their own defence within an over-all, national plan. As to who would pay, the answer was to be broadly the same: the regions and, in particular, the towns. This led to significant developments. Meetings or regional estates voted sums which, by royal authority, could be spent in those same regions. On occasions the crown presented towns with gifts of money to help in a particular crisis: sometimes a local lord did the same. But usually such a royal gift was only the paying over of part of a levy already collected for their own defence to those who had paid it. In a word, although this seemed like outside help, such sums, like that granted to the people of Rodez in 1367, were only helping the citizens to help themselves.

In large measure, money spent on local projects of urban defence had been raised locally. Loans sought from both town-dwellers and those who had property there, but lived outside the walls, frequently raised considerable sums: almost 2,000 *écus* at Tours and some 4,500 *écus* at Reims in 1358. But the major contribution (some 61 per cent at Tours in 1358) came from the imposition of local taxes (*aides*) upon a variety of goods and services: on salt, on wine, and on rents raised on property in the towns, the rate being 10 per cent at Tours in 1364, 20 per cent at Dijon in 1412, the greater sum being levied upon absentee landlords who might not otherwise contribute towards the needs of defence.

In England, too, there were examples of local measures being employed in addition to national ones. Of these murage, first raised in 1220 at a time of threatened invasion from France, was the principal one. This tax, levied upon the sale of goods entering a town, was authorised by the crown and was collected and administered locally, accounts being submitted to the king. As in France, in this case by raising a levy on local trade, an attempt was made to force contributions from the wider community. As in France, too, a direct sales tax such as murage was not the only form of levy imposed for the building of walls. In the fourteenth century taxes on local property were raised: likewise the king could remit what was owed to him in fee-farm, customs dues, or profits of justice. In 1382 the people of Colchester, in their search for saving on communal expenditure, obtained exemption from sending a representative to Parliament for the next five years (an exemption later renewed until 1410), the savings thus made being spent on the building of walls around their town.[10]

In both France and England it is clear that help was given to encourage local initiatives. It would be a mistake to think that the war was directed from and paid for by Paris or Westminster alone. The reverse of the coin should not be forgotten, for it showed that local autonomy, energy, and initiatives were all exercised for the best purpose, the defence of the common good itself.

ORDER AND CONTROL

As we have already noted, people of the late Middle Ages appear to have accepted, with a certain sense of fatalism, the destructive energies released by war. We have also seen that the period witnessed an increasing awareness of what such destruction meant to those who experienced it: moral shock and material loss. Was this desirable, either in terms of the physical violence which war appeared to breed ('there is no good war without fire'), or of the economic loss (sometimes long-lasting) which it caused, or (a point increasingly accepted) of the military effectiveness which commanders sought to achieve? The evidence seems to suggest not.

It has become fashionable to see war in terms of armies ravaging the enemy's countryside, in order to deprive him of material and economic resources, rather than as a series of 'set-piece' confrontations or battles. The enemy, Vegetius had taught, should be brought to his knees with as little risk, effort and expense as possible. This required that war be fought in a relatively disciplined and ordered manner. We must take note of how these changes took place.

The late Middle Ages witnessed a development in the formalisation of war's activities. Some writers have seen this as satisfying the well-known medieval love of symbolic action: the giving of his right glove to Sir Denis de Morbecque symbolised John II's act of surrender at the

---

[10] Turner, *Town defences*, p. 42.

battle of Poitiers, while the very formal surrender of the keys by its
leading citizens represented the capture of Harfleur by Henry V in
September 1415. Likewise the raising of unfurled banners signalled the
opening of hostilities, just as the firing of a cannon came to mark the
start of a siege. The sociologist may choose to interpret such acts in terms
of play or game, and that element cannot be totally ruled out. Yet of far
greater significance is the fact that such acts were not only symbolic but
were also regarded as creating particular legal situations which could
have effects upon decisions taken in the courts of law. Disputes as to the
legal status of a soldier claimed by another as his prisoner could hang on
the circumstances in which the man was captured or the manner in
which he was taken. Whose prisoner he was might depend to whom he
had formally surrendered, and how. A knight might take another
prisoner and assume that he was now his 'master' (with all that this
could mean in legal terms); but if the 'giving of faith' to the captor by
the captured were not done properly and formally, then the 'capture'
might be regarded as invalid and open to challenge in a court of law.[11]

The historical significance of this form of evidence (which may
appear to be mere quibbling over a matter of military custom) is
precisely that it shows us that recourse to the law was encouraged as a
means of bringing fairly widely-held conventions to bear upon the
conduct of war, and that these were being applied judicially in courts
such as the Parlement of Paris or the military or admiralty courts in both
England and France.[12] In such courts a number of different traditions,
some more formally legal than others, were brought to bear. One was
local custom, built up over decades and even centuries, upon which
many decisions in suits over merchandise taken in war time were based.
Another, more difficult to define with precision, was the tradition of the
chivalric code, which gave guidance and, sometimes, laid down principles for the conduct of the knightly class in war. But probably most
important of all was the strong influence of the 'written law', and in
particular of the specifically military law of Rome which, much modi-
fied by more recently promulgated canon law, sometimes formed the
basis of judgements handed down in, for instance, the Parlement. Here
the influence of the fourteenth-century Italian school of jurists, one of
whose tasks was to make the law of Rome, and the later law of Justinian,
relevant and applicable in their own, very different, century, was con-

---

[11] 'Si aucun prent un prisoner, qil preigne sa foy...', *Black Book of the Admiralty*, ed.
T. Twiss (R.S., London, 1871), I, 457.
[12] See Keen, *Laws of war*, ch. 2, and 'Jurisdiction and origins of the constable's court', pp.
159–69; R. G. Marsden (ed.), *Select pleas in the court of admiralty* (Seldon Soc., 6, London,
1894).

siderable. In Italian tradition law was one means of achieving the common good. Law must be practical, otherwise its influence and effectiveness would be diminished. Significantly it was to the Italian universities that Charles V of France turned in 1368–9 for advice as to whether he had a cause for resuming the war against the English in Aquitaine. Equally significant, it was to the same widely accepted precepts of Roman law that those who sought to find solutions to legal problems arising out of war between different peoples also turned. The law was 'international' in all but name.

Appeal to the old-established law, albeit an up-dated one, was a way of bringing a measure of order to war's activities. Another was the introduction of new or restated regulations concerning the conduct of both armies and individual combatants in time of war. It was the final quarter of the fourteenth century which witnessed increasingly outspoken criticism of the way contemporary war was being fought; the works of Honoré Bouvet and Philippe de Mézières are among our prime witnesses to this. The call to defend the civilian, his person, and his property, a reaction against the generally accepted ways of making war, was beginning to be heard. It is no coincidence that the best-known attempt to control the excesses of English armies, the ordinances drawn up by Richard II at Durham in 1385, should date from this time. In these regulations, a number of important matters are dealt with. The military jurisdiction of the constable and the marshal of the host is clearly established, and punishments for specific offences are set out; the need for soldiers to act only with authority of superior ('chevytaignes') is emphasised; order within the army is to be maintained; the rights of civilians are to be observed; and specific regulations regarding the capture and ransoming of prisoners are set out. A generation later, in Henry V's day, another, rather longer, set of ordinances was to be issued, 'the whiche...thinketh the Kyng to be nedefull to be cried in the oste' from a copy to be given to all commanders, 'so that thay may have playn knowlege and enfourme their men of thiez foresaide ordinauncez & articlez'.[13] It was not sufficient for the ordinances to be made; their contents had to be publicised so that all serving or present in the king's army should know what they might or might not do. There could be no doubt regarding the king's firm intention to exercise discipline within his army.

The practical ability to translate that determination into reality was increased by the development of the military indenture, one of whose major contributions was that it established a hierarchy of authority and

[13] *Black Book*, I, 453ff, 471.

command, and made all those within the system liable to the taking of
orders and the acceptance of discipline. In theory, if not always in
practice, authority in both English and French armies came to be exercised in the name of the king, or of one or more nominated to act in his
name. Further down, captains who did not have lieutenants assigned to
them often appointed such men themselves, the relationship being
formalised through the drawing up of indentures. In this way the chain
of command came into existence, and could be seen to exist. When it
was a question of applying that command, this could be done in different
ways. Captains exercised a measure of disciplinary authority which they
could use to counter or eliminate specifically unauthorised activities, and
in this they had the assistance of the marshals and of the court of the
constable of the host. Standards of competence and equipment could be
maintained by musters, and then by regular reviews, when soldiers
under a particular commander were regularly assembled (often once a
month in time of war) to be counted, inspected and passed as suitable for
service ('armez entiers'), the inspection being usually carried out at the
command of the highest authority by two independent persons, one of
whom was sometimes a civilian.[14] It was only after such an inspection
that the crown's financial agents were instructed to make payment to the
captain, and then only for those men who were present and had 'passed
muster'.

The application of such a structured system had great advantages, as
was clearly appreciated when a form of it was introduced into the
French army in 1351 as part of a package of reforms. The quality of
troops, and not merely their quantity, could thus be maintained. In this
way the men themselves, if fulfilling what was required of them, would
experience no financial loss through penalties; nor would their leaders
suffer reproach for providing soldiers who did not come up to standard,
as was sometimes the case. The inspection system had the advantage that
it held no fear for those who fulfilled their obligations, while it could
expose those who did not and who, thereby, not only diminished the
efficiency of the force in which they served, but also laid themselves
open to 'correction by the purse'.

The withholding of wages, the basic source of wealth to most soldiers,
for the breaking or non-fulfillment of an indenture was perhaps the most
effective way of applying and maintaining military standards within an
army. Important, too, were the attitudes of the crown's military officers
and of the courts to military misdemeanours. For a soldier not to be
adequately prepared for war (lacking proper weapons, for instance) was

---

[14] A similar practice was carried out in fifteenth-century Florence.

bad enough; for him to be absent without leave ('noman departe fro[m] the stale [army] withoute leve & licence of his lord or maister', as Henry V's ordinance put it)[15] was coming to be seen as not merely the infringement of a private contract to which he was party, but as something much more important and significant, little short of treason itself. This change of emphasis was coming about in the second quarter of the fifteenth century. In 1433, when Robert Stafford was involved in a suit before the Parlement of Paris, accused of having negligently failed, through absence, to prevent the capture by the French of La-Ferté-Bernard, of which he was captain, he sought (successfully, as it turned out) to defend his 'honneur' and to have the sentence of confiscation of property passed against him overturned. At the same time, and in the same court, Thomas Overton and Sir John Fastolf were locked in legal combat over a complex financial case which was concerned, on the one hand, with a matter of personal honour, on the other, and more significantly, with how money, collected in the form of taxes, should be spent.[16] How far, the question was being asked in these years, was the obligation of the king (and, by implication, that of soldiers in his pay) to defend the public welfare the all-important consideration governing military conduct? A soldier, having agreed by indenture to serve the king or his representative in return for the promise of pay, was now coming to be seen as accepting pay from public funds, so that the obligation to serve the public welfare (expressed in terms such as 'la chose publique' or 'la deffense du pais') imposed itself with greater moral weight upon his shoulders. In 1439 the English Parliament moved with the times when it passed legislation making desertion, even when no war was being fought, the breaking not simply of a private contract between soldier and captain but, more important, the breaking of a formal undertaking in which both soldier and captain were the servants of a greater, public good. In such circumstances, and with such ideas in the air, it is scarcely surprising that every effort possible should have been made to achieve and maintain proper authority over every soldier in an army. With Parliament asking questions about the spending of funds publicly voted, it became morally incumbent, as well as militarily desirable, for commanders to impose discipline from the top. Very slowly the idea of public accountability for money spent (or ill spent) was coming into being.[17]

---

[15] *Black Book*, I, 466.

[16] Allmand and Armstrong (eds.), *English suits*, pp. 220–30, 231–68.

[17] A. Curry, 'The first English standing army? Military organisation in Lancastrian Normandy, 1420–1450', *Patronage, pedigree, and power in later medieval England*, ed. C. Ross (Gloucester: Totowa, 1979), pp. 205–6.

DIPLOMACY

The delicate relationship between England and France, based since 1259 upon the treaty of Paris, needed very careful handling. None took more care than did the English who, in the second half of the thirteenth century, began to build the foundations of a diplomatic service and record-keeping system so efficiently that, in the mid-fifteenth century, Jean Juvénal des Ursins, impressed by its workings, drew his sovereign's attention to it as an example to follow. That service was based upon two essential factors: a suitable personnel, and an archive system. With regard to the first, there was an increasingly conscious effort to enable envoys to develop a specialism (for example, knowledge of the problems of one country) with the result that the same persons were sent time and again to help negotiate treaties or breaches of truce with that country. There were advantages, particularly that of continuity, in such a system: Henry V's envoys were not impressed in 1418 when they found that their French counterparts were not familiar with the terms of the treaty of Brétigny (which the English wanted to apply) nor with the Frenchmen's evident lack of exact geographical knowledge. The growing professionalism of English diplomats was further reflected in the legal training, particularly in canon and civil law, which many had received. In a world in which treaties were drawn up and negotiations often carried out in accordance with principles derived from these legal traditions, experts in such matters could have an important part to play. No embassy with powers to treat could be without its legal expert, and, if the gathering were to be a significant one, a number would be in attendance. The increasing popularity of civil law as a subject of study at Oxford and Cambridge in the late Middle Ages, and the founding, by Edward II, of the King's Hall, Cambridge, as an institution many of whose members were to train in law before entering the royal service, is evidence of the universities being aware of society's developing needs, and of their wish to supply the state with the suitably qualified personnel it needed.

Along with this expansion of personnel went the development of an archive or departmental file. In 1268, John of St Denis had already been named Keeper of Papal Bulls by Henry III in an attempt to bring order to a situation in which essential documents were subject to dispersal. A generation later a 'Keeper of the Processes and other royal records concerning the duchy of Aquitaine' was appointed, his first task being to collect, sort, and store a wide variety of diplomatic documents, and to provide royal envoys with both the necessary records and advice which would help them in their work. The importance of what was being done was underlined when, in 1294, the English lost most of their records concerning Aquitaine when these were dumped on the island of Oléron by a mutinous crew, only to be seized by the French when they later took the island. Such an administrative disaster led to the compilation, between 1320 and 1322, of a calendar of a wide variety of documents touching the duchy of Aquitaine 'in order to have a fuller memory thereof in the future',[18] the documents having already been divided into a number of classes for the sake of convenience, an index permitting ease of access to what was being sought. A collection of diplomatic documents with an essentially practical value had been created.

The organisation of diplomatic practice was being developed in accordance with the needs of the time. The day of the permanent embassy had not yet dawned; it would do so, under Italian influence, only in the second half of the fifteenth century. In the meanwhile, the most had to be made of the existing *ad hoc* system, by which embassies were despatched to fulfil a particular mission and then return home once it was completed. None the less, there can be no doubt that the status of the ambassador was rising. Envoys were increasingly chosen not merely for their social status (although that was important) but for their experience and, in some cases, for their oratorical and linguistic skills. A knowledge of the law could have an important contribution to play in an embassy's work: an ability to speak good Latin (as Thomas Bekynton, one of Henry VI's leading ambassadors, possessed) was also highly regarded, particularly among the English who mistrusted those, such as the French, who preferred to negotiate in their own language. Latin, it was felt, was a language which was generally understood, and in which ambiguities could be avoided.

The growing importance attributed to diplomacy could be seen in other ways. The sacredness of the diplomat's work ('Blessed are the peace-makers') was underlined by the scene chosen for the solemn sealing of treaties: the Anglo-Portuguese alliance of May 1386 was sealed in the chapel royal at Windsor, while that of Troyes was sealed on and proclaimed from the high altar of the cathedral on 21 May 1420 in the presence of Henry V, the English using the same seal, with change of name, as Edward III had used for the treaty of Brétigny some sixty years earlier. Adherence to the terms of so solemn an agreement could not be easily renounced: Philip, duke of Burgundy, had to seek papal dispensation from the allegiance which he had given to Henry V on the occasion just cited. The immunities and privileges accorded to envoys on their travels (privileges which many abused, claimed Philippe de

---

[18] Quoted in *A Gascon calendar of 1322*, ed. G. P. Cuttino (Camden third series, 70, London, 1949), p. viii.

Commynes, who regarded ambassadors as legalised spies) were also part of the growing recognition of the work of ambassadors, which ought to be carried out, as far as was possible, without fear of harm being done to them on their travels, particularly in the lands of an enemy. Rulers generally recognised this. Far from wishing to harm envoys, they often made a point of making expensive presents to them, perhaps as a sign of friendship, more probably in the hope of thereby obtaining a favourable report of their own country at the court of another.

The more important and influential diplomacy became, so the need to organise it with greater efficiency came to be recognised. We have noted that one important factor was for envoys to have easy and reasonably well-organised access to papers, which might include instructions given to, and memoranda drawn up by, former ambassadors. This enabled diplomacy to be carried out with continuity: envoys could see what their predecessors had said and done, what offers had been made – and perhaps rejected – by both sides, knowledge which was intended to strengthen the hand of new negotiators. Another factor of importance was that the instructions of new envoys should bear relation to the actual war situation and to the views of those who formulated policy. Until about the middle years of the fourteenth century, the English chancery issued the major formal documents, such as procurations and letters of credence, which every embassy needed before it could treat; the same department, too, was the main training ground for those sent on diplomatic missions. But the war brought change, a move towards more direct royal participation in diplomacy through the greater use of the Chamber, to store incoming documents, and of the Wardrobe, with its close proximity to the person of the king. This tendency, to some extent paralleled (as we have seen) in financial and military organisation, led to a greater control by the king and his council of the diplomatic process through documents issued under the privy seal and, under Richard II, the king's own signet. Such a system had two advantages. It enabled documents to be prepared close to the source of authority from which they emanated; while such a development also enabled a measure of flexibility, even, if need be, of speed to be introduced into the system. It became clear that negotiations with foreign states were being organised in a manner which made for the greatest degree of compatability between the complexities of administration and the desire of the king, and those whose advice he sought, to make their influence upon diplomacy properly felt. The practice of an embassy reporting back to the king (and probably to his council, too) either when its mission was completed or when it sought further instructions, and the frequent presence of the clerk from the royal household among members of an embassy, reflect clearly how the newly developing procedures were being built around the office of the king. In this manner of proceeding lay the greatest hope of co-ordinating war and diplomacy at the centre.

5

WAR, SOCIAL MOVEMENT, AND CHANGE

It has become increasingly accepted over recent years that the economic effects of war upon European society may only be seen in their true perspective when studied in the context of the long-term developments of the late Middle Ages. This approach to history sees the thirteenth century as a period of fairly general expansion and prosperity, when populations grew and the land needed to sustain them was developed. Although in many places both population and prosperity had ceased to grow by the last years of the century, the rapid decline which occurred in much of Europe in the first half of the fourteenth century shocked contemporaries. It must have seemed that nature (or was it God manipulating nature?) had turned on man to punish him.

Between 1315 and 1317 prolonged rains and unseasonal weather in many parts of northern Europe lead to dearth, lack of seed corn, a shortage of salt (which could not be properly dried when the sun failed to show itself for long periods), followed by epidemics of murrain among sheep and cattle. These years of famine which, in some places, recurred in 1321 and 1322, are now regarded by many historians as the turning point in the history of the period. For these disturbed years led to greater numbers living on the poverty line, to an increase in crime, a further decline in population (that of Flanders had decreased by 10 per cent in 1315–16), uncertainty in England about the wool trade and, very important, a marked rise in the surrender of land holdings, clear indications of a crisis and of little hope being placed in the immediate future. In France, bad and irregular harvests in the decade 1340–50 were to have considerable effects upon production. No wonder that the weather

appeared as a recurring theme in the brief record of these years given in
La petite chronique de Guyenne.

Then, in 1348 (following severe flooding in south-west France in the
previous year) there came the plague, which hit much of Europe and
never completely disappeared, recurring again, in England for example,
in 1361, 1369, and 1375. The effects were sudden and catastrophic.
Mortality rates ranged from about one-eighth to two-thirds, with long-
term adverse results. Prices rose, as did wages, when less land came under
cultivation. Populations became more mobile. For the landowning
classes such devastation could be disastrous. If some large estates survived
and, in a few cases, became even larger by the purchase of surplus land,
the troubles were to affect more modest landowners, especially those
whose estates lay in sparsely populated and already less prosperous
regions.

Other kinds of changes were taking place elsewhere. By the end of the
thirteenth century the economy of Flanders was on the downward slope,
affected by the commercial enterprise of Italy, the development of the
cloth-making industry in England, the need to import large quantities
of cereal, mainly from the Baltic, to feed a dense population, and by self-
inflicted wounds of political rivalry and war with France. Flemish
manufacturing and trade patterns were changing, and with these so did
those of other countries, notably England. It is against such a background
of change that war and its effects can be seen.

How did such factors affect those who lived in urban communities?
Plague hit towns more dramatically than it did the countryside. Furthermore, in time of war, townsfolk were in an unenviable situation. Without walls they were defenceless, at the mercy of even relatively small
forces of soldiers or freelance troops. Not unnaturally, many towns
chose to build walls, but in so doing involved themselves in cruel
expense: Rouen spent about a quarter of its municipal budget on the
building and maintenance of its defences during these years. Once built,
it might be thought, walls provided security for those living within
them. Yet they proved a powerful attraction to refugees fleeing before
armies, whilst the changed character of the war meant that they attracted
those whose aim was not merely raiding, but conquest.

The close link between town and countryside was evident both in
military terms (the town was both a refuge and a place where a garrison,
intended to protect the surrounding 'plat pays', was stationed) and in
economic ones. The countryside might rely on urban-based industries
for certain of its needs; but more so the town depended upon the rural
population to provide it with some of the basic necessities of everyday
life, notably the bulk of its food. One has only to read the account given

by the 'Bourgeois de Paris' of fresh food arriving in Paris, often by river, to appreciate the significance to the town-dweller of having ready and easy access to regular supplies, sometimes from nearby, sometimes from far away. The Parisians counted upon peace in Normandy for fish from the Channel ports, particularly Dieppe; and when Chartres, some fifty miles from the capital as the crow flies, fell to the forces of Charles VII in April 1432, the immediate effect was a sharp rise in the price of bread in Paris, since much of the corn required was grown in an area now vulnerable to the attention of enemy soldiers. The bitter language used by the 'Bourgeois' against those (usually Armagnacs) who deliberately destroyed Paris's sources of supply shows how far towns were reliant upon the countryside for many of their everyday needs, and how true was the saying that the quickest way to take a town was to ravage the country round about.

Trade and commerce were among the first to feel the effects of war. At Caen, in Normandy, the amount paid for the right to farm taxes in the port in 1326 was 2,800 *livres*; by 1368 it had fallen to 1,650 *livres*, while by 1413 it had sunk to a mere 1,100 *livres*. The trade of the town was clearly contracting. In England, the decline of Winchelsea, in Sussex, was finally settled by the French raid of 1380, from which the town never recovered; Yarmouth was to feel the effects of war at sea and increasing competition from Flanders in the second half of the fourteenth century; while on the Dorset coast Melcombe Regis, which had once been a centre of shipping and had contributed vessels to the fleet, but had twice been burned in the reigns of Edward III and Richard II, was in rapid decline by the beginning of the fifteenth century, the customs post being discontinued in 1433.

Yet if many small ports suffered from the effects of war, large ones did not necessarily do so. The hegemony of London among English ports and towns continued. So did the prosperity of Bristol, even though its imports of wine from Gascony were never to be higher than they had been in the time of Edward I. So even Bristol's trade was to change. It depended for much of its wealth upon the link with Bordeaux, to which went cloth and other everyday commodities in exchange for wine. The availability of that wine depended upon political and military good fortune, especially in the 'Haut Pays', Bordeaux's hinterland. In the years of active war in Aquitaine the volume of trade declined, only to rise again when military activity ceased. The commerce in wine, therefore, was closely linked to conditions in south-western France: the relatively low years of 1348–9, 1355–6, 1369–70, and 1374–6 coincided with years of plague and war. After the French reconquest of Aquitaine in 1453 the wine trade with Bristol suffered a sharp decline. Although it was to be revived some years later, Bristol had already learned the vital lesson. Like other ports, it was to diversify its activity to trade with Spain and Portugal; and, as the author of the *Libelle of Englyshe Polycye* wrote *c.* 1437, Bristol was one of the ports from which the fishing trade with Iceland was to be carried out.

The conveyance of produce was as much a part of commerce as was its manufacture, since it generated wealth for others than producers or growers. War had the effect of dislocating maritime activity. We have seen how merchant ships were regularly requisitioned for the transport of men, horses, and armaments for war across the sea. The long list of Norman ports from which ships came to join the French navy at Sluys in the spring of 1340 suggests that there must have been a major effect on commercial activity in the Channel, normally vital to local prosperity, during those months which the losses in both men and vessels, suffered at the hands of the English in the battle, can only have compounded. Piracy, sometimes carried out under the guise of war (the opposite was also true) made further inroads upon trade. It was war and piracy which forced up the costs of wine by compelling merchants to add significant freight charges, which rose from 8 shillings a tun in 1300 to 12 or 13 shillings in 1350, for wine being carried from Bordeaux to England, those sums helping to pay for protection at sea; in 1372–3 the Bristol *Gracedieu* carried a crew of fifty instead of twenty-six precisely for that purpose.[1] The admiration of the author of the *Libelle* for Edward III was largely based upon the measures which that king had taken for the protection of English trade against Bretons, 'the gretteste rovers and the gretteste thevys that have bene in the see many a yere'.

How was the countryside affected by war? Its importance in the life of France was well understood by contemporaries. 'If the countryside is destroyed', wrote Jean de Courtecuisse in 1413, 'all the estates of the kingdom will experience poverty.' Such was the opinion of one sensitive and careful observer, an opinion which has received much support from the recent study on the subject. Armies, with the insecurity which their presence all too easily implied, often did little good to rural economies. Being what they were, military tactics meant that the most vulnerable targets were the sources of production in the countryside: the mill, the barn (preferably full as it would be in the summer), the field of uncut corn (how far was it appreciated that a burned crop could fertilise the earth?), the fruit trees in an orchard, the vineyard on a valley side. All these could be destroyed quickly and with little cost or risk to the soldiery, for most were difficult to defend, although villages, churches,

[1] On the commerce of Bristol, see A. Crawford, *Bristol and the wine trade* (Bristol, 1984).

farm buildings, and even mills could be fortified, albeit at some expense.
Yet if the land's produce could be reaped but not sold, and as a consequence rent could not be paid, both lord and tenant would suffer. The
tenant would be the first to have to act. Having exhausted his seed-corn
to feed his family, it would not be long before he was forced to restrict
cultivation to only a part of his holding, the remainder becoming
'marginal': the final step was to abandon the land altogether, so that it
soon fell out of cultivable use. In such conditions, those who normally
made their living from land either moved to a nearby town in order to
eke out an existence as best they could or, in times of active war and
maximum insecurity, joined that desperate class of persons who took to
the woods and added their own element of fear and insecurity to a society
already suffering at the hands of the national enemy. 'See if your woes
are equal to mine, you who live in towns and castles', wrote Hugh,
prior of a religious house destroyed by the English in 1358. He was only
expressing what defenceless men and women all over France must have
been feeling at that time.

Armies destroyed property; they also frightened people. In 1418, on
the approach of the English, the family of Thomas Basin, the future
bishop and chronicler, left its home in Caudebec, near Rouen, and, after
some wanderings, settled briefly in Brittany, whence it returned once
the treaty of Troyes had restored a measure of stability to Normandy.
Others from the duchy moved further southwards: a group found itself
in Poitiers where it chose to live in the obedience of the dauphin, Charles.
The lands and properties belonging to such people, confiscated by the
Lancastrian kings, were regranted to those, both French and English,
who supported the invader. In later years it would take time to resolve
the legal problems arising from attempts to restore to their original
owners the lands which they had abandoned in the face of the
enemy.

The picture which emerges is of French rural society affected by
natural disasters and, in many places, notably the Ile de France, Normandy, Champagne, Auvergne, and the Rhône Valley, much troubled
at certain times by war. It should be stressed, however, that the effects
of war were irregular both in time and extent. In the Ile de France,
although there were bad years between 1337 and 1342, years affected by
the beginnings of greatly increased royal taxation and the effects of
debasement practised by the crown, the arrival of the English in 1346
brought the first active war to the area for almost 200 years. The years
until 1365 were difficult, with not only the plague but political problems
and the Companies never far away. The next two generations, between
1365 and 1410, saw peace in the region, but after that thirty years of

calamities set in until 1441 so that, in all, in a period of just under a century, nearly half the years were free of war. In the Bordelais, too, the periods of war were limited: 1337–40, 1345–7, 1374–9, 1405–6, 1438, 1442, and 1449–53, a small total indeed for a period of well over a century. Normandy, on the other hand, experienced some periods of war in the fourteenth century and a period of over thirty years in the fifteenth century under English rule. It was during these years, after some revival at the end of the fourteenth century, that very adverse natural conditions and plague caused economic decline to set in. Between 1415 and 1422, it has been suggested, a crisis in food supplies, the recurrence of plague, and the flight of the population before the English army, conspired to halve the population of the duchy. After 1422 there came a period of relative political and military calm which helped to restore the demographic decline; but between 1436 and 1442 Normandy, along with much of north-western Europe, suffered again from bad weather and disease which killed about one-third of the population, an Hiroshima-like effect, as one writer has put it. The result was that, in Normandy, the values of rents received in certain parts of the duchy fell by about a half, in some places by more. By aggravating economic and social conditions already rendered difficult as the result of unfavourable natural conditions and disease, armed men in both large and small numbers brought tension, fear, and material destruction to the country-side. In time of war there was little confidence in the future, little incentive or money to rebuild or even repair property which had been damaged or destroyed.

The fiscal demands made by war came, in both England and France, at a time when they could only aggravate what were already difficult economic conditions, years of low production, unemployment, and generally declining revenues. In both countries it was the 1330s and 1340s which witnessed the formation of the war economy, when public expenditure suddenly increased and measures had to be taken to make the levying of indirect taxation possible. In France, *greniers* were built to house the salt which would be a source of taxation, while in England the system of 'staples', for the channeling of wool through certain ports, thus enabling the raising of dues by the customs services (themselves a product of late thirteenth-century beginnings being fully developed to meet rising needs), came into play.

On both sides of the Channel kings demanded money which, since it represented strength, they needed quickly. But in both kingdoms money was short, and the institutions for raising it, in particular in France, were only gradually coming into existence. So recourse had to be had to artful dodgery. When a military crisis occurred, the king would coax hoarded (and usually good) metal into circulation by demanding taxes and then, having reminted and, as happened in France more often than in England, possibly debased it, the metal would be issued again as coin at a lower value than before, the king pocketing the difference. It was such a need which compelled Edward III to play with fire in his unsuccessful venture of trying to obtain control of the entire export trade in wool in 1338–9, a venture which backfired and left him almost penniless in 1340. The king had been desperate to make a large profit in a short time, for he had foolishly spent £130,000 on continental allies in search of their help against France. But Edward soon found that neither the methods which he used, nor his association with speculators, Italian bankers and monopolists, nor the economic condition of the country, would allow him to make much progress.

In France, although there was no scandal of the kind which broke out in England, the early attempts by the crown to raise money for war met with resistance. It has been calculated that the subsidy demanded in Normandy in the winter of 1347–8 cost the agricultural worker, living on his modest smallholding in the countryside, the equivalent of about thirty days paid work. Not surprisingly, the tax imposed in 1348 in Rouen was cancelled after violent opposition had been expressed; in 1351 further anti-fiscal riots occurred, and in 1355 the people of the city refused to pay the subsidies demanded by the king. In February 1382 Rouen witnessed the rising known as the 'Harelle'; among its numerous causes was a tactless attempt to raise a tax greater than that voted by the Norman estates. There can be no doubt, if one includes the notorious example of the English poll taxes raised at the end of the reign of Edward III and at the beginning of that of Richard II, that the needs of war were the cause of very considerable social unrest in these years, in England as well as in France.

Not least among those to suffer from the adverse economic effects of war were members of the landowning class. From the first decades of the fourteenth century, before the Anglo-French war had ever begun, the class had been feeling the pinch. Nature, in the form of adverse climatic conditions and disease, was causing perceptible decline in revenues derived from land. In the north of England the effects of Scottish raids (which led to the systematic levying of protection money to buy off the raiders) added to the toll of difficulties experienced by the landowners of the region in the late 1310s and 1320s. Vacancies in the North Riding occurred in greater number as a result of Scottish raids: men could no longer afford to pay their rents, and the less wealthy landlords, in particular, suffered from the troubles, a position not unknown to many French landowners in areas ravaged by war. In France, inflationary tendencies were reflected in monetary manipulations which, begun about 1290, continued, on and off, for years thereafter, so that the currency lost its accustomed stability. The effect of the bad weather on harvests also began to tell. On estates which depended largely upon the sale of cereal foods, the effects upon profits could be marked, the value of some leases falling by about half in the second and third decades of the fourteenth century. It is clear that the process of economic fluctuation, already referred to above, was having an adverse influence on seigneurial revenues by the time the war between France and England began, and that the pressure of taxation was very soon felt.

Because the records of some have survived, we can work out how the great institutional, and predominantly ecclesiastical, landlords faced their financial problems. We know less about the experiences of secular landlords, yet more than enough to know that, for many, entry into the service of the greatest of all employers, the crown, was the principal way by which they might save themselves from financial decline. Their service could take a number of forms but, in the circumstances, it was often connected with war. Employment in war had the advantage that it helped members of the traditional fighting caste to maintain their honour (by serving a war) and their rank (by making up for what was in many instances a rapidly dwindling income from land). Once in royal service, many received wages which compared favourably with their landed revenue, so that we need not be surprised, as some contemporaries were, at the willingness of the French nobility, for example, to join the king's army for pay. War service under the crown enabled many of the seigneurial class to recoup in this way what their tenants had contributed in taxation.

There is much to be said, then, for the argument that economic factors encouraged the nobility to support their kings in active war. Military service in the age of the paid army gave many opportunities to those who chose to serve. Wages, even for those with large landed revenues, were reasonably generous. Other sources of rewards (or profit, in the more modern meaning of the word) were also open to the soldier; but these were rewards which were not continually available, and whose winning required initiative on his part. The possibility of making a financial 'kill' was an essential element in securing support for any military enterprise. At the top end of the scale, the sums involved could be huge. The ransom of John II was fixed at 3,000,000 gold crowns (£500,000 sterling) in 1360, some five or six times what the English crown might receive from its ordinary revenues, including the wool subsidy, together with the lay and clerical subsidies, a staggering sum even when we recognise that, in the end, less than half of it was paid.

A ransom of this size was exceptional, as was that of 100,000 marks (£66,666. 13s. 4d.) demanded (only some £13,333 of which was received) from the Scots for their king, David II, captured at Neville's Cross, makes clear. Further down the scale, much more modest sums were demanded. Renaud le Vicomte, taken prisoner in 1358, ransomed himself for the value of two tuns of wine; while some knights, for example, Jean de Meudon, obtained licences from the crown giving them permission to trade so as to raise even the modest sums needed to pay their ransoms without losing their noble status.

In addition to prisoners, plunder and booty could be profitable. Evidence of the importance of such profits of war to the soldier comes to us in the manner in which the division of spoils was formalised. Armies and, as one English chronicler reports, even ships, had men (*butiniers*) specially appointed to collect and assess the value of booty taken in war. The purpose of this was to ensure an equitable, indeed a lawful, division of spoils. Inevitably, the matter raised the question of who was the ultimate owner of such spoils. At the end of the fourteenth century Honoré Bouvet argued that since an army was in the pay of its prince, all the booty should be his. Although a lawyer's point of view, it did bear some resemblance to the reality of practice, since convention had it that a soldier ceded a third (in Castile, a fifth) of the value of his gains to his captain who, in his turn, gave a third of his gains, and a third of what had been passed on to him by his soldiers, to the king. The practice thus ensured a reasonably fair and widespread division of the profits of war; a certain rough justice appeared to have been done, and, what was more, successful expeditions went some way towards financing themselves.

With the fifteenth-century phase of the war, the profits available to Englishmen changed somewhat. Fighting there still was. But with the establishment of the land settlement and a permanent English presence in much of northern France, the nature of war altered perceptibly. Instead of active war, garrison duty became the main task of many Englishmen serving in France, a form of war which, while it lessened the risks of death or capture, also diminished the opportunities of making the traditional profits on campaign. The main sources of profit were now to be grants of land, the application of the feudal rights of lordship, and the remuneration due to the holder of office or other position in the royal or ducal household. Such 'unmilitary' sources of benefit confirmed another important factor, that the war waged by the English in France brought advantage to both the military class and to others, administrators and clergy, who followed in the wake of armies ready to serve in the newly-won territories.

Centuries later, we can still tell how important the profit motive was to those who, in one way or another, became involved in war. The opposition to the idea of peace expressed by Thomas, duke of Gloucester, about 1390 when faced with the problem of what to do with men who knew no way of life other than war, or by the lord of Albret who spoke of the restricted opportunities of plunder in peace time, is revealing. Even more so is the legal evidence of suits, civil and criminal, heard before courts in both England and France, in which we see litigants suing one another for what were very often the sources of monetary gain, stolen or confiscated by one side and reclaimed by the other. The dispute between John Hoton and John Shakell over the ransom of the count of Denia, a Spaniard, not only occupied the Court of Chivalry between the years 1390 and 1395 (it was not settled until well on into the next century) but had already proved to be a *cause célèbre* at the Gloucester Parliament in 1378, leading to the murder in sanctuary of Shakell's brother-in-arms, Robert Hawley. The record of this suit, and others, many heard before the Parlement of Paris, emphasises the long and frequent delays to which litigants were often subject, reminding us of the considerable expense which such suits could entail. The tenacity and hope with which some litigants pursued their ends emphasise the importance of titles, revenues, and, sometimes, a measure of local influence which the profits of war might bring to men who spent much of their lives at war, and for whose defence they were prepared to incur considerable costs and effort. Early in the fifteenth century the poet, John Lydgate, put it this way:

> Now of days men
> Yerne and desiren after muck so sore
> That they good faime hav leyd...
> To wynne worldly tresour and richesse.

Was it all worth it? Was it all gain? To a fortunate few, war became a source of personal wealth. Sir Robert Knolles, a valet who became an influential knight, made his fortune in France and Spain partly as a freelance soldier, partly in the service of the crown. At the time of the Peasants' Revolt in 1381, he was reported by Froissart to have been in London 'guarding his treasure with over six score fighting men all in readiness', a fact confirmed by another chronicler, Thomas Walsingham, who described Knolles's fortune as having reached almost royal proportions. In the fifteenth century Sir John Fastolf achieved fortune from war in France, whence he sent home money to be invested in land.[2] Others made use of war's opportunities in different ways. It was not only

[2] K. B. McFarlane, 'The investment of Sir John Fastolf's profits of war', *T.R. Hist. S.*, fifth series, 7 (1957), 91–116.

soldiers who did well. Sir John Pulteney, four times mayor of London, was not the only Englishman to benefit from his ability and willingness to advance money to Edward III. The recipient of grants of lands in a number of counties and of an annual sum of 100 marks for his better support in the order of knighthood to which he was raised in 1377, Pulteney died a rich man. The provision of money also advanced the Hull merchant, William de la Pole, whose family rose from commoner to duke in four generations, although, as the Paston family correspondence suggests, not all were impressed by this rapid promotion to nobility.

In France Jacques Coeur is the most famous instance of a man who attained great wealth as a supplier of arms to Charles VII, and who built what has been termed 'virtually a palace' at Bourges, still open to the visitor today. War also gave Pierre Baille his opportunity; he rose from being a shoemaker's assistant to the heights of fiscal administration as treasurer of Maine, and then of Normandy, for the English after 1436. The family of Perrote, who came from near Caen, constituted an example of a different kind, that of a family which made good by buying lands and rents cheaply from others who had fallen upon hard times. In 1460 Colin Perrote, recently ennobled, drew up a cartulary (or inventory) of copies of the documents which concerned the lands acquired by his family.[3] It is a modest, but significant, memorial to an achievement largely made possible by a state of war, an instance of persons with the ability of finding ready money to purchase a chance of advancement when it presented itself. By the same token we may see those whose lands they bought as examples of persons against whom the wheel of fortune, in the form of war, had turned.

If some gained, others lost, for confiscation of estates was the political and economic price which had to be paid for being on the wrong side. Worse (since it could mean long years of detention) was to fall into enemy hands, for the purchase of liberty could be ruinous, and involve others than the immediate family, as Guillaume de Châteauvillain and Jean de Rodemack discovered to their cost. Nor did the thousands of Englishmen who served in France during the war all return home much better off than when they left. Even the English crown, the largest owner of lands in France acquired by conquest and confiscation, found itself considerably in debt and having to borrow to pay for the war. On paper, the value of its lands looked impressive. In practice, these constituted a diminishing asset: revenues from mints were down; those from forests, now often under the control of enemies, were also down;

---

[3] Archives départementales du Calvados, Caen, F. 1650.

tolls and fairs, because of the adverse effects of war conditions upon trade, were less than they should have been. There were no great riches to be made from these sources in such difficult times.

Such a view may appear pessimistic, to some, indeed, even partial. A generation ago a famous academic debate took place between two leading historians, K. B. McFarlane and M. M. Postan, over the question of who, if anybody, benefited from the Hundred Years War.[4] McFarlane was of the opinion that, by and large, the English crown did well out of the war; he could point to the huge sums – at least £8,000,000 – raised in taxation in England between 1336 and 1453, a large proportion of which, he argued, came from the pockets of foreigners in the form of indirect taxation on wool, fells and hides. For their part, too, ransoms were important in furnishing the king with large sums of money, for he was able to obtain those of the more important prisoners who had been obliged to pay high sums to secure their freedom. Certain members of the nobility, and others who served them, also did well out of English military enterprises in France.

So the argument ran. Yet it failed to convince Postan, and more recently views of the subject have, on the whole, not supported McFarlane. It is by no means certain that the high taxes on wool exports (so profitable to the English crown) were borne by foreign merchants who bought English wool; it seems more likely that the growers themselves paid in the form of lower prices obtained from the sale of their products. What of the other argument, that war brought in money from abroad and that the military effort was being subsidised by the enemy themselves? In this we may be more confidently assertive. While a case for this can be made for the first two or three decades of the war, McFarlane himself chose to base much of his argument upon the remarkably well-documented case of Sir John Fastolf. But the more we know about the fifteenth century, the better we recognise that Fastolf's career was exceptional, if not unique. If we look at others whom Fastolf will have known in France (although few will have been there longer than he was) we do not find his story repeated. We must recognise Fastolf's exceptional business acumen, as well as his military skill. The England of his day was not full of men like him, flaunting their wealth won the hard way in the war against France. On the contrary, most of

[4] K. B. McFarlane, 'War, the economy and social change. England and the Hundred Years War', *P&P*, 22 (1962), 3–13; M. M. Postan, 'The costs of the Hundred Years War', *P&P*, 27 (1964), 34–53. To these may be added P. Contamine, 'Le coût de la guerre de cent ans en Angleterre', *Annales*, 20 (1965), 788–91; and A. R. Bridbury, 'The Hundred Years War: costs and profits', *Trade, government, and economy in pre-industrial England. Essays presented to F. J. Fisher*, ed. D. C. Coleman and A. H. John (London, 1976), pp. 80–95.

the signs (admittedly they are seldom much more than that) suggest that few came back significantly richer than they went out. This being the case, France did not lose much bullion to departing Englishmen (if anything, the movement of cash, in the form of payments to armies, may have been the other way); nor was England notably enriched by the wealth entering from abroad. The financial advantages of war came irregularly; the few fortunes which war did provide for Englishmen (at the cost of the foreigner) were exceptional. That is not to say that they should be ignored; they should not be. It is a sense of proportion which is at issue.

Perhaps, indeed, in employing the word 'profit' when describing the motivation behind so much English military activity in France, historians have been using the wrong word, or have attributed too strong a meaning to it. Profit implies loss. When Sir Hugh Calveley came home with sufficient profit to build at Bunbury in Cheshire, or Fastolf to build at Caistor in Norfolk, they did so because they had, indeed, 'robbed' France of part of her wealth. But of the thousands of Englishmen who went to France in the fifteenth century, many were to remain there for years at a time, sometimes marrying, sometimes settling into local communities. The word which is more appropriate for them, one which they themselves used, was not 'profit' but 'livelihood', not the winning of moveable riches which could be taken away to England in an emergency, but the earning of everyday revenue which enabled them to live out their lives in new surroundings. It is the attitude of these people, now better understood, which should be appreciated. For they represent an attitude to war different to that of the soldier who set out in the hope of hitting the jackpot before returning home. In a very real sense these people represent war without the glitter. In practice their experience of war without what we would today term 'capital gains' was that shared by the majority of those who made their way to France in the hope, if not the expectation, that Dame Fortune would one day smile on them.

In short, we have to understand that the normal military career pursued by an Englishman in France was unlikely to lead to great wealth. Much of the war fought in the fifteenth century was, in fact, the guarding of towns, castles, and other strategic points. Contact with the enemy was, for long periods, limited; so, consequently, were the opportunities for sudden wealth. Not surprisingly many soldiers turned their attention to the robbing and ransoming of the civilian populations. Such activity might relieve frustration, but it did not lead to riches. It must be recognised that, other than on days of exceptional good fortune, war was little more profitable, and often a good deal more dangerous, than living at home.

Yet the sun did shine on some. In the structuring characteristic of medieval society, it was possible for men to move from one grade to another, to move up and, sometimes, down. They could improve their social and material standing in society through, for instance, education, connection and service. War was also an important way of achieving social distinction and advancement. If birth could make a man noble, so could war. In this process, reputation mattered a great deal. The desire to enhance his name in the eyes of society, and principally in those of his equals and superiors, gave an incentive to a soldier's life. Honour, fame, and renown, the desire to shine, were all fundamental to the ethos of chivalry. Fighting in wars was clearly one way, perhaps the best, of earning respect and reputation. To merit a mention in Froissart's chronicle was the equivalent of receiving a medal today. Jean de Bueil, over half a century after Froissart, wrote in a not dissimilar way – but with a difference. For him war was fought more explicitly for the public good. The soldier must not be afraid of the sweat and tears of war. If he had fighting skills which he developed and then used to good purpose, he would be among those 'esteemed by both God and the world'. Knighthood exercised for the common good was one way to eternal salvation.

On this side of eternity, too, reputation could earn its rewards. But reputation had to be won, and this meant taking an active part in war. The more action, the greater the chance of renown. Acts of heroism abound in the 'chivalric' chronicles of the period. Sir Hugh Calveley's refusal to take command of the rearguard at the battle of Auray in September 1364, and the duke of York's request to Henry V to accord him the honour of leading the English vanguard against the enemy at Agincourt reflect the fact that it was better to be seen in the van than at the rear. York, one of a handful of Englishmen to lose his life in this battle, earned the commendations of the chroniclers for what he had done.

Reputation was one form of recognition for action in war. There were more tangible rewards to be won as well, although, as the poet Guillaume de Machaut wrote in the mid-fourteenth century, no amount of riches were the equal of honour. Yet Sir Eustache de Ribemont could feel well satisfied after his encounter with Edward III outside the walls of Calais in 1348, for it led to him being awarded a diadem of silver and pearls by the king in recognition of his praiseworthy conduct. The gallantry of Sir James Audley on the battlefield of Poitiers was brought to the notice of the Black Prince who made a point of visiting Audley, recovering from his wounds, to tell him of the honour which his conduct had brought him, and to inform him that he was retaining him 'for ever to be my knight with 500 marks of yearly revenue', which sum Audley, 'with great nobleness', immediately bequeathed to four esquires in his own service, the incident (recalled by Froissart) underlining both Audley's generosity (an act of true nobility) and the fact that feats of war could lead to recognition expressed in material terms.

On the French side, where knights and esquires were sometimes given important military positions, it has been remarked that a career in arms in the second half of the fourteenth century most certainly encouraged, and indeed accelerated, social advance, so that esquires became knights-bachelor, and these rose to the rank of knights-banneret. The most famous instance of such advance is that of Bertrand du Guesclin, who bettered himself by receiving the county of Longueville from the hands of Charles V in 1364, that of Trastamara from Henry of Trastamara in the following year, and the duchy of Molina in 1368. His appointment as Constable of France in 1370, on an occasion when, according to Froissart, he expressed doubts regarding his worthiness to give commands to men of inherited nobility, was but the culmination of a career which had brought this man 'de grant entreprise' to the top of the command structure and to the level of nobility which all acknowledged. When du Guesclin died in 1380, he was honoured, as none had been before, by being buried at the abbey of Saint-Denis, the royal mausoleum, a sure sign of recognition that he had served his king and his country with success. It should be noted, however, that the astonishing social promotion of du Guesclin was entirely exceptional. Perhaps the nearest to him may have been John Hawkwood, whose career as a leader of mercenaries ended in the service of the Florentine republic and burial in a place of honour in the cathedral there.

Some Englishmen, too, did well out of military achievement. We have already noted Sir Robert Knolles and Sir John Fastolf. Sir John Chandos, knighted in 1339 and one of the original knights of the Garter, became lord of Saint-Sauveur-le-Vicomte in Normandy in 1360; Sir Hugh Calveley won both a wife and a castle in Spain, although neither, it must be said, brought him much comfort; while in the fifteenth century Walter, Lord Hungerford, liked to style himself 'lord of Heytesbury and Homet', the first title being English, the second French. All five were among those Englishmen who had privately-appointed heralds or pursuivants,[5] a social phenomenon upon which Nicholas

---

[5] See the list in *The complete peerage* (London, 1949), XI, app. C.

Upton commented in *c.* 1440 when he wrote of those who had become noble by virtue of their skill, hard work, and courage, as well as through other virtues which might ennoble a man.

Examples of individual advancement could be multiplied. Nobility, the highest social level to which a man might aspire, could be achieved in a number of ways, but in all an essential element was the approval of others. As has been well noted, the years at the end of the Hundred Years War formed a specially critical period when talent could more than make up for a lack of birth.[6] Thus a number achieved advancement by merit and personal acceptance of the fact by their equals and superiors. Such was inherent in the very concept of advancement. Froissart recounts the telling story of Crockart, who came to France from Germany, and became the leader of a group of freelance soldiers. Having made much money from his activities of taking and ransoming towns in Brittany, he was offered a knighthood, a wife, and a pension by king John II, all of which he refused. Returning to the scenes of his early life, he flaunted the wealth which war had brought him. But, Froissart tells us with a sense of approval, the nobles whom he had once known were not impressed. Crockart failed to find acceptance from those whose ranks he had hoped to join. In his case, war had not won him what he most desired: advancement in the form of recognition that his activities and achievements merited admission to the rank of nobleman. The point should not be lost on us.[7]

---

[6] Contentamine, *Guerre, état et société*, p. 417.
[7] Froissart, *Chroniques*, v, 227–9: Allmand, *Society at war*, pp. 88–9.

6

WAR, PEOPLE, AND NATION

A notable feature of the history of both France and England in the fourteenth and fifteenth centuries is a marked increase in public participation in war. In each country, as events in the late 1350s in France and in the late 1440s in England amply demonstrated, the conflict and its many implications, social, political, and economic, provoked reactions of deep intensity, especially in France, where the element of civil war provoked deeper feelings than in England. Questions about the war, in particular regarding its human and financial commitment, were asked quite openly. Was the cost of the commitment worth it? What advantage did it bring? Who, the nation or merely individuals, benefited from it all? The commitment of Henry IV's four sons to the war is seen by the fact that three of them died in France in the service of the English crown. This was natural enough, since the war was regarded as a struggle between rival kings over the crown of France. According to the traditional view taken of their place in society, the nobility would have been expected to support their king in the furtherance of his claim. Yet in England noble support was not always whole-heartedly forthcoming. There is something of this in the reminder given by William de la Pole, duke of Suffolk, to Henry VI in 1450, that his own father had died at the siege of Harfleur, his brother only a few weeks later at Agincourt, while two of his relatives had met their death at Jargeau in 1429. This suggests that Suffolk was proud of his family's war record; but it also hints at the fact that the record may have been exceptional.[1] What was

---

[1] On this matter see N. Saul, *Knights and esquires: the Gloucestershire gentry in the fourteenth century* (Oxford, 1981), ch. 2, and S. M. Wright, *The Derbyshire gentry in the fifteenth century* (Derbyshire Rec. Soc., VIII, 1983), pp. 8–11.

needed was an awakening of a conscious and continuous interest in the affairs of the war among the different elements of the population.

The sustaining of public involvement was rapidly becoming part of the growing art of the management of war. Although the word 'propaganda' did not come into use until the mid-nineteenth century, we may none the less use it conveniently to describe a number of activities which had one aim in common, to encourage and secure the widest possible involvement of a nation in war. As we have seen, wars needed justification on legal and moral grounds. Just as diplomats provided themselves with the evidence, often of an historical nature, to sustain their demands and negotiating positions, so such material could be woven into tracts to support or rebut a claim such as that of successive English kings to the crown of France. These works, often written by the learned and well-informed for people of their own kind at the urging of their royal masters, had but a limited effect: their form (frequently legal and often pedantic) and language (all too often Latin) scarcely made them easy reading; it is likely, more often than not, that they were read by the converted, and that few were brought 'oute of doute' or over to their author's point of view as a result of their reasoned arguments. Yet such tracts (of which it is probable that many more were written in France than in England), although formal in character and unlikely ever to have enjoyed more than a very limited circulation, serve to emphasise how important it was to have defenders of a cause who could justify the need to pursue or defend claims through war.

Such claims, even when pitched in legal language, were often based on history or a particular reading of past events. As the Florentines wrote their history in the fifteenth century under humanistic influence to show themselves to be the heirs of Rome, or the Habsburgs used genealogies to justify their claims to be heirs both of an historic empire and the duchy of Austria, so the late medieval kings of France sought to bolster their position by a claim to be the true heirs of Clovis and even, as some would have it, to be the claimants to the throne of England as heirs to William, duke of Normandy and king of England! Once again, such history was only for the literate, indeed for the well-educated.

There were other ways, however, of conveying a relatively simple message more directly and in a manner more likely to appeal to the unlearned and unsophisticated. From a variety of sources we learn that the door of the parish church often served as a communal notice-board. It was for display on church doors in northern France that the English prepared illustrated genealogies, accompanied by verses, to stress the right of Henry VI to be king of France, through direct descent from St Louis in both the male and female line. To an age accustomed to the use and meaning of signs and symbols, the juxtapositioning of the arms of

England and France witnessed by the crowds present at Henry VI's
English coronation in 1429, and at his return to London after his French
coronation early in 1432, was an easy and natural way of using the
language of heraldry and armorial bearings to make a political point. In
January 1450, after the reconquest of Normandy, the French council
ordered the arms of England found in the castle and palace at Rouen to
be removed, since they formed visible memorials of the English usurp-
ation of the duchy. By the following May glaziers and stone masons
had got to work, and the offending signs of the English presence had
disappeared.

Propaganda could also be used to awaken people's consciousness of
the events of war, to publicise these (particularly when they could be
interpreted favourably) in the hope of giving encouragement and lifting
morale. The return of the Black Prince to London after his victory at
Poitiers, bringing with him the king of France as his prisoner, was the
occasion for triumphant celebrations. In October 1416, Henry V ordered
the clergy of his chapel to commemorate the first anniversary of his
victory at Agincourt; while in 1450 Charles VII, perhaps influenced by
Italian practice, ordered the striking of a medal to record the successes
recently achieved against the English. The advantages to be gained from
bringing before the public mind memories of notable victories were not
merely to recall success. Victories were the supreme justification of title,
an expression of the divine will, the way, as the English chancellor told
Parliament in 1377, that God honoured a country, as he had honoured
Israel, his own heritage, a title which England could now assume.[2]
Following this train of thought, it is not surprising that Bishop Brinton
of Rochester could remind congregations in 1375 and 1378 that God had
usually been English. It was therefore right that Englishmen should fight
for their country.[3]

But, as the bishop added, if God could honour a people, he could also
withdraw his support to punish it for its waywardness. To remedy this,
men and women should turn to prayer, as kings ordered the clergy to
exhort their people to do in moments of special need. In one large
English diocese, that of Lincoln, special prayers were requested over fifty
times during the course of the Hundred Years War, and on two-thirds
of these occasions the intention was linked, directly or indirectly, with
war or peace.[4] As all realised, the power of the pulpit was considerable,

[2] *Rotuli parliamentorum*, II, 362.

[3] *Sermons of Thomas Brinton*, I, 47; II, 339.

[4] A. K. McHardy, 'Liturgy and propaganda in the diocese of Lincoln during the Hundred Years' War', *Religion and national identity*, ed. S. Mews (Oxford, 1982), pp. 216–
17; R. Barber, *The life and campaigns of the Black Prince* (Woodbridge, 1986); Hewitt,

particularly when a patriotic sermon was preached in English by an effective speaker. In 1420, Bishop Fleming of Lincoln ordered that an English version of his thoughts on the theme of war should be made available, and a copy affixed to the door of every church in his diocese. Episcopal records, extant for England but, sadly, not for France, enable us to see how things were done. The faithful were specially encouraged to acts of good works, to fasting and penance, to attendance at Mass, and to participation in that communal act of religious devotion so characteristic of this period, the procession. We may be sure that the age, with its belief in divine intervention in war and in the efficacy of prayer, quickly saw how England's fortune could advantageously be affected by the sincerity of prayer.

Requests for participation in such acts of devotion had another side to them. In an age lacking means of modern communication, the task of the priest in his pulpit was to inform, making available news about events both inside and outside the country. News was always welcome, particularly in time of war. And since good news was doubly welcome, English commanders sent home from France and elsewhere reports of their successes (when they could) for these to be circulated not only through meetings of the county courts and at markets, but also along the ecclesiastical network of church pulpits and places, such as St Paul's Cross in London, which served as important centres of open-air preaching and, hence, of publicity. There can be no doubt that the Church had an important role to play in what has been described as 'a rudimentary publicity system which was particularly used for spreading military news',[5] as well as for creating a sense of community feeling through the use it allowed to be made of its personnel and facilities to publicise and support a national war.

Public opinion also expressed, and was sometimes consciously encouraged to express, itself through other uses of the word, spoken and sung. The old tradition of recalling feats of arms in song and verse persisted. The Welsh, Adam of Usk reported, recounted the deeds of Sir Edmund Mortimer in song at feasts;[6] while in France, as late as the reign of Louis XI, itinerant singers were encouraged for overtly political

---

Organization of war, pp. 158–66; J. R. Maddicott, 'The county community and the making of public opinion in fourteenth-century England', *T.R.Hist.S.*, fifth series, 28 (1978), 34–5, 38.

[5] A. E. Prince, 'A letter of Edward, the Black Prince, describing the battle of Najera in 1367', *E.H.R.*, 41 (1926), 417. Such letters were sometimes incorporated into the chronicles. See *The Anonimalle Chronicle, 1333–1381*, ed. V. H. Galbraith (Manchester, 1927; repr. 1970), p. xxxv; and A. Gransden, *Historical writing in England II: c. 1307 to the early sixteenth century* (London, 1982), index under 'newsletters'.

[6] *Chronicon Adae de Usk, A.D. 1377–1421*, trans. E. M. Thompson (2nd edn, London, 1904), pp. 77, 247.

reasons. Writers who have rightfully achieved literary reputation also contributed to the creation of this kind of political literature. Many of the ballads of Eustache Deschamps, for instance, had war (or its effects) as their theme, or expressed the sense of national consciousness growing in France in the fourteenth century; while in Spain both the civil wars and those of reconquest against the Moors proved a fertile inspiration for verses and ballads of a political nature composed by minstrels serving in the army. The 'Agincourt Carol' had a long and honourable ancestry.

Battles, in particular, lent themselves well to accounts in dynamic language, the words playing on the glorious deeds and courage of one side and the inevitable defeat of the other. The language of political literature needs to be emphasised. It helped to justify action, to boost morale, to encourage a hostile attitude towards the enemy who, since he usually lost battles, was given the role of whipping-boy caught in a war of words, to be taunted, abused, slandered, and ridiculed through the use of a special vocabulary of emotion and of hostility. Strangely, the French (and some Scots, too) thought that the English had tails ('Engloiz couez', as the *Ballade contre les anglais* of 1429 put it);[7] they acted in 'an arrogant manner' ('orgouilleuse maniere') and had come to France falsely ('faucement') to take the crown of France. On the other side, the French were regarded as usurpers of that crown, a people who acted deceptively, broke truces to which they were bound, a 'stiff-necked people' who refused to see when the judgement of God had gone against them. The language was very different from that of an earlier age (and even that of the spirit of Froissart) in that, contrary to chivalric tradition, it gave little credit to the loser or the enemy when it was his due. Rather it was a language applied in blanket terms. Hence Englishmen had a curious propensity for killing their kings: Frenchmen were effeminate and deceitful. In this way a whole people, seen by an outsider, was condemned in a few words. Their very separateness, identity, and characteristics were recognised by others who, in their turn, had another identity imposed upon them. The way a nation was seen by another had a part in creating the sense of national consciousness of each.

Much of this propaganda literature, in particular that in verse form, must be placed in the category of 'author unknown'. Yet the Hundred Years War saw the active encouragement in England of a group of writers who produced verse to order, much of it of a strongly nationalist character. Laurence Minot, a Yorkshireman who wrote that Edward III had attacked the French king in 1340 'to shac him by the berd', was a man with the ability to use simple language to striking effect, whose

[7] Ed. P. Meyer, *Romania*, 21 (1892), 50–2.

lively commemorative verses reflect a deliberate attempt to whip up an emotionally satisfying feeling against the disdained enemy, Frenchman or Scot. Thomas Hoccleve, who worked in the Privy Seal office for much of his life, could make his position regarding England's enemies quite clear: 'I am an Englyssh-man & am thi foo.' The Benedictine monk, John Lydgate, in the course of a long career as a writer of political and patriotic literature, composed verses for many purposes, including a dynastic poem, *The Kings of England*, in which he stressed the long historic link between France and successive kings of England, a prelude to the statement of their claim to that country's crown. If Lydgate's style was far removed from that of Minot, their intentions were not so far apart. Together with their masters, both men knew that verses had their role to play in creating an atmosphere favourable to English aspirations in time of war. As the words which the author of the *Vow of the Heron* put into the mouth of Edward III indicate, war was fought elsewhere than simply on the battlefield: 'I will make war upon him [Philip VI] both in deeds and in words' ('Je le guerreray et en fais et en dis').[8] Propaganda was part of that war of words.

What makes a nation? What, in particular, made the French nation in the last two centuries of the Middle Ages? A glance at the wider European setting will reveal that this was an age which witnessed the death of old 'universal' values, whether papal or imperial, and the rise of 'national' ones in their place. If there were still a long road to be travelled in Italy and Germany, developments would occur more quickly in France, England, and Iberia.

In France, in particular, the idea of nation and nationhood took a notable step forward during the period. The use of a phrase such as 'Mother France' ('Mère France'), as Alain Chartier used it in 1422, does not mean that the idea that all Frenchmen had a common mother was generally accepted. Historians have emphasised that the idea of nationhood grew only slowly during this period; that in legal matters local custom ruled, and that even the Parlement of Paris (France's supreme court dispensing justice directly for the king, whose body members claimed to carry to its burial) functioned in such a way as to emphasise the very localism of French society. Legal particularism was one thing; another was the close connexion between the titles of the great feudatories, the areas from which they took them, and the exercise of real power which they enjoyed within them, facts which helped to develop a local patriotism at the expense of the national one.

[8] *Political poems and songs relating to English history composed during the period from the accession of Edward III to that of Richard II*, ed. T. Wright (R.S., London, 1859), I, 7.

Particularism was furthered by the practice of encouraging meetings of local estates, whose continued existence can be read as a recognition of the desires of most French people to see them dealing with local matters, especially taxation, which could then be employed in the furtherance of local defence. There was, too, the very size of the country and the physical location of the capital, well 'off-centre': Paris was a long way from Bayonne or Brest. Inevitably, distances militated against the hegemony of Paris and the court; inevitably, too, for that very reason one of the main themes of French history has long been to see the centre struggling to assert itself against the periphery in an attempt to gain political control. The process, although successful, was a slow one.

Much modern writing has stressed the significance of the conscious encouragement of provincial loyalties and the growth of autonomy in certain areas of France. The development of the Burgundian dominion was an extraordinary example of this. There were other areas, too, which were not insignificant in this respect. One factor which enabled the kings of England to win favour and exercise a measure of effective control over Normandy in the fifteenth century was their appeal to a sense of local patriotism, in this case based largely on a revival and defence of Norman institutions which had all but disappeared in the years following the conquest of the duchy by the French king in the thirteenth century. Brittany constituted an even more dramatic instance of the reluctance of a *pays* to allow itself to be forced into submission. At the end of the Middle Ages the sense of Breton identity was very marked. It was found in the works of local writers; in a sense of the duchy having its own roots and history and, of course, its ducal house, against which it was possible to commit treason; in its own march or frontier which, in the east, was the river Couesnon which runs into the sea near the Mont-Saint-Michel, thus marking the border of the duchy with its neighbouring one of Normandy. This was provincialism in the strictest meaning of the word. It was, at the same time, one of those factors which militated strongly against the creation of a French nation.

What factors could weaken these tendencies? Basically, they were three in number: monarchy, history, and war. Monarchy, in every sense a truly living institution, provided the country's leadership. More than any other institution, it came to symbolise the unity of France. The thirteenth century had seen developments which were important in this respect. The reign and person of St Louis (1226–70) had done much to advance the cause of royal prestige and power. Louis's piety and personal life, which were to lead to his canonisation in 1297, were taken as being a clear sign of divine approval of the monarchy of France, a point underlined with the placing of a reliquary containing the newly canonised monarch's skull in the Sainte Chapelle in Paris which Louis himself had founded to receive the relics from Christ's crown of thorns. Then, about 1300, as part of a great publicity drive associated with the reign of Philip the Fair (1285–1314) Guillaume Nogaret had written of that king's personal piety which made him into the 'principal pillar supporting the Roman church and the Catholic faith', while the Dominican friar, Guillaume de Sanqueville, almost transformed Philip into a Christ-figure, or a leader for all French people.

What, in our own time, Marc Bloch was to call the religion of monarchy took off even more strongly in the reign of Charles V (1364–80). One of the motifs prominent in much of the art of these years was that of monarchy. This can be seen in manuscript illuminations of the crowned king receiving gifts, or in the king's sceptre, a magnificent piece topped with a figure of Charlemagne, enthroned, holding his own sceptre and orb, the whole placed in an open *fleur de lys*, and including an inscription which begins 'Saint Charles the Great…' ('Sanctus Karolus Magnus…'). The sceptre was one of the items which Charles V bequeathed to the abbot of the monastery of Saint-Denis, north of Paris, to form part of the regalia for the coronation of future French kings. The creation of a new *ordo*, or order of service, for Charles V's coronation, which placed much emphasis upon both the power and the responsibilities of majesty, underlines the fact that kingship was a political theme of much importance at this time.[9]

We noted earlier in this chapter the importance of armorial bearings as symbols of a political claim. The age also attributed great significance to the outward symbols and trappings of monarchical authority. The royal entry (*entrée royale*) into towns other than Paris was a development of the second half of the fourteenth century. In October 1389 Charles VI made his formal entry into Lyon, walking under a canopy similar to that which protected the Host in Corpus Christi processions, essentially a mark of respect to him who walked beneath it. When, in November 1449, Charles VII took possession of the recently re-conquered city of Rouen, he did so in a manner intended to impress, riding a horse draped in cloth of gold worked with *fleur de lys*, his sword borne before him, his party preceded by a white palfrey, symbol of sovereignty. Such ceremonies were important, reflecting, as they were intended to do, the need of the king's subjects to see their lord, the chief agent of unity within the country, and the need of the king to assert his lordship in far-

---

[9] R. A. Jackson, 'The Traite du sacre of Jean Golein', *Proceedings of the American Philosophical Society*, 113 (1969), 305–24.

flung parts of his kingdom.[10] The *fleur de lys* referred to in the Rouen
entrée was the symbol of the monarchy and of France which all would
have understood, especially since Charles V had taught that it had
originally been sent down from heaven as a sign of divine approbation.

A further sign was the sacred banner (*oriflamme*) which might
accompany the king to war, kept at the royal abbey of Saint-Denis,
which became the royal mausoleum and something of a mystical centre
of royalty (St Louis had decreed that only kings, not members of their
families, might be buried there, giving added significance to the burial
of Bertrand du Guesclin among this royal company). Nor should we
forget the claim of the king of France to be regarded not merely as a
king but as an emperor: 'the king is emperor in his kingdom' ('rex in
regno suo est imperator'), as the much-quoted tag went. To emphasise
this the figure of Charlemagne on Charles V's sceptre (the two men, it
will be noted, shared a name) wore not an open, royal, crown but a
closed, imperial one, and was flanked by two imperial eagles. The cult
of Charlemagne at the French court in the late fourteenth century, in
which the old emperor was shown with a halo, suggests very strongly
that everything was being done to hint that the king was being imbued
with something of the former imperial authority.

'There is no nation', one of France's leading historians has recently
claimed, 'without a national history',[11] thereby stressing the political
value which could be attached to making a people aware of its history,
or common experience. Not for the first time, the study of the past in
the late Middle Ages became a means of expressing, channelling, and
developing a sense of national consciousness, in this case an awareness of
how France had arisen and developed, what she was, and where she
might go. If it could be shown that France (and not simply parts of
France) had a natural, indubitable, and historic past which could be
recorded, then the study of that past could make a considerable contribution towards the creation of the present and the future. Paris (the man)
had been the son of Priam, king of Troy: through the tribe of the Parisi
he had given his name to the capital of France – or so the story went.
The Trojan legend had slowly developed since the seventh century, and
in the course of the Middle Ages few countries refused to be associated
with it or with the figure of Brutus whose travels, after he had left Troy
and gone to Greece, brought him to Gaul and then, finally, to Albion,
where he founded Troja Nova, the New Troy, which became

[10] B. Guenée and F. Lehoux (eds.), *Les entrées royales françaises de 1328 à 1515* (Paris, 1968);
D. Styles and C. T. Allmand, 'The coronations of Henry VI', *H.T.*, 32 (May, 1982),
28–33.   [11] Guenée, *States and rulers*, p. 58.

London. The Trojan origins were seized upon at different times, but the late Middle Ages used them to create an ancient and respectable stock from which nations had since descended in Germany, Wales, Scotland, Brittany, England and France. In England the Trojan origins had been dealt with by Geoffrey of Monmouth in 1135; in France it was in the *Historia regum francorum*, written well over half a century afterwards, that the story resurfaced; it was one which was maintained well to the fore of French historical writing for a long time to come.

If one tradition was based on Troy, another was founded on Rome and, in particular, on the imperial past. This tradition, as we have seen, was not limited to France, although in France it was not the people who owed their being to the Romans (Troy had been responsible for that) but rather their rulers, who were descended from the emperors of Rome. The emphasis on descent was also to be seen in the interest which men had in genealogies and pedigrees. The Middle Ages were familiar with Christ's genealogy as found in the Tree of Jesse of Isaiah and in the pedigrees traced in the gospels of Matthew and Luke. The establishment of a line of kings gave ancestry to the most recent of monarchs, as well as providing continuity to their people. In the Declaration of Arbroath of 1320, due importance was given to the 113 kings of royal stock who had ruled the Scottish nation in line unbroken by a single foreigner. In France, when the dynasty was being challenged by the English, it was essential to prove legitimacy through ancestry. As Jean Golein wrote at the end of the fourteenth century, popes and emperors were elected, but the kingdom of France belonged to her kings by inheritance through male heirs, the descendants of a holy and sacred lineage. The tracing of ancestry was not simply a family affair. In this case it was concerned with the royal office and the wider family, the nation. It had thus become a matter of state.

Legitimacy and the inheritance of an unbroken succession was one thing. The whole matter had another dimension which has been stressed in recent writing; the long Christian tradition of the country called France to which the words of St Peter, 'a chosen race, a royal priesthood, a consecrated nation, a people set apart' (1 Peter 2) might be said to apply. In the Declaration of Arbroath, the Scots were able to refer to themselves as a 'holy people' confirmed by an apostle, Andrew. The English, in their turn, could claim that Christianity had been brought to them by Joseph of Arimathea; that the great Constantine, through his mother, Helena, was a grandson of King Coel, and that he had been born in York; and that England had more parishes than had France.[12]

[12] J. -P. Genet, 'English nationalism: Thomas Polton at the Council of Constance', *Nottingham Medieval Studies*, 28 (1984), 67–8.

Yet all this was nothing in comparison with the proud boast of late medieval French kings to be descended from Clovis, said to be a saint as well as the first Merovingian king; from Charlemagne, Frank, emperor and saint (he had been canonised in 1165, four years after Edward the Confessor); and from St Louis, paragon of the royal virtues, all this giving a sense of the continuity of Christian rule and holy blood going back almost one thousand years. The influence of this way of seeing matters was to be well illustrated in Louis XI's decision, taken in 1469, to declare a feast of 'monseigneur Saint Charles, notre predecesseur comme roi de France', with a public holiday to commemorate it. There were other patrons, too, of whom France had a notable series: St Denis, third-century bishop of Paris, but also something of an historic, even mythical, creation; St Louis, of happy memory; and St Michael, archangel, appropriately a soldier, first brought to prominence in the fourteenth century, and finally assigned an order of chivalry by Louis XI. With such protectors, how could the nation or its dynasty fail?

The monarchy would thus have powerful reasons for ensuring that history be written and used to good purpose. The *Historia regum francorum* was already being composed at Saint-Denis late in the twelfth century, and this tradition continued until the end of the Middle Ages. In the mid-fourteenth century Richard Lescot, monk of the abbey, styling himself 'historiographer royal', wrote an historical treatise against England and another on the exclusion of the female line upon which the English claim to the crown of France was based. By the fifteenth century the *Grandes chroniques de France*, written with royal approval, were being cited almost as if they were the Bible itself; while it was in the same century that another monk of the abbey, Jean Chartier, was styling himself 'historiographer of the French', which suggests that he was producing work of a certain kind, in all likelihood to order. In this way the old Dionysian tradition of writing history favourable to the monarchy and its role as the leader and unifier of French society was continued. But this was not left to the monks alone. Members of the royal entourage were also actively encouraged to partake in this exercise. Charles V persuaded his chancellor, Pierre d'Orgemont, to write the history of both himself and his father, John II. Under Charles VII, the royal chancellery continued to provide historians, when Noël de Fribois and Nicole Gilles, both royal notaries and secretaries, each produced a successful history of France in which, granted the position of the writers and the access to documents which their work at the centre of power accorded them, they were able to make use of documentation taken from the royal archives. The virtual invention of the Salic Law occurred in the mid-fifteenth century when, on the orders of Charles VII, a search was instigated at Saint-Denis, Reims, and elsewhere for texts upon which a treatise, the *Grand traité*, could be composed with a view to diffusing a myth which excluded any but the existing royal line, descended, as it was, through the male, from the throne of France.

It is arguable that it was the long war with England which was the most influential single factor to contribute to the growing awareness of French nationhood in this age. With the country open to attack from the English, the needs of defence came before all others. To meet the threat, which came from a number of directions, the French crown had, in the face of strongly-held feelings of local loyalty, to create a national effort which would both depend upon and reflect a developing sense of nationhood. Yet, over a period of a century or more, this was achieved. First, it was necessary to emphasise the inclusiveness of the word 'Francia' to describe the whole kingdom, and not simply those areas ruled by the crown. This was already being done in the thirteenth century, and it was in that century, too, that the idea of the *communis patria*, the motherland with the king at its head, came to be increasingly employed. From the same inspiration, that of Roman law, there emerged the idea of the common good (*res publica*) embracing, in this case, all French people, with the king as their head (*caput*). This notion of *res publica* (translated variously as 'la chose publique', 'le bien publique', 'l'utilité publique', or 'le bien commun') beloved of lawyers, doubtless influenced the great canonist, Guillaume Durand (d. 1296), when he wrote that all should be ready to contribute 'to the defence of the country and the crown' ('pro defensione patrie et corone'). Similarly, the popularity of the late-Roman writer, Vegetius, was partly due to the stress which he had placed upon communal responsibility for defence and the need to serve the common good.

The threat of external attack played a crucial role in obliging France to take stock of her defensive needs, in forcing her to face them in a communal way, and in creating an awareness that all French people belonged to the same nation, or *patria*, owing allegiance and obedience to the same king. But this was not enough. At this stage we should insist upon another factor (already studied in an earlier chapter) which formalised this new-found unity, namely the development of institutions, and principally those which emerged from war, the army and the national fiscal system. As we have seen the period witnessed the creation of a royal army, owing its existence, its pay, and its command structure to the king, but increasingly regarded as the defender of the good of France as a whole. The growth of the army as an instrument of state, its development as the effective symbol of the country's strength, controlled and sometimes led in person by the king, marks the rise of an institution which directly reflects the growing sense of French unity. When Charles VII instituted the *francs-archers* in 1448, he decided that every community should provide one man who would render military service in return for exemption from certain taxes. The essential point is sometimes forgotten; through the *francs-archers* the French army would represent the whole nation, seen now as a geographical expression, since (in theory) every community was to be represented in it.

Complementary to the building up of the new army was the creation of a national taxation system, recognition that the army's needs had to be met: no taxation, no army; no army, no defence. If the common good came under attack, the crown called upon necessity to justify the imposition of taxation which, after the publication of an ordinance by Charles VI in October 1383, established the principle that all, wherever they lived, were henceforth to pay *aides*, ignorance of the ordinance not excusing any person from its terms. Even royal decrees could be used to educate men in the needs of France as a whole.

Two further factors may also be taken into account. It was during the fourteenth century that the two great privileged bodies, nobility and clergy, came to be included (albeit slowly) in the everwidening circle of those who paid taxation and who, like other members of the larger community, became more closely subject to its practices. Secondly, we cannot ignore the influence of the need to collect the ransom of John II upon the growing sense of political unity. For the ransom had the effect of making it necessary to collect taxation with regularity over many years throughout the country, and thereby rallying the whole people around the king in his need, a symbolical and practical sign of the involvement of the nation in achieving the release of its head and leader, honourably captured in battle while seeking his country's deliverance from enemy attacks.

What was the connexion between war, the growing sense of French nationalism, and treason? In spite of attempts by lawyers in the royal service to establish a clear-cut definition of treason which would secure condemnation before the law, 'there was never any precise delimitation of the crime.'[13] Yet one thing remains clear. Treason grew out of particular political situations, and was regarded as a political offence against both king and people. For this reason, some brief remarks must be made about it here.

Termed *lèse majesté*, or the injuring of majesty, treason was a concept which, in the late Middle Ages, could be used to defend the crown both in time of war and social unrest, and in a period when there might be

[13] S. H. Cuttler, *The law of treason and treason trials in later medieval France* (Cambridge, 1981), p. 1.

opposition to the extension of its theoretical and practical claims. But treason was more than that. It was also seen as a crime against the common good of society as a whole, which might suffer from a stab in the back which treacherous acts such as giving information to, or plotting with, the enemy could constitute. Treason was thus an act which threatened both the king and the body politic.

The time of war against England marked the point when men began to be prosecuted for treason. In 1343 Olivier III de Clisson was tried and executed 'pour pluseurs traïsons et autres crimes perpetrez par lui contre le roy et la coronne de France, et aliances qu'il avoit faites au roy d'Angleterre, anemi du roy et du royaume de France' ('for several acts of treason and other crimes carried out by him against the king and the crown of France, and alliances which he had made with the king of England, enemy of the king and the kingdom of France').[14] Three years later one Simon Pouillet met the same fate for uttering public support for the English king's claim to be king of France. Thus began a long line of trials of those who plotted against the king. We do well to remember that the quarrel between the French and English kings was fundamentally a quarrel over a matter of succession, and that it was precisely this which had prompted Pouillet to speak the words which cost him his life. We should also note that the common good of France was being increasingly associated with the well-being of the person of the king and of the office which he exercised. An attack on him, as lord, was an attack on the people; if he prospered, so would they. It is hardly surprising that in such circumstances consorting or plotting with the 'anciens ennemis' would be regarded as treason.

Attitudes towards treason could be harsh. Yet it is clear that the situation resulting from the war against England allowed for much discretion in the matter. Individuals might be prosecuted and punished. But in situations in which territorial borders and spheres of political influence were subject to not infrequent change resulting from military campaigns and treaties, it was difficult to accuse the populations of whole areas of disloyalty or treason. French legal records of the period contain much evidence of the problems thus caused. Both the transfer of large areas, particularly in south-western France, from one obedience to the other by virtue of the treaty of Brétigny, and the English conquest of large parts of northern France in the fifteenth century, brought about clashes of loyalty in the minds of the people involved, creating situations in which certain acts might be regarded as treasonable. This was particularly liable to happen in areas adjacent to frontiers: the friend of one day might technically have become an enemy by the next, and all

[14] M. Langlois and Y. Lanhers (eds.), *Confessions et jugements de criminels au Parlement de Paris*, (*1319–1350*) (Paris, 1971), p. 151.

relationship with him (or her: lovers were separated by living in opposing obediences) construed as treason. In the language of the day, France was a country of 'war and divisions' ('guerre et divisions'), symbolised by those who wore the white cross, the red cross and the cross of St Andrew (Valois, English, and Burgundian supporters respectively). The element of civil conflict in the war led to feelings of great bitterness and the taking of extreme and sometimes very violent measures against those who were political, rather than national enemies, with the effect that accusations of treason were frequently hurled by one side against the other.

There were, in addition, other problems. Could all French people be certain that the English king had no legitimate claim whatever to the crown of France? God, after all, had appeared to back him by helping him to victory on the battlefield, a view which undoubtedly caused many to accept English rule, albeit with resignation. Further, there were those, Jean Juvénal des Ursins, Thomas Basin, and the anonymous 'Bourgeois de Paris' among them, who felt that English rule compared favourably with that of the Valois. Not surprisingly, at the end of the war, des Ursins was to urge Charles VII to take a lenient view of acts which had arisen not out of a conscious desire to betray him but rather out of circumstances which had obliged men, in a divided France, to live outside the jurisdiction of him whose claim to legitimacy, denied by the terms of the treaty of Troyes, had recently been spectacularly vindicated by the expulsion of the English. Consequently, although a large part of the population of Normandy appeared to have 'collaborated' with the English by living under their rule, it was not prosecuted when those who had lived in the Valois jurisdiction returned to the duchy after 1450. As if in reply to the idea that traitors were those who failed to resist the enemy (as surrendering a castle without resistance was regarded as treacherous conduct) the argument that French people had been forcibly subjected to English rule in spite of themselves was generally accepted. Now, the pursuit of the common good demanded the re-establishment of social peace as soon as possible. Besides, one of the attributes of kingship, as des Ursins more than once reminded the king, was the exercise of mercy, which the texts of letters of pardon pronounced to be preferable to the rigours of justice. The strict application of penalties for technical treason in what had been a form of civil war would have been to have taken a sledgehammer to crack the nut. At the end of the war, the cause of the common good and of the unity of France would best be furthered by a policy of reconciliation. The alternative was still further division. After so many years of 'guerre et divisions', none would want that.

7

WAR AND LITERATURE

———— · ————

What can be learned by turning to contemporary writings which, in one way or another, touched on the theme of war? If we regard literature as a mirror, we see reflected in it something of the growing awareness of what war was, what it was doing to society, and how change was coming about.[1] It was through literature that society thought aloud, commented on changing moral and political values, and reacted to developments of which it disapproved. No one writer could be the common voice on all matters which concerned the public; his importance might lie in him being a voice in the wilderness. But some notice of what people wrote, how, and when they did so, can give the historian an idea of reactions to events and developments.

There are at least two ways of recounting the same event: in war these reflect the points of view of the attacker and of the attacked. Chroniclers (like football correspondents today) tended to describe the events of war from the point of view of the attacker, but for whom there would have been no action to report. It was upon action that the greatest of the late medieval war correspondents, Jean Froissart, depended. Not over-concerned with seeking explanations for the causes of war, Froissart's prime interest was to report action in terms which would evoke the spirit of chivalry among his readers, making them wish that they themselves had taken part in the actions described. Seen through his eyes, and through those of his successors who wrote not so well but in a similar chivalric tradition, war was noble because it brought out the best in

[1] See L. R. Muir, *Literature and society in medieval France. The mirror and the image, 1100–1500* (London, 1985).

those men, mostly knights, whose exploits came to fill his pages. Courage, honour, perseverance, and loyalty were among the military virtues to which Froissart wished to draw attention through his writings. He was less concerned with the outcome of a battle than with the way in which individuals or groups fought. This was so because his purpose was didactic: he wanted the episodes which he described to serve as examples for others to follow.

Froissart's message caught on. 'One good man', wrote the anonymous recorder of the deeds of Jean le Maingre, *dit* Bouciquaut, about 1410, 'is worth a thousand who are not', his stated aim being to praise chivalry by describing the life and military career of one such man.[2] Both Froissart and the Bouciquaut author were writers who saw war through the eyes of the individual whose deeds ('Faits' or 'Gesta') were in the mainstream of chivalric literature. Hardly less so was the text of the deeds of Henry V, written by a clerical member of his household. In this work the king, striving for justice through war, is confronted by the forces of evil (the heresy and social dangers of Lollardy, and the treason of some of his closest associates) over which he triumphs (the very vocabulary used has a military ring about it) before winning an even greater victory at Agincourt. Adjectives such as 'epic' and 'heroic' are not out of place in describing this approach to the reporting of war seen through the actions of one or more individuals.

Froissart excelled in the description of the large-scale military encounter, the battle. But he was also aware that war had its other side, less noble and less admirable, in which those who had not chosen to fight, but had none the less got involved, were caught up. France (it was natural that it should be France, on whose land the war was mainly fought) produced a number of writers who depicted that less-than-admirable side of war. One such was Jean de Venette, who could not refrain from describing the campaigns fought in the war's first decades in terms of the physical sufferings imposed upon society by unlicensed soldiery. The priest in Venette saw many of the acts carried out under the guise of war as little other than sin; what sticks in the reader's mind is the bitterness behind so much of what the chronicler wrote.

There was bitterness, too, in the personal record of events kept by an anonymous Parisian clerk for almost the whole of the first half of the fifteenth century; but it was a bitterness which differed a little from that of Venette in that it reflected a deep disappointment at the political failure of those at the head of French society to save their country from the unfavourable effects of war. In other ways the war reflected through the

---

[2] *Le livre des fais du bon messire Jean le Maingre, dit Bouciquaut, mareschal de France et gouverneur de Jennes*, ed. D. Lalande (Paris: Geneva, 1985), p. 238.

pages of this disillusioned Parisian is of very great interest. He was not concerned with analysing political events, which he merely recorded as having taken place, although he sometimes added a comment on their consequences and effects. The real importance of the work lies in other fields. The author had much sympathy for those who suffered the physical and moral effects of war (he underlined the futility of wholesale destruction of crops and property, and the effects of this upon the poor in days of rising prices), but he was also mindful of the degrading effects which war had upon the soldier. It was one thing for men from one country to fight those from another. But the war in Fance was a civil war, an act of treason by one section of the community against another, a point of view which made him reflect that while the nobility might have wished for war, the common people, desiring only peace, had never done so. It was here that his criticism of the nation's leadership was expressed most vigorously; far from uniting the country, it had only divided it.

The historian, then, can search the texts of chronicles for reflections of opinion regarding war and what it was doing to society. But more useful, and certainly more significant, are those works, difficult to place in a particular category, written more specifically as contributions to an on-going public debate about the effects of war, particularly upon French society. By 1390 the war, after half a century, had seen the growth to adulthood of two generations. It is not surprising that the most significant works of this nature should have been produced during the long generation which began in the 1380s and ended in the 1410s. Between them, these works represent some of the worries and concerns of literate people who looked about them and did not wholly like what they saw.

Nor are the views of certain well-known Englishmen without significance in this respect. To John Wyclif war was an evil thing. To his contemporary, John Gower, the poet, it was motivated largely by greed and was not properly justified even if waged against the Saracens: how could a man kill another whose very face his own reflected?[3] Geoffrey Chaucer, although no pacifist, expressed doubts about the war which, by the late fourteenth century, had lasted so long with seemingly so little result. Two generations later, in 1436, when the conflict still seemed no nearer being resolved, John Lydgate, one-time court poet and monk of Bury St Edmunds, who was not in principle against war ('withouten werre be-forn as I yow told / We may nat save nor keepe wele our right') could none the less plead that 'al wer & striff be sett a-side'. In

[3] Gower, *Confessio amantis*, trans. Tiller, p. 148.

his *Debate of the Horse, Goose and Sheep*, a dispute between the three as to which was the most useful and important, the horse emphasised his role in war. So did the goose, as the provider of feathers for arrows. The sheep, by contrast, has appeared to critics as the representative of peace.[4] That is so. But an interpretation of the poem also allows us to see in the sheep Lydgate's vision of the meek and uncomplaining non-combatant who is the chief sufferer in time of conflict, and whose enemies are the more aggressive horse and goose.

What had the poets to say on the subject of war? There was nothing new in the fact that, like the troubadours, poets should comment upon war as they might upon any matter of public interest. Their task was to enquire what was wrong with the world, to express their feelings with truth, and thus to improve the lot of mankind in general. Just as poets such as Guillaume de Machaut, Eustache Deschamps, and Geoffrey Chaucer (in his *Tale of Melibee*) wrote about the proper exercise of power by the ruler, so they also voiced criticisms (often those of an increasingly vocal and literate middle class) against war which can be seen as part of a wider literature of complaint.

Two themes, particularly in French poetry, stand out. One was the need to pursue the war with vigour and proper organisation, so as to protect the people from death, a frequent and favourite theme in the poetry of the day. In this way there could be peace, and the public good could be achieved. The second was criticism of those who ignored or abandoned their responsibilities to that good, and of the consequent need of the king to take a firm lead to ensure the achievement and maintenance of peace. As Lydgate wrote, 'Rem publicam ye must of riht preferre / Alwey consideryng that pees is bet than were'.[5]

How were the themes treated in literature other than poetry? There can be no doubt that, by the late fourteenth century, a general desire for peace was manifesting itself very clearly in both France and England. John Gower, Christine de Pisan, John Lydgate, and Alain Chartier all wrote works in which the word 'Peace' or 'Paix' appeared in the title, while in 1395 Philippe de Mézières addressed a plea to Richard II to bring the war against France to an end. Half a century later Jean Juvénal des Ursins could urge his sovereign, Charles VII, along the 'road to peace' ('la voye de paix'); the war against England, he claimed, had gone on for too long. How did these men envisage peace? All wanted the fighting to stop; at the same time all recognised that, in itself, such a cessation of hostilities would not necessarily bring true and lasting peace. What Mézières, Pisan, and des Ursins had in common (besides

---

[4] *Minor poems of John Lydgate*, ed. H. N. MacCracken (E.E.T.S., London, 1934), II, 539–66.   [5] Ibid., II, 556.

their Frenchness) was their recognition that it was the responsibility of the crown to achieve peace. It is evident that to them peace meant not merely an absence of war; it involved a proper balance in the social structure, the abolition of abuses both legal and fiscal (critics still had a very long way to travel along this particular road) and the curbing of the tyranny of the soldier whose activities neither the crown nor anybody else was any longer able to control. In his plea for peace, Mézières described his vision of an orchard surrounded by a wall, called Tuition, a kind of Eden ruled by a King of Peace ('rex pacificus') who 'stood for authority and the common good...so loved and looked up to that he might have been the father of each and all'.[6] To Christine de Pisan, too, the need for good rule was paramount; it would bring the orders of society together in harmony and peace ('well ioyned and assembled all in on[e]').[7] To des Ursins, writing in the war's declining years, something must be done (the fact that he still needed to write on this theme shows how unsuccessful earlier efforts had been); even if it required the making of territorial concessions, the calamities of war must be ended so that the people (des Ursins wrote as a bishop with experience of a diocese on a 'frontier' area) should suffer no more. Justice and peace, he exclaimed in the vein of the psalmist, should embrace; as the attributes of God, they were a king's best gift to his people.[8]

Lydgate's other theme was that of the *res publica*, or common good. Appeal to the concept went back a very long way in the Middle Ages, in particular in works on government, in which it was often placed against that of the particular interest, or tyranny. Whom did men of the fourteenth and fifteenth centuries regard as tyrants? In England and France it was not the king (whatever could be said of Richard II) but the soldier who was seen as the main public malefactor, who sought the fulfilment of his own interest at the cost of that of others. How had this come about?

The most important attempt to face up to this question, with its implications for all groups of society, was undoubtedly that of Honoré Bouvet, prior of Selonnet, a Benedictine monastery in the south of France, who wrote his *Tree of Battles* in the 1380s. Bouvet had a good working knowledge of civil and, in particular, canon law, and it was to the law that he turned for a solution to the problem. War, he argued, was not wrong when used for legitimate ends, nor when it was initiated

---

[6] *Letter to King Richard II. A plea made in 1395 for peace between England and France*, ed. and trans. G. W. Coopland, (Liverpool, 1975), pp. 54–6.

[7] *The middle English translation of Christine de Pisan's 'Livre du corps de policie'*, ed. D. Bornstein (Heidelberg, 1977), p. 165.

[8] *Ecrits politiques de Jean Juvénal des Ursins*, ed. P. S. Lewis (S.H.F., 2 vols., Paris, 1978–85), II, 166.

and controlled by a prince. It was wrong, however, when it degenerated into a private affair fought without proper authority, as was too often the case at a time when the Companies roamed in France, and in particular the south, seeking their private advantage. It was this development in war which Bouvet condemned so strongly. The knight, with his love of the individual exploit, who was, at exactly the same moment, receiving the praise of Froissart, also came in for criticism. So, too, did the merchant who, attacked and deprived of his cargo upon the high seas, procured letters of marque from his sovereign which enabled him to seek compensation by seizing the lawful property of a fellow national of his attacker, either at sea or in port. According to the law of arms and common practice, such acts of retribution were legitimate. Yet, Bouvet argued, was it just that an innocent merchant, whose only association with the original miscreant was a shared nationality, should suffer the consequences of another's illegal act? Was the cause of justice and peace well served if such a practice were allowed to continue, for the issue of letters of marque did little more than legalise piracy?

Aware of the implications of his criticisms, Bouvet asked what rights the non-combatant, whether woman, child, farmer, priest, or student travelling to his place of study, had in time of war? The purpose of discussing such questions was obvious. Bouvet was trying to limit the physical effects of war to those who actively took part in it; as far as possible the bystanders should remain innocent of those effects. In his view, the soldier was allowed too much freedom, and was too little subject to the discipline of the law. For the law under which the soldier acted, the law of arms, although intended to give some protection to all parties, none the less gave the soldier a privileged position by emphasising his rights over those of others. A soldier must be within society, not outside it.

Bouvet, 'one of the first to argue for the rights of non-combatants',[9] was standing up for the overwhelming majority whom many saw as the victims of the soldiery. It was their good which he equated with the public good, the good which knighthood should be defending, not abusing under cover of the law of arms. Only the person who exercised sovereignty over both the soldier and the general community should apply the laws of war: and he should do so with vigour, to see justice done in the name of the public interest. The emphasis which emerges from Bouvet's *Tree* is of the law being strongly administered by the ruler for the benefit of all, not simply for a few, and of a vision of the soldier as a servant, not as a master, of the community. In this way, as

[9] R. L. Kilgour, *The decline of chivalry as shown in the French literature of the late Middle Ages* (Cambridge, Mass., 1937), p. 168.

Lydgate pleaded, and as Mézières had done before him, the common good ('le bien du peuple') would be preferred to a particular one.

In essence what Bouvet was advocating was not new. 'The name of knight is an honour, but it involves hard work', John of Salisbury had written in the twelfth century, and some three hundred years later his view was to be quoted with approval by Jean Juvénal des Ursins.[10] A country's chivalry, he wrote, must defend its other members, and even its king, in the name of the public good. The knight and, by implication, even the common soldier, was the servant of that good; both, too, should be ready to submit to the discipline of the law. The alternative was that a particular interest, a form of tyranny, might prevail. The firm attitude of the Romans of old was much read about and praised at the end of the Middle Ages. The Bouciquaut author stressed how far Jean le Maingre had applied the rules and discipline of chivalry as the ancients had done, and Jean de Waurin was to praise Henry V's discipline in the very same terms. Medieval society felt it had much to learn from the ancient world in matters military.

Nowhere is this better seen than in the popularity in this period of the late fourth-century handbook on war, the *De re militari* of Vegetius. The twelfth and thirteenth centuries had witnessed an increasingly intellectual approach to war: the knight must be not only a fighter but a thinker endowed, above all, with foresight ('prudence'). He must always be ready for whatever might happen, in particular the unexpected, and he could prepare himself for this in several ways. He could read about the science of war in a work such as that of Vegetius, which told him how to organise a fighting force, how to succeed in certain situations such as sieges, and how, through training, to make himself ready to fight. The popularity of Vegetius's manual was undoubted, many manuscript copies surviving to this day.[11] Beginning with that made into Anglo-Norman for the future Edward I in the mid-thirteenth century, translations were made into the growing vernacular languages, Italian, German, French (four), Catalan and, finally, English. Some have chosen to regard the *De re militari* primarily as a handbook for war, to be kept within reach for ease of rapid consultation in battle or siege. Be that as it may, the work is much more than that. It is the expression of a basic philosophy on the waging of war, intended as much as food for thought as directive to action. Not only do the works (military, philosophical and religious) with which it is bound tell us something of how it was

---

[10] *Ecrits politiques*, ed. Lewis, II, 240–1. See also 'iste nomen militis est nomen honoris et laboris' (*Sermons of Thomas Brinton*, ed. Devlin, I, 167).

[11] C. R. Shrader, 'A handlist of extant manuscripts containing the *De re militari* of Flavius Vegetius Renatus', *Scriptorium*, 33 (1979), 280–305.

regarded by men of the Middle Ages; the names of the work's owners, which include those of bishops and monks, as well as kings, princes and soldiers, reveal to us who may have read it and been influenced by its content.

What did Vegetius have to teach the late Middle Ages on the waging of war? Rather than the details of techniques or organisation, we should be seeking generalities and principles; it is these which were important. Crucial was the understanding that war was fought to achieve a political end. The need to achieve victory was, therefore, paramount, so that a soldier's value was to be judged by his effectiveness rather than by the fine deeds, however notable, which he carried out. Victory, too, should be won in as brief a time as possible, with a minimum of effort and the least possible loss of life. Advance information of the enemy's plans and movements would enable commanders to act with foresight, and if spies could tell them what they needed to know, then they should be used, a point endorsed by Philippe de Mézières.[12] It is clear that, in the system advocated by Vegetius, the commander who planned in advance, and who used his experience of war to the best effect, would be at an advantage over the enemy. Henry V was admired for the elaborate preparations which he carried out before invading France. Equally, and to the contrary, Philippe de Commynes criticised the failure of Duke Charles of Burgundy to capture Beauvais in the summer of 1472 not because God was on the side of the defenders (which Commynes thought he was) but because Charles had come to the siege with ladders which were too short for scaling the town's walls and with an insufficiency of cannon shot with which he could easily have battered down the defences. As Commynes commented wryly, the duke 'had not come prepared or equipped for such an eventuality', so that success was rightly denied him.[13]

Nor would numbers necessarily ensure victory. Men had constantly before them the success in battle of Judas Maccabeus, who did not rely on the size of his army to defeat the enemy. What mattered were other factors. One was the quality of leadership. The recurrence of the theme of the Nine Worthies (great military leaders of the past, of whom Maccabeus had been one) serves as a reminder of the importance attached to this factor. As we saw earlier, men were coming to recognise that the ability to lead was not always an attribute of birth. Authority in an

---

[12] J. R. Alban and C. T. Allmand, 'Spies and spying in the fourteenth century', *War, literature and politics in the late Middle Ages*, ed. C. T. Allmand (Liverpool, 1976), pp. 73–101.
[13] Philippe de Commynes, *Memoirs. The reign of Louis XI, 1461–83*, trans. M. Jones (Harmondsworth, 1972), p. 208.

army, commented the Bouciquaut author, should be given to only the most sensible, the most expert in arms, and the most experienced ('les plus sages et les plus expars aux armes et les plus acoustumez').[14] The intention was not to deny the nobility its traditional position of command, but rather to ensure a reasonable chance of victory through having armies led by men of above-average military ability to exercise effective discipline and leadership over them.

To present a commander with at least a sporting chance, the army placed under him must be composed, as far as possible, of troops who were properly prepared to fight. Training, an important theme in the Roman war canon, could lead to the soldier facing battle both better prepared in the use of his arm and psychologically at an advantage over an enemy less well trained. The insistence of Edward III that Englishmen should train at the butts suggests that the teachings of Vegetius were in the process of taking effect. William Worcester, writing in the mid-fifteenth century, had clearly learned the message (which he probably got from Christine de Pisan who, in her turn, had taken it from Honoré Bouvet) when he wrote 'that there is none erthely thing more forto be allowed than a countre or region whiche be furnisshed and stored withe good men of armes well lerned and exercited', by which he meant trained.[15] Indeed, in another passage in the same work, Worcester attributed the English loss of Normandy to the fact that the army was not properly prepared to face the French who, in such conditions, were the natural victors in the contest.

One final, and all important, lesson was to be learned from Vegetius and other classical writers. Since war was waged for the general good, defence should be a common obligation. In Italy, notably in Florence in the first years of the fifteenth century, the classical view of civic obligation in matters touching the common welfare, which stressed the citizen's duty to help his state in moments of danger, was gaining ground. With its implied rejection of the mercenary, the soldier temporarily hired from outside to fulfil a particular military objective, and its stress on the need for self-sufficiency, the view was also to find greater acceptance north of the Alps, particularly in France. The story, recalled by Alain Chartier in his *Quadrilogue invectif* of 1422, of the women of Rome who helped in the defence of the Capitol by allowing their hair to be cut and twisted into ropes 'to help the public necessity' had its broad parallel in the role played by the women of Beauvais against the

---

[14] *Bouciquaut*, ed. Lalande, p. 402.
[15] William Worcester, *The Boke of Noblesse addressed to King Edward IV on his invasion of France in 1475*, ed. J. G. Nichols (Roxburghe Club, 1860), p. 27.

Burgundian besiegers in 1472, a role which was to win them social and civic privileges from the king.[16]

In the context of a growing awareness of national consciousness, the obligation to take part in the protection of a town or city was easily extended to the defence of the wider common interest, the country. Taxation for war, after all, had been justified by that very argument, and constituted one form of national response to a military crisis, the severity of which would be judged by the king. 'If you ask your people for money for reform', Jean Juvénal des Ursins told Charles VII in 1440, 'they will vote it very willingly' ('tres voulentiers le vous octroyent'). Des Ursins was certainly not against taxation; far from it. The king, he was to write a few years later, can take part of his people's possessions required to maintain the public good, since the raising of money to satisfy public necessity is legitimate. But as both Philippe de Mézières and Jean de Montreuil before him had emphasised, no more than was really necessary should be demanded, and taxes levied for war should be used for that purpose alone.[17] Mézières's comments on royal fiscal practice show him to have been much concerned with contemporary developments. Taxes, he wrote more than once, were high, if not insupportable, and were having a devastating social and economic effect, draining the country's well-being. At a period of truce, when God had temporarily ceased to punish his people, the king should also show mercy. The invitation not to impose taxation during that period was all too obvious.

Although the anonymous author of the poem *Against the King's Taxes* (c.1340), taking the part of the English rural community, had stressed the evil effects of taxation, what emerged from the works of these commentators was not opposition to taxation but deep hostility to misappropriation and misuse. In the England of 1340 it was being said that 'not half the tribute raised in the land reaches the king'.[18] Fifty years later in France, Mézières could voice much the same criticism: money was not being properly collected, but was being diverted into the wrong hands. What he meant by this is clear. Writing like a fourteenth-century Jeremiah, Mézières could point out that the life of luxury being led at court was swallowing up the money intended for defence and re-

---

[16] *Quadrilogue invectif*, ed. Droz, p. 31; R. Vaughan, *Valois Burgundy* (London, 1975), p. 156.

[17] *Ecrits politiques*, ed. Lewis, I, 320–1: Philippe de Mézières, *Le songe du vieil pèlerin*, ed. G. W. Coopland (Cambridge, 1969), II, 66; Jean de Montreuil, *Opera. II. L'oeuvre historique et polémique*, ed. N. Grévy-Pons, E. Ornato, and G. Ouy (Turin, 1975), 220/424.

[18] J. Coleman, *English literature in history, 1350–1400. Medieval readers and writers* (London, 1981).

conquest, in a word for the public good. Gifts, pensions, buildings and other forms of expensive living were draining the funds needed for war. The theme was thus already familiar when it was taken up by Jean Juvénal des Ursins in 1452. In a moral tone he pointed out how John II may have been punished (by defeat and capture) in 1356 because wrongful use had been made of taxes, a thing which a king, in all conscience, should not allow to happen. More recently, he admonished Charles VII, money raised for war had been used to pay for jousting and luxury in a period of truce, something which was bringing no advantage to the public welfare. Both critics were indignant about a phenomenon developing before their very eyes, but which they were powerless to stop, namely the levying of taxes when there was no war to justify them.

A second matter troubled them. Mézières, Montreuil, and des Ursins were united in their indictment of the growing body of royal officials needed to administer the collection and expenditure of public money. Describing them as extravagant upstarts whose corrupt ways and practices enabled them to become rich to the point when they could buy the lands of knights impoverished by the rising costs of war, Mézières denounced their abuses and demanded that they should give proper account of their stewardship. The theme was again to find a place in the writings of des Ursins: money, he wrote, which had been raised for purposes of war was being spent on high living and building by royal administrators who were, in any case, far too numerous and grossly overpaid from public funds which, very significantly, he termed the 'blood of the people' ('le sanc du peuple').

Reform was needed. Let royal officers, both Mézières and des Ursins wrote, be made regularly accountable not to one another, but to the king himself. Mézières favoured a large measure of decentralisation in the collection and redistribution of war taxes: people would be more ready to pay if they knew that collectors had been chosen locally and if they could see how the money was being spent. Besides, the number of officials could thus be considerably reduced. And, in order to re-establish public confidence, each locality should appoint a suitable person to hear disputes regarding the levying of such taxes with, of course, right of appeal from his decisions. Such proposals, Mézières thought, would find general approval; the only persons to object would be the royal officers and a few others who had hitherto controlled the use of taxes, and who stood to lose from any change to a system whose development they had turned to their advantage over a period of half a century or so.

Some literature could be a vehicle of criticism and complaint, intended to show what was wrong with a society heavily involved in war over a long period of years. Other literature was, in the widest meaning of the word, didactic: it was a spur to action, a guide to ensure that things were done – and well done – for the good of society. Victory in battle might be won with divine favour; equally, God helped those who helped themselves. There were 'reasonable' lessons to be considered about the conduct of war which, at worst, could help avoid defeat, at best, might bring victory. Man was learning to break out of a fatalistic spirit and to make his own contribution to events more positively and powerfully.

The military and historical literature of the period helped him do this. Just as the Bouciquaut author wrote (in much the same vein as Froissart and others had done) 'to recall to mind the acts of good men so that they may give courage and inspiration to noblemen who hear them to try to follow them and do likewise', so he reported that Jean le Maingre liked to hear readings from books about God and the saints 'and from the *Fais des rommains* and authentic histories'.[19] This work, which dated from the early thirteenth century, and had originally been planned as a history of Rome, proved to be a best seller, drawing upon some of the main historical writers of Rome, and presenting history as a series of deeds with, as might be expected of a work intended for a chivalric audience, warlike action taking the limelight. Three other works concerned with war were also popular. The *Facta et dicta memorabilia* of the first-century writer, Valerius Maximus, like the *Fais des rommains*, was much used as a source of good stories and didactic points; while the *Stratagemata* of Frontinus, of the same period, was a compilation of military maxims illustrated by reference to historical events culled from a wide group of classical writers. The last and, as has been suggested, the most influential was Vegetius's *De re militari* of the late fourth century, a book whose philosophical message was at least as important as its military one.

All four works were translated into the developing vernacular languages, and thus came to be read in their own right. Jean Gerson recommended that the dauphin should have copies of Valerius Maximus, Frontinus, and Vegetius in his library, while rulers such as Edward I, Edward III, and Charles V owned manuscripts of Vegetius. The first French translation was commissioned late in the thirteenth century by the knight, Jean de Brienne, count of Eu, and the English one was prepared for Thomas, Lord Berkeley, in 1408; while among the other military owners of Vegetius's work were Sir John Fastolf and Antonio da Marsciano, the fifteenth-century Italian *condottiere*, who had a good collection of military books.[20]

---

[19] *Bouciquaut*, ed. Lalande, pp. 410, 416.

[20] M. Mallett, 'Some notes on a fifteenth-century *condottiere* and his library: Count Antonio da Marsciano', *Cultural aspects of the Italian Renaissance. Essays in honour of Paul Oskar Kristeller*, ed. C. H. Clough (Manchester: New York, 1976), pp. 202–15.

But it was not necessary to own the works themselves to appreciate the main points they were making. In the twelfth century John of Salisbury, who owned a copy of Vegetius, had incorporated substantial extracts from his work into his own *Policraticus*; Vincent of Beauvais was to do the same, and their example was followed by Giles of Rome, whose *De regimine principum*, written late in the thirteenth century, was perhaps the most popular contribution to the large and still developing 'Mirror' (or 'How to be a Good Prince') literature of the Middle Ages. As Aquinas had pointed out, a ruler had to defend his people; to do so he must be able and ready to fight, and it was in the provision of advice as how best to fulfil this obligation that the work of Giles of Rome was so useful. When Christine de Pisan wrote her *Livre du corps de policie* in the same tradition early in the fifteenth century, she also quoted Valerius Maximus and Vegetius frequently, while in her very popular *Livre des fais d'armes et de chevalerie*, destined to be translated into English by William Caxton, she relied on the same two authors, adding to them Frontinus and, most significantly, Honoré Bouvet, whose ideas thus reached a wider public.

In this way war literature, whether of ancient or more recent times, whether it consisted of whole texts or 'moralised' ones, in which the distilled wisdom of past historians or writers on war, significantly termed 'the seyng of the masters of philosophie', was incorporated into updated works, came to have a practical influence. In all cases the aim was unashamedly didactic: people read or were read to (as Charles the Bold, in camp before Neuss in 1474, had read to him, 'Valerius Maximus, Livy or some book about Alexander the Great or of battles') partly for distraction, partly for what they could learn.[21]

Learn what? About the art of war? It has to be recognised that since the examples which they read came from the very distant past, it was more the generalities of military experience than the niceties of military art, the general rather than the particular, which they could obtain from books. But since, too, the popular form of didactic literature for princes contained much advice on the place of war in the polity, there were things here which the ruler, as well as the soldier, might usefully learn. Much of this literature was ultimately about the good of the state, its rule, and its defence against outside enemies. It was 'les choses pourfitables pour le royaume et la chose publique d'icellui' which concerned writers such as Mézières and, in particular, Bouvet. The title of Bouvet's work, the *Tree of Battles*, suggests a more than passing interest in war. Yet, in the final analysis, his greater concern was with peace, a peace in which the soldier was not allowed to practise violence for his own end, but used his strength and training for the good of the whole community.

---

[21] Cited by R. Vaughan, *Charles the Bold* (London, 1973), p. 163.

CONCLUSION

How to conclude? After a long period of war, both England and France had to recover from the ordeal. In England it was the monarchy which was, to all appearances, the loser, its claim to rule France unceremoniously repelled. The contrast with the triumphant years of Edward III and Henry V could not have been greater, as anyone reading the very different accounts of events in London in 1415 and 1450 will quickly recognise. On the second of these occasions betrayal, as well as the bitter sense of defeat, hung heavily in the air. Englishmen who had lived, worked, or fought in Normandy felt let down. Even the pride of those who had never seen France had suffered as the result of recent reversals of fortune, for which Sir John Fastolf, who had left France ten years earlier, had to bear some of the odium of the Kentish rebels who attacked London in July 1450.

Before long, the losses in France would be turned to another purpose, a call to arms in support of the dynastic ambitions of Richard, duke of York, who had twice held high command in Normandy under Henry VI, during which time his eldest son Edward (who would assume the royal mantle in 1461) had been born in Rouen. The link between those who had been with York in France and those who supported him in his quarrel with Henry VI is not, in all cases, clear. But the fact remains that when conflict broke out in England in 1455, many of those who came out in York's support had fought in France in the previous generation or so, and were ready to put their experience at his service.

Like a football pitch at the end of a long season, France needed much careful tending, in particular in certain areas of that pitch.

Quant Angloys furent dehors
Chascun se mist en ses efforts
De bastir et de marchander
Et en biens superabonder.[1]

(Once the English had gone
All tried very hard
To build and to trade
And to produce all manner
of goods again.)

By a happy coincidence, which probably had little to do with the ending of the war, the economy of France, which had seen so many crises in the past 150 years (and not least since 1430 or so), began to improve. The weather got better; the effects of recurring epidemics were diminished; and a measure of greater stability (the result of peace) returned to the country. Yet it would be wrong to imagine that all became normal again overnight; it did not. None the less, on a wider European level economic historians have observed a distinct move in the direction of recovery characteristic of the period *c.* 1450 to *c.* 1480. In this, an upsurge in commercial activity was to play an important part. Admittedly, trade between France and England, a pawn of politics, had come almost to a standstill in the 1450s; but in the 1460s, given official encouragement, it began to recover. The treaty of Picquigny of 1475 was to be dubbed the 'merchants' peace' because of the positive help which it gave to international commerce, which itself reflected two factors in France's recovery: confidence in the future which was seen in the capital invested in commerce and agriculture; and the greater security to be found on France's roads and rivers, which made the conveying of goods a less risky undertaking. It was in these, much more favourable, economic and social conditions that the French population, which had fallen by about two-thirds in the past century and a half, began to mark a considerable rise.

The decade or so after 1450 also saw the resolution of another major problem, that of the restoration of property confiscated by the Lancastrian kings and given to their supporters who had, by now, largely left for England. By good management and the adoption of a flexible approach to the law (the matter was one which might have given rise to many disputes which both legal claims and emotional memories could easily have fuelled), this potential problem was soon defused, and

---

[1] Cited by M. Mollat, *Le commerce maritime normand à la fin du moyen âge* (Paris, 1952), p. 75.

a major step in the 're-establishment of social peace' in a country so recently divided was successfully carried out.[2]

Linked to these steps to restore the economy and the social order were other developments, the products of a century or so, which were greatly to influence the future. One such was the evolution of the army, and its place within society. The Hundred Years War had been the cause of great developments in this regard, the most significant ones occurring in France. If, in 1350, the French army was, institutionally, less advanced than that of England, by 1450 the reverse was certainly the case. This was due to a number of factors. As events in 1449–50 showed, France's ability to rid her territory of the enemy depended upon her army; England had never experienced this need, and had therefore not developed such a force which, in France, was an arm of the growing French state, under the control of the crown, benefitting from a primitive form of career structure. By the time the English came to be driven out, France had taken her first, active steps towards the creation of a permanent army which would exist in periods of both war and peace.

Nor was France alone. The dukes of Brittany employed soldiers on a permanent basis from the mid-fifteenth century, while in the 1470s a series of ordinances issued by Charles, duke of Burgundy, established in detail the organisation of the new permanent ducal army whose members, when not needed in war, could serve in garrisons and in the service of the developing artillery trains. By contrast, England had not yet advanced down the road towards the establishment of a permanent army; while Scotland had no paid contract armies at all, relying on the service of able-bodied men freely given in time of crisis.[3]

Costs of maintaining an army were high. Taxes went up by leaps and bounds, the *taille* increasing threefold between 1470 and 1484. There appeared to be good reasons for this. Wages had to be paid, and training cost money. Weapons had to be provided: cannon, which only the state could afford, had to be forged, and gunpowder manufactured. The army had to be fed and billeted, which meant the erection of new buildings or the modification of existing ones. These were only beginnings, yet they were expensive ones. And, as in all organisations, a bureaucracy had to be set up which, inevitably, contributed its share (some thought too great a share) towards the growing cost of employing a permanent army.

[2] A. Bossuat 'The re-establishment of peace in society during the reign of Charles VII', *The recovery of France in the fifteenth century*, ed. P. S. Lewis (London, 1971), pp. 60–81.

[3] M. Jones, 'L'armée bretonne, 1449–1491: structures et carrières', *La France de la fin du xve siècle: renouveau et apogée*, ed. B. Chevalier and P. Contamine (Paris, 1985), pp. 147–65; Vaughan, *Charles the Bold*, ch. 6; A. Grant, *Independence and nationhood. Scotland, 1306–1469* (London, 1984), p. 34.

It was the lawyer, Sir John Fortescue, who emphasised the different styles of making laws and raising taxes which characterised France and England in the fifteenth century. France, he said, was ruled with regal authority ('dominium regale'), England in a manner tempered by the consent of the ruled ('dominium politicum et regale'). To what extent did these traditions affect another factor closely associated with war, the development of taxation?

Recent work has shown what was happening in England in the first half of the fourteenth century. Taxation to meet the needs of war had to be voted if the need were proved. That much was settled early in the period. Taxation was raised nationally, and it was spent as the king wished to spend it, although advice on the matter might be given. In the middle years of the century, in 1356, the wool subsidy was voted for the coming six years, the sum raised to be used for the defence and safeguard of trade. This vote was an important one, for it went beyond immediate needs, and showed that the representatives who met in Parliament were appreciative of developments which, before long, would make taxes permanent, albeit voted in Parliament.

It is important to stress that the demands of war did not always lead to a situation of 'confrontation politics' between king and people, even though Parliaments were frequently haunted by the problems arising out of the need to provide money for war. In practice, the nation's peril was normally recognised and its obligation to respond in fiscal terms was met, something which was helped by the presence in Parliament of men who fought in the war and were able to give an active lead in the voting of taxes. It was only in other matters, those which concerned the country's broader welfare, and which were dealt with after those of defence had been considered, that differences of opinion between king and people might arise. But serious bargaining, and the making of 'political' concessions by one side or the other over matters regarding war did not take place. Both king and Parliament, in their different ways, reflected the unity of the nation. If the unity were threatened, they acted in concert. The traditional English view of Parliament as a meeting place where the king struck deals with his people, who thereby forced him to rule with consent (the 'constitutional' argument) needs some modification.[4]

In France, by contrast, two different traditions had developed. One was the general manipulation of the coinage by the crown which enabled

[4] See the work of G. L. Harriss, *King, Parliament and public finance in medieval England to 1369* (Oxford, 1975), and his 'War and the emergence of the English Parliament, 1297–1360', *J.Med.H.*, 2 (1976), 35–56. See also the appreciation by J.-P. Genet, 'Les débuts de l'impôt national en Angleterre', *Annales*, 34 (1979), 348–54.

certain kings, notably Philip IV, Charles IV, Charles VI, and Charles VII to debase coinage in their favour. Such methods were unpopular; but for short periods they worked. The other traditon was that of raising taxes through the votes of assemblies, not, normally, assemblies on a national scale as was the custom in England, but meetings convened at provincial level, at which local interests often had the better of national ones. In contrast with the situation in England, the weakness of the French estates is well known, so that the monarchy found relatively little difficulty in obtaining the sums which it sought.[5] When combined with the undoubted authority of the crown in the matter of money supply (what Richelieu would one day call 'puissance du prince') this made for a situation in which the effective power of the crown to obtain money for war, in particular in times of justifiable necessity, was very considerable.

Not surprisingly, then, although Philip IV once experienced opposition when taxes voted him for the needs of defence were not reimbursed when the necessity which had justified the royal demand had passed, some fifty years later the climate had so changed that taxation in France had become all but permanent. The causes of this development are not difficult to find: a state of almost continuous war had, as its corollary, permanent taxation, while the need to raise the ransom of King John II, and combat the *routiers* who threatened the internal stability of France (both evidence of grave necessity), led to regular taxation which few opposed. When, nearly a century later, Charles VII took the further step of creating a permanent army, at a time when the country was, once more, under threat from foot-loose soldiers, he did so knowing that, in an historical situation which had long been developing in favour of the monarchy, he could safely count on raising the money to support it. Jean Juvénal des Ursins might chide him for raising taxes 'sans le consentement de vos trois estas': but even des Ursins must have known that his protest would have no effect.

What such developments in France might lead to was a matter over which opinions differed. In the mind of Jean Juvénal des Ursins, they provoked a distinct sense of unease, although he conceded that an army might bring order to a divided society, with beneficial results to the economy. The cost, in financial terms, would be a high one. To Fortescue, an army of this kind could be an instrument of tyranny, both

[5] P. S. Lewis, 'The failure of the French medieval estates', *P&P*, 23 (1962), 3–24; reprinted in the author's *Essays in later medieval French history* (London, 1985), pp. 105–26. See also A. R. Myers, 'The English Parliament and the French estates general in the middle ages', *Album Helen Maud Cam. Studies presented to the international commission for the history of representative and parliamentary institutions XXIV* (Louvain: Paris, 1961), pp. 139–53.

through the unbridled behaviour of the soldiery and the cost of taxation required to support them. Thomas Basin was inclined to agree; in his view the nobility itself provided the king with a sufficiently adequate army. As for Philippe de Commynes, he emphasised that what people had against the concept of the permanent army was not its permanence but its cost, which caused great hardship and a dramatic rise in the level of taxation in the third quarter of the fifteenth century. Tyranny there might be; but it would be fiscal rather than military.

War and its needs – the judgement of historians is almost unanimous – made huge and ever-growing demands upon the finances of nations. Indeed, it may be argued that the development of public finance was to prove to have been one of the major changes caused by the Hundred Years War. But it had some unforeseen and undesirable results. Mézières and des Ursins were not alone in voicing their complaint that it was the extension of the state's ability to tax, on the grounds of the needs of war, which led to the lavish patronage of the courts, royal and princely, to which men attached themselves in the hope of winning work, favour, and material rewards. As des Ursins told Charles VII, money raised to pay for the public good but then spent on other things, such as luxury goods, should rest uneasily on the royal conscience.

The Hundred Years War may have been neither a turning point nor a watershed, but it did have important effects upon the society of the time, not least in the social and economic fields. Those who have argued that the war was profitable to one side and loss-causing to the other have not gained much support. Certainly, individuals gained from war. But whole groups? That is far less evident. None the less, some historians have recently tended to the argument that war caused a 'redistribution' of wealth in France and England, in which, for instance, the clergy, bowing to pressure to contribute to the costs of war and, in particular, to those of local defence, found themselves paying very substantial sums in direct taxes, thereby placing their wealth at the disposal of the wider community.

Taxation, then, was a prime means of 'redistribution'. In time of war, not only did royal taxation increase, but so, too, did royal expenditure. And since expenditure on war was very varied (involving, for instance, both the purchase of materials and food in large quantities, and the payment of wages on an even bigger scale), many came to benefit, in one way or another, from this increase in public spending. Because it gave the crowns of both France and England control of greatly increased sums of money, war also gave them more power and influence in the patronage which they could exercise. Having received money to meet a military emergency, kings had no formal legal obligation to account for it. None the less, this was a very sensitive matter and, in 1377, the Commons insisted on the appointment of two treasurers for war to help allay suspicion of mis-spending. In France, in the meanwhile, the criticisms made on how money was spent make it evident that there was much jockeying and in-fighting at the court to ensure that, however it was spent, whether on the financing of military expenditure or on the wages of the burgeoning number of administrators and office-holders, those with influence should get their share.

Money was power, and men struggled for possession of it, the courts of kings being the principal focal points of that struggle. The nobility, often in economic difficulty as a result of declining revenues and the high cost of going to war, turned to a new means of making ends meet, war in the service of the crown, with whom the nobility, particularly that of France, now entered a new relationship. Even in England members of the nobility were unlikely to protest too strongly against the taxes which both they and their tenants had to pay for war. For that very same war would ensure that money would come back to them, for some in larger sums than they had paid out in taxation.

War provided opportunities to the nobility of the two countries. There would be chances of winning booty, ransoms, and other material benefits. War gave members of the nobility the opportunity of achieving reputation, both among their equals and others. It presented them, too, with the chance of fulfilling one of the roles which justified their very existence and privileged position: the task of defending a people in time of imminent danger. And all this was to be done at the country's expense, through taxation, much of which was received by the nobility in the form of wages or pensions for the fulfilment of military and administrative duties. One can understand why war might be popular among those who fought it under such conditions.

Equally, one can appreciate the disgust of those who felt let down (as many did in France in 1356) when the nobility, paid out of public funds, allowed itself to be defeated by the English. The widening gap, apparent in the social commentaries of the late fourteenth century, between the fighting nobility and the growing army of office-holders, on the one hand, and the 'ordinary' people, on the other, shows how war could become a divisive factor in late medieval society.

'Redistribution' and change did not stop at the level of the nobility. The increasingly wide involvement of many groups and occupations in war also meant that their members stood to lose and gain from war's activities. We know that whole communities died, or at least declined, as the direct result of the effects of war upon their main, economic, activities, which might be trade or fishing. Others, including some large ones, had to redirect their commercial enterprise in response to political changes caused by war. For some years after 1453 the wine trade of Gascony was virtually denied to the English, so that a port such as Bristol began to seek other markets. Likewise the Gascons, still left with wines to sell, began to supply a wider market than before, to their evident advantage. There is good reason for thinking that war had a positive effect in broadening out the trading patterns of late medieval Europe.

War was also an opportunity to those who used the conditions arising out of war for their own profit. These were the early entrepreneurs, the purveyors who supplied the armies, or the builders who, like those who helped Edward I to construct his castles in north Wales, made considerable profits out of war and its needs. Others took advantage of depressed prices to buy up land. As France recovered in the years after the defeat of the English, royal employees living in Paris (they often had the money) bought up land and properties going at knock-down prices in some of the regions adjacent to the capital. These were the men who wanted to register their advancement by investing in land in the country, a phenomenon which has been noted as occurring in England as well, as the careers of several war captains, such as Sir John Fastolf and Sir William Oldhall, clearly show.

Finally, we may note that French historians of our time have increasingly emphasised the effects which war had upon the growth of the modern state. For France a convincing case can be made in this respect. There is no doubt that the period of conflict against England witnessed a growing awareness of what constituted 'France', her national identity, her growing territorial integrity, and the authority which her rulers could exercise over her. France was now a nation, whose king was no longer a feudal lord but the ruler of a *regnum*, with subjects rather than vassals. The requirements of national defence could now be imposed upon all Frenchmen, in whatever part of the kingdom they lived: so much was implied by the establishment of the *francs-archers* in 1448. The war against England had become a national war, directed by the state which became visible and personified in the men who, appointed by the king, institutionalised war by organising, co-ordinating, and channelling the nation's effort.

Was the war as influential in this respect in England? As already suggested,[6] there is good reason for saying that the administrative system which the English kings used to organise war against France was fundamentally the same as that created well before Edward I began his wars against the Welsh, the Scots, and the French in the late thirteenth

---

[6] Ch. 4, pp. 108–9 above.

century. What is important and impressive is how this system, based upon the Exchequer and the Wardrobe, was made to expand, but without its original character experiencing fundamental change. Equally, we must recognise that English society had a homogeneity which, because it can be dated to the legal and administrative developments of the twelfth century, already existed long before the Hundred Years War began. It is true that the growth of Parliament as an institution in the fourteenth century was accelerated by the opportunities which the war (in particular its mismanagement) presented. Yet little could have been achieved in this respect had the fundamental basis of parliamentary power and authority, the fact that, in some way, it represented the nation, not already been established in the reigns of Edward I and Edward II.

'Whether one likes it or not, war has played for better or for worse a fundamental part in the whole process of historical change.'[7] None would dispute the general validity of this opinion. But in comparing two societies, even two neighbouring societies, over a period of time, we must be ready to note not merely comparisons, but contrasts, too. History and geography both had a vital role in deciding how the kingdoms of France and England would develop. In more than one respect, in law and institutions, for example, England established a good lead over France. Even the developments which took place in thirteenth-century France were not effective enough, or of the kind needed, to counter the powerful English thrusts of the early phase of the Hundred Years War. France lacked that sense of unity which England, a smaller country, already possessed. She lacked the will to act as one, and, as a consequence, the machinery to do this in an emergency was lacking, too. It is to the credit of the French monarchy that, in the vital half-century spanning the years *c.* 1330 – *c.* 1380, the will to create a war machine with the ability to work both in low gear (without the need to be started 'from cold' every time war was undertaken) and in high became a reality. Originally at a disadvantage, the French nation joined with its monarchy to place itself on a war-footing. Since the conflict was settled largely in its territory, one may say that the French people had little choice but to react in this way. By contrast, the English employed more traditional methods to galvanise and organise themselves for war. Was it because the French moved more with the times and employed methods which looked more to the future that they had the last laugh? Perhaps so.

[7] M. Howard, *The causes of war and other essays* (London, 1983), p. 151.

SELECT BIBLIOGRAPHY

The list of works which follows is necessarily selective. The interests of the English-speaking reader have been the first and main ones to be considered. Those who may wish to take their reading further should be referred to the excellent bibliographies contained in P. Contamine, *War in the Middle Ages* (Oxford, 1984) and B. Guenée, *States and rulers in later medieval Europe* (Oxford, 1985).

I THE CAUSES AND PROGRESS OF THE HUNDRED YEARS WAR

Allmand, C. T., *Henry V* (London, 1968)
  Lancastrian Normandy 1415–1450. The history of a medieval occupation (Oxford, 1983)
Buchan, A., *Joan of Arc and the recovery of France* (London, 1948)
Burne, A. H., *The Crécy war* (London, 1955)
  The Agincourt war (London, 1956)
Chaplais, P., 'The making of the treaty of Paris (1259) and the royal style', *E.H.R.*, 67 (1952), 235–53.
  'Le traité de Paris de 1259 et l'inféodation de la Gascogne allodiale', *M.A.* (1955), 121–37
  'Le duché-pairie de Guyenne: l'hommage et les services féodaux de 1259 à 1303', *A.M.*, 69 (1957), 5–38
  'Le duché-pairie de Guyenne: l'hommage et les services féodaux de 1303 à 1377', *A.M.*, 70 (1958), 135–60
  'La souveraineté du roi de France et le pouvoir législatif en Guyenne au début du xive siècle', *M.A.* (Livre jubilaire, 1963), 449–69
  'Les appels gascons au roi d'Angleterre sous le règne d'Edouard 1er', *Economies et sociétés au moyen âge. Mélanges offerts à Edouard Perroy* (Paris, 1973), pp. 382–99

[The above-listed articles are reprinted in the author's *Essays in medieval diplomacy and administration* (London, 1981)]

'English arguments concerning the feudal status of Aquitaine', *B.I.H.R.*, 21 (1948), 203–13

Contamine, P., *La guerre de cent ans* (Paris, 1968)

Cuttino, G. P., 'The process of Agen', *Speculum*, 19 (1944), 161–78

'Historical revision: the causes of the Hundred Years' War', *Speculum*, 31 (1956), 463–77

Fowler, K. A., *The age of Plantagenet and Valois* (London, 1967)

Grant, A., *Independence and nationhood. Scotland, 1306–1469* (London, 1984)

Griffiths, R. A., *The reign of king Henry VI* (London, 1981)

Jacob, E. F., *Henry V and the invasion of France* (London, 1947)

The fifteenth century, 1399–1485 (Oxford, 1961)

Jones, M., *Ducal Brittany, 1364–1399* (Oxford, 1970)

Keen, M. H., *England in the later Middle Ages* (London, 1972)

Kicklighter, J. A., 'French jurisdictional supremacy in Gascony: one aspect of the ducal government's response', *J. Med. H.*, 5 (1979), 127–34

'English Bordeaux in conflict: the execution of Pierre Vigier de la Rousselle and its aftermath, 1312–24', *J. Med. H.*, 9 (1983), 1–14

Labarge, M. W., *Gascony, England's first colony, 1204–1453* (London, 1980)

Lander, J. R., 'The Hundred Years War and Edward IV's 1475 campaign in France', *Tudor men and institutions: studies in English law and government*, ed. A. J. Slavin (Baton Rouge, 1972), pp. 70–100; reprinted in the author's *Crown and nobility, 1450–1509* (London, 1976), ch. 9

Leguai, A., *La guerre de cent ans* (Paris, 1974)

Le Patourel, J., 'Edward III and the kingdom of France', *History*, 43 (1958), 173–89

'The Plantagenet dominions', *History*, 50 (1965), 289–308

'The king and the princes in fourteenth-century France', *Europe in the late Middle Ages*, ed. J. R. Hale, J. R. L. Highfield, and B. Smalley (London, 1965), pp. 155–83

'The origins of the war', *The Hundred Years War*, ed. K. A. Fowler (London, 1971), pp. 28–50

[The above-listed articles are reprinted in the author's *Feudal empires: Norman and Plantagenet* (London, 1984)]

'France and England in the Middle Ages', *Feudal empires*, ch. 18

Lucas, H. S., *The Low Countries and the Hundred Years War, 1326–1347* (Ann Arbor, 1929; repr. Philadelphia, 1976)

McKisack, M., *The fourteenth century, 1307–1399* (Oxford, 1959)

Maddicott, J., 'The origins of the Hundred Years War', *H.T.*, 36 (May, 1986), 31–7

Palmer, J. J. N., *England, France, and Christendom, 1377–99* (London, 1972)

'The war aims of the protagonists and the negotiations for peace', *The Hundred Years War*, ed. K. A. Fowler (London, 1971), pp. 51–74

Perroy, E., *The Hundred Years War* (English trans., London, 1951)

Prestwich, M., *The three Edwards. War and the state in England, 1272–1377* (London, 1980)

Russell, P., *The English intervention in Spain and Portugal in the time of Edward III and Richard II* (Oxford, 1955)

Saul, N., 'Henry V and the dual monarchy', *H.T.*, 36 (May, 1986), 39–42

Templeman, G., 'Edward III and the beginnings of the Hundred Years War', *T.R. Hist. S.*, fifth series, 2 (1952), 69–88

Vale, M. G. A., *English Gascony, 1399–1453* (Oxford, 1970)

2 APPROACHES TO WAR

Allmand, C. T., *Society at war. The experience of England and France during the Hundred Years War* (Edinburgh, 1973)

Barber, R., *The knight and chivalry* (London, 1970)

Barnes, J., 'The just war', *The Cambridge history of later medieval philosophy*, ed. N. Kretzmann, A. Kenny, and J. Pinborg (Cambridge, 1982), pp. 771–84

Barnie, J., *War in medieval society. Social values and the Hundred Years War, 1337–99* (London, 1974)

Benson, L. D., *Malory's Morte Darthur* (Cambridge, Mass: London, 1976), chs 7–9

Bond, B., 'The "just war" in historical perspective', *H.T.*, 16 (1966), 111–19

Bornstein, D., *Mirrors of courtesy* (Hamden, 1975)

Contamine, P., *Guerre, état, et société à la fin du moyen âge. Etudes sur les armées des rois de France, 1337–1494* (Paris: The Hague, 1972), ch. 7.

'L'idée de guerre à la fin du moyen âge: aspects juridiques et éthiques', *Comptes-rendus de l'académie des inscriptions et belles-lettres* (1979), 70–86; reprinted in the author's *La France aux XIVe et XVe siècles. Hommes, mentalités, guerre, et paix* (London, 1981), ch. 13

'Notes sur la paix en France pendant la guerre de cent ans', *La France aux XIVe et XVe siècles*, ch. 14

'Froissart: art militaire, pratique, et conception de la guerre', *Froissart: historian*, ed. J. J. N. Palmer (Woodbridge: Totowa, 1981), pp. 132–44

Coopland, G. W. (trans), *The Tree of Battles of Honoré Bonet* (Liverpool, 1949)

Ferguson, A. B., *The indian summer of English chivalry* (Durham, N. Carolina, 1960)

Gist, M. A., *Love and war in the middle English romances* (Philadelphia: London, 1947), chs 6–8

Haines, K., 'Attitudes and impediments to pacifism in medieval Europe', *J. Med. H.*, 7 (1981), 369–88

Hale, J. R., *War and society in renaissance Europe* (London, 1985), ch. 1

'War and public opinion in Renaissance Italy', *Italian Renaissance studies*, ed. E. F. Jacob (London, 1960), pp. 94–122

'The military education of the officer class in early modern Europe', *Cultural*

aspects of the Italian Renaissance. Essays in honour of Paul Oskar Kristeller, ed.
C. H. Clough (Manchester: New York, 1976), pp. 440–61
'War and public opinion in the fifteenth and sixteenth centuries', *P&P*, 22
(1962), 18–32
[The above-listed essays are reprinted in the author's *Renaissance war studies*
(London, 1983)]

Huizinga, J., *The waning of the Middle Ages* (London, 1924; repr. 1955)

Jarrett, B., *Social theories of the Middle Ages, 1200–1500* (London, 1926), ch. 7

Johnson, J. T., *Ideology, reason, and the limitation of war. Religious and secular
concepts, 1200–1740* (Princeton, 1975)

Kantorowicz, E., '*Pro patria mori* in medieval political thought', *A.H.R.*, 56
(1951), 472–92; reprinted in the author's *Selected studies* (New York, 1965),
pp. 308–24

Keen, M., *The laws of war in the late Middle Ages* (London: Toronto, 1965)
Chivalry (New Haven: London, 1984)
'Brotherhood in arms', *History*, 47 (1962), 1–17
'Chivalrous culture in fourteenth-century England', *Historical Studies*, 10, ed.
G. A. Hayes-McCoy (Dublin, 1976), 1–24
'Chivalry, nobility, and the man-at-arms', *War, literature, and society in the late
Middle Ages*, ed. C. T. Allmand (Liverpool, 1976), pp. 32–45
'Huizinga, Kilgour, and the decline of chivalry', *Medievalia et Humanistica*,
new series, 8 (1977), 1–20
'Chivalry, heralds, and history', *The writing of history in the Middle Ages.
Essays presented to R. W. Southern*, ed. R. H. C. Davis, J. M. Wallace-
Hadrill, R. J. A. I. Catto, and M. Keen (Oxford, 1981), pp. 393–414

Kilgour, R. L., *The decline of chivalry as shown in the French literature of the late
Middle Ages* (Cambridge, Mass., 1937)

McFarlane, K. B., 'A business-partnership in war and administration, 1421–
1445', *E.H.R.*, 78 (1963), 151–74; reprinted in the author's *England in the
fifteenth century* (London, 1981), ch. 8

McNeill, W. H., *The pursuit of power* (Oxford, 1983), ch. 3

Markus, R. A., 'Saint Augustine's views of the "just war"', *The church and war*,
ed. W. J. Sheils (Oxford, 1983), pp. 1–13

Mathew, G., *The court of Richard II* (London, 1968), ch. 13
'Ideals of knighthood in late fourteenth-century England', *Studies in medieval
history presented to F. M. Powicke*, ed. R. W. Hunt, W. A. Pantin, and R.
W. Southern (Oxford, 1948), pp. 354–62

Porter, E., 'Chaucer's knight, the alliterative *Morte Arthure*, and medieval laws
of war: a reconsideration', *Nottingham Medieval Studies*, 27 (1983), 56–78

Riley-Smith, J., 'Crusading as an act of love', *History*, 65 (1980), 177–92

Russell, F. H., *The just war in the Middle Ages* (Cambridge, 1975)

Tuck, J. A., 'Why men fought in the Hundred Years War', *H.T.*, 33 (April,
1983), 35–40

Vale, J., *Edward III and chivalry. Chivalric society and its context, 1270–1350* (Woodbridge, 1982)

Vale, M. G. A., *War and chivalry. Warfare and aristocratic culture in England, France, and Burgundy at the end of the Middle Ages* (London, 1981)

Wright, N. A. R., 'The *Tree of Battles* of Honoré Bouvet and the laws of war', *War, literature, and politics in the late Middle Ages*, ed. C. T. Allmand (Liverpool, 1976), pp. 12–31

3 THE CONDUCT OF WAR

Military objectives

Brill, R., 'The English preparations before the treaty of Arras: a new interpretation of Sir John Fastolf's "report", September 1435', *Studies in Medieval and Renaissance History*, 7 (1970), 213–47

Burne, A. H., 'John of Gaunt's grande chevauchée', *H.T.*, 9 (1959), 113–21

Contamine, P., *War in the Middle Ages* (Oxford, 1984)

Delbrück, H., *History of the art of war, within the framework of political history. III: The Middle Ages* (Westport: London, 1982)

Gillingham, J., 'Richard I and the science of war in the Middle Ages', *War and government in the Middle Ages. Essays in honour of J. O. Prestwich*, ed. J. Gillingham and J. C. Holt (Woodbridge: Totowa, 1984), pp. 78–91

    The Wars of the Roses. Peace and conflict in fifteenth-century England (London, 1981)

Goodman, A., *The Wars of the Roses. Military activity and English society, 1452–97* (London, 1981)

Hewitt, H. J., *The Black Prince's expedition of 1355–1357* (Manchester, 1958)

McNeill, W. H., *The pursuit of power* (Oxford, 1983), ch. 3

Newhall, R. A., 'Henry V's policy of conciliation in Normandy, 1417–1422', *Anniversary essays in medieval history of students of C. H. Haskins*, ed. C. H. Taylor (Boston, 1929), pp. 205–29.

Oman, C., *A history of the art of war in the Middle Ages* (2nd edn, London, 1924)

Palmer, J. J. N., 'The war aims of the protagonists and the negotiations for peace', *The Hundred Years War*, ed. K. A. Fowler (London, 1971), pp. 51–74

Phillpotts, C., 'The French plan of battle during the Agincourt campaign', *E.H.R.*, 99 (1984), 59–66

Vale, M. G. A., 'Sir John Fastolf's "report" of 1435: a new interpretation reconsidered', *Nottingham Medieval Studies*, 17 (1973), 78–84

Vaughan, R., *Valois Burgundy* (London, 1975), ch. 7

Verbruggen, J. F., *The art of warfare in western Europe during the Middle Ages* (Amsterdam, 1977)

Land forces

Alban, J. R., 'English coastal defence: some fourteenth-century modifications within the system', *Patronage, the crown, and the provinces in later medieval*

England, ed. R. A. Griffiths (Gloucester: Atlantic Highlands, 1981), pp. 57–78

Contamine, P., *Guerre, état, et société à la fin du moyen âge. Etudes sur les armées des rois de France, 1337–1494* (Paris: The Hague, 1972)

Hewitt, H. J., *The Black Prince's expedition of 1355–1357* (Manchester, 1958)
The organization of war under Edward III, 1338–62 (Manchester, 1966)
'The organisation of war', *The Hundred Years War*, ed. K. A. Fowler, (London, 1971), pp. 75–95

Howard, M., *War in European history* (Oxford, 1976), chs 1 and 2

Hudson, W., 'Norwich militia in the fourteenth century', *Norfolk Archaeology*, 14 (1901), 263–320

Lewis, N. B., 'The English forces in Flanders, August–November 1297', *Essays in medieval history presented to F. M. Powicke*, ed. R. W. Hunt, W. A. Pantin, and R. W. Southern (Oxford, 1948), pp. 310–18

Lloyd, S., 'The lord Edward's crusade, 1270–2: its setting and significance', *War and government in the Middle Ages. Essays in honour of J. O. Prestwich*, ed. J. Gillingham and J. C. Holt (Woodbridge: Totowa, 1984), pp. 120–33

Lot, F., and Fawtier, R., *Histoire des institutions françaises au moyen âge* (Paris, 1958), II, 511–35

Lourie, E., 'A society organized for war: medieval Spain', *P&P*, 35 (1966), 54–76

McGuffie, T. H., 'The long-bow as a decisive weapon', *H.T.*, 5 (1955), 737–41

Morgan, P. J., *War and society in medieval Cheshire, 1277–1403* (Chetham Soc., third series, 33, Manchester, 1987)

Morris, J. E., *The Welsh wars of Edward I* (Oxford, 1901)
'The archers at Crécy', *E.H.R.*, 12 (1897), 427–36

Powicke, M., *Military obligation in medieval England* (Oxford, 1962)

Prestwich, M., *War, politics, and finance under Edward I* (London, 1972), chs 3 and 4
'English armies in the early stages of the Hundred Years War: a scheme in 1341', *B.I.H.R.*, 56 (1983), 102–13
'Cavalry service in early fourteenth-century England', *War and government in the Middle Ages. Essays in honour of J. O. Prestwich*, ed. J. Gillingham and J. C. Holt (Woodbridge: Totowa, 1984), pp. 120–33

Prince, A. E., 'The army and navy', *English government at work*, ed. J. F. Willard and W. A. Morris (Cambridge, Mass., 1940), I, 332–93
'The strength of English armies in the reign of Edward III' *E.H.R.*, 46 (1931), 353–71
'The payment of army wages in Edward III's reign', *Speculum*, 19 (1944), 137–60

Sherborne, J. W., 'Indentured retinues and English expeditions to France, 1369–80', *E.H.R.*, 79 (1964), 718–46
'John of Gaunt, Edward III's retinue and the French campaign of 1369', *Kings and nobles in the later Middle Ages. A tribute to Charles Ross*, ed. R. A. Griffiths and J. Sherborne (Gloucester, 1986), pp. 41–61

Vaughan, R., *Charles the Bold* (London, 1973), ch. 6
  Valois Burgundy (London, 1975), ch. 7

Leadership

Allmand, C. T., 'The Black Prince', *H.T.*, 26 (1976), 100–8
  'Henry V the soldier, and the war in France', *Henry V. The practice of kingship*,
    ed. G. L. Harriss (Oxford, 1985), pp. 117–35
Barber, R., *Edward, prince of Wales and Aquitaine* (London, 1978)
  The life and campaigns of the Black Prince (Woodbridge, 1986)
Contamine, P., *Guerre, état, et société à la fin du moyen âge. Etudes sur les armées des
    rois de France, 1337–1494* (Paris: The Hague, 1972), chs 3, 6, 14, and app.
    1–4
  'The French nobility and the war', *The Hundred Years War*, ed. K. A. Fowler
    (London, 1971), pp. 135–62; reprinted in the author's *La France aux XIVe
    et XVe siècles. Hommes, mentalités, guerre, et paix* (London, 1981), ch. 10
Fowler, K. A., *The king's lieutenant. Henry of Grosmont, first duke of Lancaster,
    1310–1361* (London, 1969)
Haines, R. M., '"Our master mariner, our sovereign lord": a contemporary
    preacher's view of king Henry V', *Medieval Studies*, 38, (1976), 85–96
Harvey, J. H., *The Black Prince and his age* (London, 1976)
Henneman, J. B., 'The military class and the French monarchy in the late
    Middle Ages', *A.H.R.*, 83 (1978), 946–65
Hewitt, H. J., *The Black Prince's expedition of 1355–1357* (Manchester, 1958)
Jones, M., 'Edward III's captains in Brittany', *England in the fourteenth century.
    Proceedings of the 1985 Harlaxton symposium*, ed. W. M. Ormrod (Wood-
    bridge, 1986), pp. 99–118
McFarlane, K. B., *The nobility of the later Middle Ages* (Oxford, 1973)
Pollard, A. J., *John Talbot and the war in France, 1427–1453* (London, 1983)
Powicke, M., 'Lancastrian captains', *Essays in medieval history presented to B.
    Wilkinson*, ed. T. A. Sandquist and M. R. Powicke (Toronto, 1969), pp.
    371–82
  'The English aristocracy and the war', *The Hundred Years War*, ed. K. A.
    Fowler (London, 1971), pp. 122–34
Prestwich, M., *The three Edwards. War and state in England, 1272–1377* (London,
    1980), ch. 5

Mercenaries

Bayley, C. C., *War and society in Renaissance Florence. The De Militia of Leonardo
    Bruni* (Toronto, 1961), chs 1 and 3
Bridge, J. C., 'Two Cheshire soldiers of fortune in the fourteenth century',
    Journal of the Chester and North Wales Archaeological Society, new series, 14
    (1908), 112–65
Bueno de Mesquita, D. M., 'Some condottieri of the trecento and their relations
    with political authority', *P.B.A.*, 32 (1946), 219–41

Carr, A. D., 'A Welsh knight in the Hundred Years War: Sir Gregory Sais', *Transactions of the honourable society of Cymmrodorion* (1977), 40–53

Chamberlain, E. R., 'The "English" mercenary companies in Italy', *H.T.*, 6 (1956), 334–43

Contamine, P., 'Les compagnies d'aventure en France pendant la guerre de cent ans', *Mélanges de l'école française de Rome*, 87 (1975), 365–96; reprinted in the author's *La France aux XIVe et XVe siècles. Hommes, mentalités, guerre et paix* (London, 1981), ch. 7

Gaupp, F., 'The condottiere John Hawkwood', *History*, 23 (1938–39), 305–21

Housley, N., 'The mercenary companies, the papacy, and the crusades, 1356–1378', *Traditio*, 38 (1982), 253–80

Jones, T., *Chaucer's knight: the portrait of a medieval mercenary* (London, 1980)

Mallett, M., *Mercenaries and their masters. Warfare in Renaissance Italy* (London, 1974)

    'Venice and its condottieri, 1404–1454', *Renaissance Venice*, ed. J. R. Hale (London, 1973), pp. 121–45

Temple-Leader, J., and Marcotti, G., *Sir John Hawkwood (L'Acuto). The story of a condottiere* (London, 1889)

Timbal, P.-C., *La guerre de cent ans vue à travers les registres du Parlement (1337–1369)* (Paris, 1961), ch. 5

Trease, G., *The condottieri: soldiers of fortune* (London, 1970)

Waley, D., '*Condotte* and *condottieri* in the thirteenth century', *P.B.A.*, 61 (1976), 337–71

Wright, N. A. R., '"Pillagers" and "brigands" in the Hundred Years War', *J. Med. H.*, 9 (1983), 15–24

Fortification and artillery

Brown, R. A., Colvin, H. M., and Taylor, A. J., *The history of the king's works*, vols. 1 and 2 (London, 1963)

Cipolla, C. M., *Guns and sails in the early phase of European expansion, 1400–1700* (London, 1965)

Clephan, R. C., 'The ordnance of the fourteenth and fifteenth centuries', *Archaeological Journal*, 68 (1911), 49–138

Contamine, P., 'Les fortifications urbaines en France à la fin du moyen âge: aspects financiers et économiques', *R.H.*, 260 (1978), 23–47; reprinted in the author's *La France aux XIVe et XVe siècles. Hommes, mentalités, guerre et paix* (London, 1981), ch. 5

    'Les industries de guerre dans la France de la Renaissance: l'exemple de l'artillerie', *R.H.*, 271 (1984), 249–80

Fawtier, R., 'Documents inédits sur l'organisation de l'artillerie royale au temps de Louis XI', *Essays in medieval history presented to T. F. Tout*, ed. A. G. Little and F. M. Powicke (Manchester, 1925; repr. New York, 1967), pp. 367–77

Finó, J. F., *Forteresses de la France médiévale* (3rd edn, Paris, 1977)

Hale, J. R., 'The early development of the bastion: an Italian chronology, *c.*1450–*c.*1534', *Europe in the late Middle Ages*, ed. J. R. Hale, J. R. L. Highfield and B. Smalley (London, 1965), pp. 466–94; reprinted in the author's *Renaissance war studies* (London, 1983), ch. 1

Jones, M., 'The defence of medieval Brittany', *Archaeological Journal*, 138 (1981), 149–204

Kenyon, J. R., 'Early artillery fortification in England and Wales', *Fort*, 1 (1976), 22–5

  'Artillery and the defences of Southampton, circa 1360–1660', *Fort*, 3 (1977), 8–13

  'Early gunports: a gazeteer', *Fort*, 4 (1977), 4–6

O'Neill, B. J. St J., *Castles and cannon* (Oxford, 1960)

Pepper, S., 'The underground siege', *Fort*, 10 (1982), 30–8

Rigaudière, A., 'Le financement des fortifications urbaines en France du milieu du XIVe siècle à la fin du XVe siècle', *R.H.*, 273 (1985), 19–95

Timbal, P.-C., *La guerre de cent ans vue à travers les registres du Parlement (1337–1369)* (Paris, 1961), ch. 3

Tout, T. F., 'Firearms in England in the fourteenth century', *E.H.R.*, 26 (1911), 666–702; reprinted in *The collected papers of T. F. Tout*, (Manchester, 1934), II, 233–75

  Chapters in the administrative history of medieval England, IV (Manchester, 1928)

Turner, H. L., *Town defences in England and Wales. An architectural and documentary study A.D. 900–1500* (London, 1970)

Vale, M. G. A., 'New techniques and old ideals: the impact of artillery on war and chivalry at the end of the Hundred Years War', *War, literature and politics in the late Middle Ages*, ed. C. T. Allmand (Liverpool, 1976), pp. 57–72

Naval objectives

Ford, C. J., 'Piracy or policy: the crisis in the Channel, 1400–1403', *T.R. Hist. S.*, fifth series, 29 (1979), 63–78

Hewitt, H. J., *The organization of war under Edward III, 1338–1362* (Manchester, 1966), ch. 1

Holmes, G. A., 'The "Libel of English Policy"', *E.H.R.*, 76 (1961), 193–216

Pistono, S. P., 'Henry IV and the English privateers', *E.H.R.*, 90 (1975), 322–30

  'The petition of Jacob de Smet: a plea for reprisals against the English, 1403', *Bulletin de la commission royale d'histoire* [Brussels], 142 (1976), 341–51

Prestwich, M., *War, politics and finance under Edward I* (London, 1972), ch. 6

Richmond, C. F., 'The keeping of the seas during the Hundred Years War: 1422–1440', *History*, 49 (1964), 283–98

  'The war at sea', *The Hundred Years War*, ed. K. A. Fowler (London, 1971), pp. 96–121

Russell, P., *The English intervention in Spain and Portugal in the time of Edward III and Richard II* (Oxford, 1955)

Saul, A., 'Great Yarmouth and the Hundred Years War in the fourteenth century', *B.I.H.R.*, 52 (1979), 105–15

Sherborne, J. W., 'The battle of La Rochelle and the war at sea, 1372–5', *B.I.H.R.*, 42 (1969) 17–29

Stanford-Reid, W., 'Sea power in the Anglo-Scottish war, 1296–1328', *M.M.*, 46 (1960), 7–23

Warner, G., *The Libelle of Englyshe Polycye. A poem on the use of sea-power, 1436* (Oxford, 1926)

Naval forces

Carpenter-Turner, W. J., 'The building of the *Gracedieu*, *Valentine*, and *Falconer* at Southampton, 1416–1420', *M.M.*, 40 (1954), 55–72

'The building of the *Holy Ghost of the Tower*, 1414–1416, and her subsequent history', *M.M.*, 40 (1954), 270–81

Evans, J. (trans.), *The unconquered knight. A chronicle of the deeds of Don Pero Niño, count of Buelna* (London, 1928)

Hewitt, H. J., *The organization of war under Edward III, 1338–62* (Manchester, 1966), ch. 4

Kepler, J. S., 'The effects of the battle of Sluys upon the administration of English naval impressment, 1340–1343', *Speculum*, 48 (1973), 70–7

Lot, F., and Fawtier, R., *Histoire des institutions françaises au moyen âge* (Paris, 1959), II, 536–44

Mallett, M., *The Florentine galleys in the fifteenth century* (Oxford, 1967)

Nicolas, N. H., *History of the royal navy* (2 vols., London, 1847)

Oppenheim, M., *A history of the administration of the royal navy and of merchant shipping in relation to the navy* (London: New York, 1896; repr. 1961), ch. 1

Prince, A. E., 'The army and navy', *English government at work, 1327–1336*, ed. J. F. Willard and W. A. Morris (Cambridge, Mass., 1940), I, 376–93

Richmond, C. F., 'English naval power in the fifteenth century', *History*, 52 (1967), 1–15

Roncière, C. de la, *Histoire de la marine française. II: La guerre de cent ans* (3rd edn, Paris, 1914)

Rose, S. (ed.), *The navy of the Lancastrian kings: accounts and inventories of William Soper, keeper of the king's ships, 1422–1427* (London, 1982)

Runyan, T. J., 'Ships and mariners in later medieval England', *Journal of British Studies*, 16 (2) (1977), 1–17

'Merchantmen to men-of-war in medieval England', *New aspects of naval history*, ed. C. L. Symonds (Annapolis, 1981), pp. 33–40

Sherborne, J. W., 'The Hundred Years War. The English navy: shipping and manpower, 1369–1389', *P&P*, 37 (1967), 163–75

'English barges and balingers of the late fourteenth century', *M.M.*, 63 (1977), 109–14

Tinniswood, J. T., 'English galleys, 1272–1377', *M.M.*, 35 (1949), 276–315

Waites, B., 'The fighting galley', *H.T.*, 18 (1968), 337–43

4 THE INSTITUTIONS OF WAR
Central organisation

Contamine, P., *Guerre, état et société à la fin du moyen âge. Etudes sur les armées des rois de France, 1337–1494* (Paris: The Hague, 1972)

Curry, A., 'The first English standing army? Military organisation in Lancastrian Normandy, 1420–1450', *Patronage, pedigree, and power in later medieval England*, ed. C. D. Ross (Gloucester: Totowa, 1979), pp. 193–214

Goodman, A., *The Wars of the Roses. Military activity and English society, 1452–97* (London, 1981), part 2

Hewitt, H. J., *The organization of war under Edward III, 1338–62* (Manchester, 1966)

'The organisation of war', *The Hundred Years War*, ed. K. A. Fowler (London, 1971), pp. 75–95

Mallett, M., and Hale, J. R., *The military organization of a Renaissance state. Venice, c. 1400–1617* (Cambridge, 1984)

Newhall, R. A., *The English conquest of Normandy, 1416–1424. A study in fifteenth-century warfare* (Yale, 1924: repr. New York, 1971)

Muster and review. A problem of English military administration, 1420–1440 (Cambridge, Mass., 1940)

Prestwich, M., *War, politics and finance under Edward I* (London, 1972), ch. 7

Recruitment

Contamine, P., *Guerre, état et société à la fin du moyen âge. Etudes sur les armées des rois de France, 1337–1494* (Paris: The Hague, 1972), chs 2, 5, 10 and 12

Goodman, A., *The Wars of the Roses. Military activity and English society, 1452–97* (London, 1981), ch. 6

'The military subcontracts of Sir Hugh Hastings, 1380', *E.H.R.*, 95 (1980), 114–20

'Responses to requests in Yorkshire for military service under Henry V', *Northern History*, 17 (1981), 240–52

Hewitt, H. J., *The organization of war under Edward III, 1338–62* (Manchester, 1966), ch. 2

Jones, M., 'An indenture between Robert, Lord Mohaut, and Sir John de Bracebridge for life service in peace and war, 1310', *Journal of the Society of Archivists*, 4 (1972), 384–94

Lewis, N. B., 'An early indenture of military service, 27 July 1287', *B.I.H.R.*, 13 (1935–36), 85–9

'The organisation of indentured retinues in fourteenth-century England', *T.R. Hist. S.*, fourth series, 27 (1945), 29–39; reprinted in *Essays in medieval history*, ed. R. W. Southern (London, 1968), pp. 200–12

'The last medieval summons of the English feudal levy, 13 June 1385', *E.H.R.*, 73 (1958), 1–26

'The recruitment and organization of a contract army, May to November 1337', *B.I.H.R.*, 37 (1964), 1–19

'The summons of the English feudal levy, 5 April 1327', *Essays in medieval history presented to B. Wilkinson*, ed. T. A. Sandquist and M. R. Powicke (Toronto, 1969), pp. 236–49

'The feudal summons of 1385', *E.H.R.*, 100 (1985), 729–43; comment by J. J. N. Palmer, ibid., 743–6

Lewis, N. B. (ed.), 'Indentures of retinue with John of Gaunt, duke of Lancaster, enrolled in chancery, 1367–1399', *Camden Miscellany XXII* (Camden fourth series, 1, London, 1964), pp. 77–112

Palmer, J. J. N., 'The last summons of the feudal army in England', *E.H.R.*, 83 (1968), 771–5 (See also under Lewis, N. B., above)

Powicke, M., *Military obligation in medieval England. A study in liberty and duty* (Oxford, 1962)

Prestwich, M., *War, politics and finance under Edward I* (London, 1972), ch. 2

Prince, A. E., 'The indenture system under Edward III', *Historical essays in honour of James Tait*, ed. J. G. Edwards, V. H. Galbraith, and E. F. Jacob (Manchester, 1933), pp. 283–97

Timbal, P.-C. (ed.), *La guerre de cent ans vue à travers les registres du Parlement (1337–1369)* (Paris, 1961), ch. 1

Walker, S., 'Profit and loss in the Hundred Years War: the subcontracts of Sir John Strother, 1374', *B.I.H.R.*, 58 (1985), 100–6

Supplies

Burley, S. J., 'The victualling of Calais, 1347–65', *B.I.H.R.*, 31 (1958), 49–57

Contamine, P., *Guerre, état et société à la fin du moyen âge. Les armées des rois de France, 1337–1494* (Paris: The Hague, 1972), chs 4, 11 and app. 11

Given-Wilson, C. J., 'Purveyance for the royal household, 1362–1413', *B.I.H.R.*, 56 (1983), 145–63

Goodman, A., *The Wars of the Roses. Military activity and English society, 1452–97* (London, 1981), ch. 7

Hewitt, H. J., *The organization of war under Edward III, 1338–62* (Manchester, 1966), chs 3 and 4

Jones, W. R., 'Purveyance for war and the community of the realm in late medieval England', *Albion*, 7 (1975), 300–16

Maddicott, J. R., *The English peasantry and the demands of the crown, 1294–1341*, *P&P* supplement, 1 (Oxford, 1975)

Newhall, R. A., *The English conquest of Normandy, 1416–1424. A study of fifteenth-century warfare* (New Haven, 1924), ch. 6

Prestwich, M., *War, politics and finance under Edward I* (London, 1972), ch. 5

'Victualling estimates for English garrisons in Scotland during the early fourteenth century', *E.H.R.*, 82 (1967), 536–43

Timbal, P.-C. (ed), *La guerre de cent ans vue à travers les registres du Parlement (1337–1369)* (Paris, 1961), ch. 2

Taxation and fiscal institutions

Brown, E. A. R., 'Cessante causa and the taxes of the last Cepetians: the political applications of a philosophical maxim', *Studia Gratiana*, 15 (1972), 565–87

'Customary aids and royal fiscal policy under Philip VI of Valois', *Traditio*, 30 (1974), 191–258

Bryant, W. N., 'The financial dealings of Edward III with the county communities, 1330–1360', *E.H.R.*, 83 (1968), 760–71

Contamine, P., 'Guerre, fiscalité royale et économie en France (deuxième moitié du xve siècle)', *Proceedings of the seventeenth international economic congress*, ed. M. Flinn (Edinburgh, 1978), II, 266–73

Fryde, E. B., 'Edward III's wool monopoly of 1337: a fourteenth-century royal trading venture', *History*, 37 (1952), 8–24

'Parliament and the French war', *Essays in medieval history presented to B. Wilkinson*, ed. T. A. Sandquist and M. R. Powicke (Toronto, 1969), pp. 250–69

'The financial policies of the royal governments and popular resistance to them in France and England, *c.*1270–*c.*1420', *Revue belge de philologie et d'histoire*, 57 (1979), 824–60

[The above-listed articles are reprinted in the author's *Studies in medieval trade and finance* (London, 1983)]

Genet, J.-P., 'Les débuts de l'impôt national en Angleterre', *Annales*, 34 (1979), 348–54

Given-Wilson, C., *The royal household and the king's affinity. Service, politics and finance in England 1360–1413* (New Haven: London, 1986)

Harriss, G. L., *King, parliament, and public finance in medieval England to 1369* (Oxford, 1975)

'War and the emergence of the English Parliament, 1297–1360', *J. Med. H.*, 2 (1976), 35–56

Henneman, J. B., *Royal taxation in fourteenth-century France. The development of war financing, 1322–1356* (Princeton, 1971)

Royal taxation in fourteenth-century France. The captivity and ransom of John II, 1356–1370 (Philadelphia, 1976)

'Financing the Hundred Years War: royal taxation in France in 1340', *Speculum*, 42 (1967), 275–98

'The Black Death and royal taxation in France, 1347–1351', *Speculum*, 43 (1968), 405–28

'The French ransom and two legal traditions', *Studia Gratiana*, 15 (1972), 613–30

'Nobility, privilege and fiscal politics in late medieval France', *French Historical Studies*, 13 (1983), 1–17

Hilton, R. N., 'Resistance to taxation and to other state impositions in medieval England', *Genèse de l'état moderne. Prélèvement et distribution*, ed. J.-Ph. Genet and M. Le Mené (Paris, 1987), pp. 169–77

Lewis, P. S., 'The failure of the French medieval estates', *P&P*, 23 (1962), 3–24; reprinted in the author's *Essays in later medieval French history* (London, 1985), pp. 105–26

Lot, F., and Fawtier, R., *Histoire des institutions françaises au moyen âge* (Paris, 1958), II, 183–285

Maddicott, J. R., *The English peasantry and the demands of the crown, 1294–1341*, *P&P* supplement, 1 (Oxford, 1975)

Miller, E., 'War, taxation, and the English economy in the late thirteenth and early fourteenth centuries', *War and economic development. Essays in memory of David Joslin*, ed. J. M. Winter (Cambridge, 1975), pp. 11–31

Miskimin, H. A., *Money and power in fifteenth-century France* (New Haven: London, 1984)

Morris, W. A., and Strayer, J. R., *English government at work, 1327–1336*, II (Cambridge, Mass., 1947)

Nederman, C. J., 'Royal taxation and the English church: the origins of William of Ockham's *An Princeps*', *J.E.H.*, 37 (1986), 377–88

Ormrod, W. M., 'The English crown and the customs, 1349–63', *Econ. H.R.*, 2nd series, 40 (1987), 27–40

Prestwich, M., *War, politics and finance under Edward I* (London, 1972), ch. 8
    'War and taxation in England in the XIIIth and XIVth centuries', *Genèse de l'état moderne. Prélèvement et redistribution*, ed. J.-Ph. Genet and M. Le Mené (Paris, 1987), pp. 181–92

Sherborne, J. W., 'The cost of English warfare with France in the later fourteenth century', *B.I.H.R.*, 50 (1977), 135–50

Spiegel, G. M., '"Defence of the realm": evolution of a Capetian propaganda slogan', *J. Med. H.*, 3 (1977), 115–33

Strayer, J. R., 'Notes on the origin of English and French export taxes', *Studia Gratiana*, 15 (1972), 399–421
    'Defence of the realm and royal power in France', *Studi in onore di Gino Luzzato* (Milan, 1949), I, 289–96; reprinted in the author's *Medieval statecraft and the perspectives of history* (Princeton, 1971), 291–9

Strayer, J. R., and Taylor, C. H., *Studies in early French taxation* (Cambridge, Mass., 1939)

Tout, T. F., *Chapters in the administrative history of medieval England*, III, IV (Manchester, 1928)

Wolfe, M., *The fiscal system of Renaissance France* (New Haven: London, 1972)

Order and control

Allmand, C. T., 'War and the non-combatant', *The Hundred Years War*, ed. K. A. Fowler (London, 1971), pp. 163–83

Allmand, C. T., and Armstrong, C. A. J., *English suits before the Parlement of Paris, 1420–1436* (Camden fourth series, 26, London, 1982)

Armstrong, C. A. J., 'Sir John Fastolf and the law of arms', *War, literature and politics in the late Middle Ages*, ed. C. T. Allmand (Liverpool, 1976), pp. 46–56; reprinted in the author's *England, France and Burgundy in the fifteenth century* (London, 1983), pp. 123–33

Barnard, F. P. (ed.), *The essential portions of Nicholas Upton's De studio militari, before 1446, translated by John Blount, Fellow of All Souls (c. 1500)* (Oxford, 1931)

Contamine, P., *Guerre, état et société à la fin du moyen âge. Etudes sur les armées des rois de France, 1337–1494* (Paris: The Hague, 1972), chs 4, 7 and 16

Coopland, G. W. (trans.), *The Tree of Battles of Honoré Bonet* (Liverpool, 1949)

Fowler, K. A., 'Les finances et la discipline dans les armées anglaises en France au xive siècle', *Les Cahiers Vernonnais*, 4 (1964), 55–84

Holland, T. E. (ed.), John of Legnano, *Tractatus de bello, de represaliis et de duello* (Oxford, 1917)

Keen, M. H., *The laws of war in the late Middle Ages* (London: Toronto, 1965)

  'Treason trials under the law of arms', *T.R. Hist. S.*, fifth series, 12 (1962), 85–103

  'The jurisdiction and origins of the constable's court', *War and government in the Middle Ages*, ed. J. Gillingham and J. C. Holt (Woodbridge, 1984), pp. 159–69

Marsden, R. G. (ed.), *Select pleas in the court of admiralty* (Selden Soc., 6, London, 1894)

Newhall, R. A., *Muster and review. A problem of English military administration 1420–1440* (Cambridge, Mass., 1940)

  'Discipline in an English army of the fifteenth century', *The Military Historian and Economist*, 2 (1917), 141–51

  'Bedford's ordinance on the watch of September 1428' *E.H.R.*, 50 (1935), 36–60

Porter, E., 'Chaucer's knight, the alliterative *Morte Arthure*, and medieval laws of war: a reconsideration', *Nottingham Medieval Studies*, 27 (1983), 56–78

Rowe, B. J. H., 'Discipline in the Norman garrisons under Bedford, 1422–35' *E.H.R.*, 46 (1931), 194–208

Squibb, G. D., *The high court of chivalry* (Oxford, 1959), ch. 1

Timbal, P.-C. (ed), *La guerre de cent ans vue à travers les registres du Parlement (1337–1369)* (Paris, 1961), ch. 4

Twiss, T. (ed.), *The Black Book of the Admiralty* (R. S., London, 1871), vol. 1

Wright, N. A. R., 'The *Tree of Battles* of Honoré Bouvet and the laws of war', *War, literature, and politics in the late Middle Ages*, ed. C. T. Allmand (Liverpool, 1976), pp. 12–31

Diplomacy

Allmand, C. T., 'Documents relating to the Anglo-French negotiations of 1439', *Camden Miscellany XXIV* (Camden fourth series, 9, London, 1972), pp. 79–149

  'The Anglo-French negotiations, 1439', *B.I.H.R.*, 40 (1967), 1–33

  'Diplomacy in late medieval England', *H.T.*, 17 (1967), 546–53

Broome, D., 'The ransom of John II, king of France, 1360–70', *Camden Miscellany XIV* (Camden third series, 37, London, 1926)

Chaplais, P., *English medieval diplomatic practice, Part I* (2 vols., London, 1982)

  'Règlements des conflits internationaux franco-anglais au xive siècle (1293–1377)', *M.A.*, 57 (1951), 269–302; reprinted in the author's *Essays in medieval diplomacy and administration* (London, 1981), ch. 9

Cuttino, G. P., *English diplomatic administration, 1259–1339* (Oxford, 2nd edn, 1971)

English medieval diplomacy (Bloomington, 1985)

Déprez, E., 'La conférence d'Avignon (1344). L'arbitrage pontificale entre la France et l'Angleterre', *Essays in medieval history presented to T. F. Tout*, ed. A. G. Little and F. M. Powicke (Manchester, 1925; repr. New York, 1967), pp. 301–20

Dickinson, J. G., *The congress of Arras. 1435. A study in medieval diplomacy* (Oxford, 1955)

Ferguson, J., *English diplomacy, 1422–1461* (Oxford, 1972)

Fowler, K. A., 'Truces', *The Hundred Years War*, ed. K. A. Fowler (London, 1971), pp. 184–215

Hewitt, H. J., *The organization of war under Edward III, 1338–62* (Manchester, 1966), ch. 6

Keen, M., 'Diplomacy', *Henry V. The practice of kingship*, ed. G. L. Harriss (Oxford, 1985), pp. 181–99

Le Patourel, J., 'The treaty of Brétigny, 1360', *T.R. Hist. S.*, fifth series, 10 (1960), 19–39

Lucas, H. S., 'The machinery of diplomatic intercourse', *English government at work, 1327–1336*, ed. J. F. Willard and W. A. Morris (Cambridge, Mass., 1940), I, 300–31

Palmer, J. J. N., *England, France and Christendom, 1377–99* (London, 1972)

'The Anglo-French peace negotiations, 1390–1396', *T.R. Hist. S.*, fifth series, 16 (1966), 81–94

'English foreign policy, 1388–99', *The reign of Richard II. Essays in honour of May McKisack*, ed. F. R. H. du Boulay and C. M. Barron (London, 1971), pp. 75–107

Perroy, E., 'Historical revision. Franco-English relations, 1350–1400', *History*, 21 (1937), 148–54; reprinted in the author's *Etudes d'histoire médiévale* (Paris, 1979)

Queller, D. E., *The office of ambassador in the Middle Ages* (Princeton, 1967)

5 WAR, SOCIAL MOVEMENT, AND CHANGE

Allmand, C. T., 'War and profit in the late Middle Ages', *H.T.*, 15 (1965), 762–9

Beresford, M. W., *New towns of the Middle Ages. Town plantation in England, Wales and Gascony* (London, 1967)

Bois, G., *The crisis of feudalism. Economy and society in eastern Normandy, c.1300–1550* (Cambridge, 1984)

Bolton, J. L., *The medieval English economy, 1150–1500* (London, 1980)

Boulton D'A. J. D., *Knights of the crown. Monarchical orders of knighthood in later medieval Europe, 1325–1520* (Woodbridge, 1987)

Boutruche, R., 'The devastation of rural areas during the Hundred Years War and the agricultural recovery of France', *The recovery of France in the fifteenth century*, ed. P. S. Lewis (New York: London, 1972), pp. 23–59

Bridbury, R., *Economic growth. England in the later Middle Ages* (new edn, Hassocks, 1975)

'The Hundred Years War: costs and profits', *Trade, government and economy in pre-industrial England. Essays presented to F. J. Fisher*, ed. D. C. Coleman and A. H. John (London, 1976), pp. 80–95

Carus-Wilson, E. M., 'The effects of the acquisition and of the loss of Gascony on the English wine trade', *B.I.H.R.*, 21 (1947), 145–54; reprinted in the author's *Medieval merchant venturers* (London, 1954)

'Evidences of industrial growth on some fifteenth-century manors', *Econ. H.R.*, 12 (1959), 190–205; reprinted in *Essays in economic history*, ed. Carus-Wilson (London, 1962), II, 151–67

Contamine, P., *Guerre, état et société à la fin du moyen âge. Etudes sur les armées des rois de France, 1337–1494* (Paris: The Hague, 1972)

'La guerre de cent ans en France: une approche économique', *B.I.H.R.*, 47 (1974), 125–49

'The French nobility and the war', *The Hundred Years War*, ed. K. A. Fowler (London, 1971), pp. 135–62

[The above-listed articles are reprinted in the author's *La France aux XIVe et XVe siècles. Hommes, mentalités, guerre et paix* (London, 1981)]

'Le coût de la guerre de cent ans en Angleterre', *Annales*, 20 (1965), 788–91

Crawford, A., *Bristol and the wine trade* (Bristol, 1984)

Fawtier, R., 'La crise d'une société durant la guerre de cent ans. A propos d'une livre recent', *R.H.*, 203 (1950), 53–8

Fowler, K. A., 'War and change in late medieval France and England', *The Hundred Years War*, ed. K. A. Fowler (London, 1971), pp. 1–27

Hatcher, J., *Plague, population and the English economy, 1348–1530* (London, 1977)

Hay, D., 'The divisions of the spoils of war in fourteenth-century England', *T.R. Hist. S.*, fifth series, 4 (1954), 91–109

'Booty in border warfare', *Transactions of the Dumfriesshire and Galloway Natural History and Antiquarian Society*, third series, 31 (1954), 145–66

Henneman, J. B., 'The military class and the French monarchy in the late Middle Ages', *A.H.R.*, 83 (1978), 946–65

Hicks, M. A., 'Counting the cost of war: the Moleyns ransom and the Hungerford land-sales 1453–87', *Southern History*, 8 (1986), 11–35

James, M. K., 'The fluctuations of the Anglo-Gascon wine trade during the fourteenth century', *Econ. H.R.*, second series, 4 (1951), 170–96; reprinted in *Essays in economic history*, ed. E. M. Carus-Wilson (London, 1962), II, 125–50, and in M. K. James, *Studies in the medieval wine trade*, ed. E. M. Veale (Oxford, 1971), pp. 1–37

Jones, M., 'Henry VII, Lady Margaret Beaufort and the Orléans ransom', *Kings and nobles in the later Middle Ages. A tribute to Charles Ross*, ed. R. A. Griffiths and J. Sherborne (Gloucester, 1986), pp. 254–73

Kershaw, I., 'The great famine and agrarian crisis in England, 1315–1322', *P&P*, 59 (1973), 3–50

Lewis, P. S., 'Decayed and non-feudalism in later medieval France', *B.I.H.R.*, 37 (1964), 157–84

'Une devise de chevalerie inconnue, créée par un comte de Foix? Le *Dragon*', *A.M.*, 76 (1964), 77–84

'Of Breton *alliances* and other matters', *War, literature and politics in the late Middle Ages*, ed. C. T. Allmand (Liverpool, 1976), pp. 122–43

[The above-listed articles are reprinted in the author's *Essays in later medieval French history* (London, 1985)]

Lucas, H. S., 'The great European famine of 1315, 1316, and 1317', *Speculum*, 5 (1930), 341–77; reprinted in *Essays in economic history*, ed. E. M. Carus-Wilson (London, 1962), II, 49–72

McFarlane, K. B., *The nobility of later medieval England* (Oxford, 1973)

'"Bastard feudalism"', *B.I.H.R.*, 20 (1945), 161–80

'The investment of Sir John Fastolf's profits of war', *T.R. Hist. S.*, fifth series, 7 (1957), 91–116

'War, the economy and social change. England and the Hundred Years War', *P&P*, 22 (1962), 3–13

'A business-partnership in war and administration, 1421–1445', *E.H.R.*, 78 (1963), 290–308

[The above-listed articles are reprinted in the author's *England in the fifteenth century*, (London, 1981)]

McRobbie, K., 'The concept of advancement in the fourteenth century in the chroniques of Jean Froissart', *Canadian Journal of History*, 6 (1971), 1–19

Miller, E., *War in the North* (Hull, 1960)

Nicholas, D., 'Economic reorientation and social change in fourteenth-century Flanders', *P&P*, 70 (1976), 3–29

Perroy, E., 'A l'origine d'une économie contractée: les crises du XIVe siècle, *Annales*, 4 (1949), 167–82

'Gras profits et rançons pendant la guerre de cent ans. L'affaire du comte de Denia', *Mélanges d'histoire du moyen âge dédiés à la mémoire de Louis Halphen* (Paris, 1951), pp. 573–80

'Social mobility among the French *noblesse* in the later Middle Ages', *P&P*, 21 (1962), 25–38

[The above-listed articles are reprinted in the author's *Etudes d'histoire médiévale* (Paris, 1979)]

Postan, M. M., 'Some social consequences of the Hundred Years War', *Econ. H.R.*, 12 (1942), 1–12

'The costs of the Hundred Years War', *P&P*, 27 (1964), 34–53

Powicke, M., 'The English aristocracy and the war', *The Hundred Years War*, ed. K. A. Fowler (London, 1971), pp. 122–34

Prestwich, M., *War, politics and finance under Edward I* (London, 1972), ch. 13

Renouard, Y., 'L'ordre de la Jarretière et l'ordre de l'Etoile. Etude sur la genèse des ordres laïcs de chevalerie et sur le développement progressif de leur caractère national', *M.A.*, 55 (1949), 281–300

Rogers, A., 'Hoton versus Shakell: a ransom case in the court of chivalry, 1390–5', *Nottingham Medieval Studies*, 6 (1962), 74–108; 7 (1963), 53–78

Saul, A., 'Great Yarmouth and the Hundred Years War in the fourteenth century', *B.I.H.R.*, 52 (1979), 105–15

Saul, N., *Knights and esquires: the Gloucestershire gentry in the fourteenth century* (Oxford, 1981)

Scammell, J., 'Robert I and the north of England', *E.H.R.*, 73 (1958), 385–403

Sherborne, J. W., *The port of Bristol in the Middle Ages* (Bristol, 1965)

Strayer, J. R., 'The costs and profits of war: the Anglo-French conflict of 1294–1303', *The medieval city*, ed. H. A. Miskimin, D. Herlihy and A. L. Udovitch (New Haven: London, 1977), pp. 269–91

Tuck, J. A., 'Northumbrian society in the fourteenth century', *Northern History*, 6 (1971), 22–39

'War and society in the medieval north', *Northern History*, 21 (1985), 33–52

Vale, M. G. A., *War and chivalry. Warfare and aristocratic culture in England, France and Burgundy at the end of the Middle Ages* (London, 1981)

'A fourteenth-century order of chivalry: the "Tiercelet"', *E.H.R.*, 82 (1967), 332–41

6 WAR, PEOPLE, AND NATION

Barber, R., *The life and campaigns of the Black Prince* (Woodbridge, 1986)

Barnie, J., *War in medieval soceity. Social values and the Hundred Years War, 1337–99* (London, 1974)

Bean, R., 'War and the birth of the nation state', *Journal of Economic History*, 33 (1973), 203–21

Beaune, C., *Naissance de la nation France* (Paris, 1985)

Bellamy, J. G., *The law of treason in England in the later Middle Ages* (Cambridge, 1970)

Bossuat, A., 'L'idée de nation et la jurisprudence du Parlement de Paris au xve siècle', *R.H.*, 204 (1950), 54–61

Bryant, L. M., 'La cérémonie de l'entrée à Paris au moyen âge, *Annales*, 41 (1986), 513–42

Cuttler, S. H., *The law of treason and treason trials in later medieval France* (Cambridge, 1981)

'A patriot for whom? The treason of Saint-Pol, 1474–75', *H.T.*, 37 (January, 1987), 43–8

Daly, K., 'A rare iconographic theme in a Bodleian Library manuscript: an illustration of the *Reditus regni ad stirpem Karoli magni* in MS Bodley 968', *Bodleian Library Record*, 11 (1982–5), 371–81

Duncan, A. A. M., *The Scots nation and the Declaration of Arbroath* (London, 1970)

Edwards, J. G., 'The treason of Thomas Turberville, 1298', *Essays in medieval history presented to F. M. Powicke*, ed. R. W. Hunt, W. A. Pantin, and R. W. Southern (Oxford, 1948), pp. 296–309

Fergusson, J., *The Declaration of Arbroath* (Edinburgh, n.d.)

Galbraith, V. H., 'Nationality and language in medieval England', *T.R. Hist. S.*, fourth series, 23 (1941), 113–28; reprinted in the author's *Kings and chroniclers. Essays in English medieval history* (London, 1982), ch. 14

Genet, J.-P., 'English nationalism: Thomas Polton at the council of Constance', *Nottingham Medieval Studies*, 28 (1984), 60–78

Giesey, R. E., 'The juristic basis of the dynastic right to the French throne', *Transactions of the American Philosophical Society*, new series, 51 (5) (1961)

Gransden, A., *Historical writing in England, II: c.1307 to the early sixteenth century* (London, 1982)

'Propaganda in English medieval historiography', *J. Med. H.*, 1 (1975), 363–82

'The uses made of history by the kings of medieval England', *Culture et idéologie dans la genèse de l'état moderne* (Collection de l'école française de Rome, 82, 1985), pp. 463–78

Grévy-Pons, N., 'Propagande et sentiment national pendant le règne de Charles VI: l'exemple de Jean de Montreuil', *Francia*, 8 (1979), 127–45

Griffiths, R. A., 'Edward I, Scotland and the chronicles of English religious houses', *Journal of the Society of Archivists*, 6 (1979), 191–9

Grosjean, G., *Le sentiment national dans la guerre de cent ans* (Paris, 1928)

Guenée, B., *States and rulers in later medieval Europe* (Oxford, 1985)

'Etat et nation en France au moyen âge', *R.H.*, 237 (1967), 17–30

Haines, R. M., 'Church, society and politics in the early fifteenth century as viewed from an English pulpit', *Church, society, and politics*, ed. D. G. Baker (Oxford, 1975), pp. 143–57

'"Our master mariner, our sovereign lord": a contemporary preacher's view of King Henry V', *Medieval Studies*, 38, (1976), 85–96

Hallam, E. M., *Capetian France, 987–1328* (London, 1980)

'Philip the Fair and the cult of Saint Louis', *Religion and national identity*, ed. S. Mews (Oxford, 1982), pp. 201–14

Hay, D., 'History and historians in France and England during the fifteenth century', *B.I.H.R.*, 35 (1962), 111–27

Hewitt, H. J., *The organization of war under Edward III, 1338–62* (Manchester, 1966), ch. 7

Huizinga, J., 'Patriotism and nationalism in European history', *Men and ideas. History, the Middle Ages, the Renaissance* (London, 1960), pp. 97–155

Jones, M., '"Mon pays et ma nation": Breton identity in the fourteenth century', *War, literature and politics in the late Middle Ages*, ed. C. T. Allmand (Liverpool, 1976), pp. 144–68

'"Bons bretons et bons francoys": the language and meaning of treason in later medieval France', *T.R. Hist. S.*, fifth series, 32 (1982), 91–112

Keeny, B. C., 'Military service and the development of nationalism in England, 1272–1327', *Speculum*, 22 (1947), 534–49

Kirkland, D., 'The growth of national sentiment in France before the fourteenth century', *History*, 23 (1938–39), 12–24

Lewis, P. S., 'Two pieces of fifteenth-century political iconography', *J.W.C.I.*, 27 (1964), 317–20

'War propaganda and historiography in fifteenth-century France and England', *T.R. Hist. S.*, fifth series, 15 (1965), 1–21

[The above-listed articles are reprinted in the author's *Essays in later medieval French history* (London, 1985)]

McHardy, A. K., 'Liturgy and propaganda in the diocese of Lincoln during the Hundred Years War', *Religion and national identity*, ed. S. Mews (Oxford, 1982), pp. 215–27

'The English clergy and the Hundred Years War', *The church and war*, ed. W. J. Sheils (Oxford, 1983), pp. 171–8

McKenna, J. W., 'Henry VI of England and the dual monarchy: aspects of royal political propaganda, 1422–1432', *J.W.C.I.*, 28 (1965), 145–62

'How God became an Englishman', *Tudor rule and revolution. Essays for G. R. Elton from his American friends*, ed. D. J. Guth and J. W. McKenna (Cambridge, 1982), pp. 25–43

Owst, G. R., *Preaching in medieval England. An introduction to sermon manuscripts of the period c.1350–1450* (Cambridge, 1926; repr. New York, 1965)

Literature and the pulpit in medieval England (Cambridge, 1933; repr. Oxford, 1961)

Post, G., 'Two notes on nationalism in the Middle Ages', *Traditio*, 9 (1953), 281–320

Prince, A. E., 'A letter of Edward, the Black Prince, describing the battle of Najera in 1367', *E.H.R.*, 41 (1926), 415–18

Richardson, M., 'Henry V, the English chancery, and chancery English', *Speculum*, 55 (1980), 726–50

Rickard, P., *Britain in medieval French literature* (Cambridge, 1956)

Robbins, R. H. (ed.), *Historical poems of the XIVth and XVth centuries* (New York, 1959)

Rowe, B. J. H., 'King Henry VI's claim to France: in picture and poem', *The Library*, fourth series, 13 (1932), 77–88

Scattergood, V. J., *Politics and poetry in the fifteenth century* (London, 1971), ch. 3

Spiegel, G. M., '"Defense of the realm": evolution of a Capetian propaganda slogan', *J. Med. H.*, 3 (1977), 115–33

Stones, E. L. G., and Simpson, G. G., *Edward I and the throne of Scotland, 1290–1296* (2 vols., Oxford, 1978)

Stones, E. L. G., 'English chroniclers and the affairs of Scotland, 1286–1296', *The writing of history in the Middle Ages. Essays presented to R. W. Southern*, ed. R. H. C. Davies, J. M. Wallace-Hadrill, R. J. A. I. Catto and M. H. Keen (Oxford, 1981), pp. 323–48

Strayer, J. R., 'Defense of the realm and royal power in France' *Studi in onore di Gino Luzzato* (Milan, 1949), I, 289–96

'France: the holy land, the chosen people, and the most Christian king', *Action and conviction in early modern Europe. Essays in memory of E. H. Harbison*, ed. T. K. Rabb and J. E. Seigel (Princeton, 1968), pp. 3–16

[The above-listed articles are reprinted in the author's *Medieval statecraft and the perspectives of history* (Princeton, 1971)]

Styles, D., and Allmand, C. T., 'The coronations of Henry VI', *H.T.*, 32 (May, 1982), 28–33

Taylor, F., and Roskell, J. S., *Gesta Henrici Quinti: the deeds of Henry V* (Oxford, 1975)

Tout, T. F., 'The English Parliament and public opinion, 1376–1388', *The collected papers of T. F. Tout* (Manchester, 1934), II, 173–90

Warner, G. (ed.), *The Libelle of Englyshe Polycye. A poem on the use of sea power 1436* (Oxford, 1926)

Wright, T., *Political poems and songs relating to English history composed during the period from the accession of Edward III to that of Richard III* (2 vols., R.S., London, 1859–61)

7 WAR AND LITERATURE

Barnie, J., *War in medieval society. Social values and the Hundred Years War* (London, 1974), ch. 5

Bayley, C. C. (ed.), *War and society in Renaissance Florence. The De Militia of Leonardo Bruni* (Toronto, 1961)

Birdsall, J. and Newhall, R. A. (trans.), *The chronicle of Jean de Venette* (New York, 1953)

Blayney, M. (ed.), *Fifteenth-century English translations of Alain Chartier's 'Le traité de l'esperance' and 'Le quadrilogue invectif'* (E.E.T.S., London, 1974)

Bornstein, D. (ed.), *The middle English translation of Christine de Pisan's 'Livre du corps de policie'* (Heidelberg, 1977)

Byles, A. T. P. (ed.), *The book of the ordre of chyualry of William Caxton* (E.E.T.S., London, 1926)

Christine de Pisan, *The book of fayttes of armes and of chyualrye* (E.E.T.S., London, 1932)

Coleman, J., *English literature in history, 1350–1400. Medieval readers and writers* (London, 1981)

'A political analysis of literary works *c.*1280–1400: ideology and perception of "The State" in England', *Culture et idéologie dans la genèse de l'état moderne* (Collection de l'école française de Rome, 82, 1985), pp. 433–62

Coopland, G. W. (trans.), *The Tree of Battles of Honoré Bonet* (Liverpool, 1949)

Philippe de Mézières, *Le songe du vieil pèlerin* (2 vols., Cambridge, 1969)

Philippe de Mézières, *Letter to king Richard II. A plea made in 1395 for peace between England and France* (Liverpool, 1975)

Coulton, G. G., *The chronicler of European chivalry* (London, 1930)

Droz, E. (ed.), Alain Chartier, *Le quadrilogue invectif* (2nd edn, Paris, 1950)

Dyboski, R., and Arend, Z. M. (eds.), *Knyghthood and bataile* (E.E.T.S., London, 1935)

Fowler, K. A., 'Froissart, chronicler of chivalry', *H.T.*, 36 (May, 1986) 50–4

Gauvard, C., 'Christine de Pisan, a-t-elle eu une idée politique?', *R.H.*, 250 (1973), 417–30

Grévy-Pons, N., Ornato, E., and Ouy, G. (eds.), Jean de Montreuil, *Opera. II*:

l'oeuvre historique et polémique (Turin, 1975); *III: textes divers* (Paris, 1981)

Guenée, B., 'La culture historique des nobles: le succès des *Faits des romains* (XIIIe–XVe siècles)', *La noblesse au moyen âge. Essais à la mémoire de Robert Boutruche*, ed. P. Contamine (Paris, 1976), pp. 261–8

Kilgour, R. L., *The decline of chivalry as shown in the French literature of the late Middle Ages* (Cambridge, Mass., 1937)

Kingsford, C. L., *English historical literature in the fifteenth century* (Oxford, 1913)

Lalande, D. (ed.), *Le livre des fais du bon messire Jean le Maingre, dit Bouciquaut, mareschal de France et gouverneur de Jennes* (Paris: Geneva, 1985)

Lewis, P. S., 'Jean Juvénal des Ursins and the common literary attitude towards tyranny in fifteenth-century France', *Medium Aevum*, 34 (1965), 103–21; reprinted in the author's *Essays in later medieval French history* (London, 1985), pp. 169–87

Lewis, P. S. (ed.), *Ecrits politiques de Jean Juvénal des Ursins* (S.H.F. 2 vols., Paris 1978–1985)

Muir, L. R., *Literature and society in medieval France. The mirror and the image, 1100–1500* (London, 1985)

Palmer, J. J. N. (ed.), *Froissart: historian* (Woodbridge: Totowa, 1981)

Pope, A. K., and Lodge, E. C. (eds.), *Life of the Black Prince by the herald of Sir John Chandos* (Oxford, 1910)

Robbins, R. H. (ed.), *Historical poems of the XIVth and XVth centuries* (New York, 1959)

Scattergood, V. J., *Politics and poetry in the fifteenth century* (London, 1971)

Vale, M. G. A., *War and chivalry. Warfare and aristocratic culture in England, France and Burgundy at the end of the Middle Ages* (London, 1981)

CONCLUSION

Allmand, C. T., *Lancastrian Normandy, 1415–1450. The history of a medieval occupation* (Oxford, 1983), ch. 11

'The aftermath of war in fifteenth-century France', *History*, 61 (1976), 344–57

'Local reaction to the French reconquest of Normandy: the case of Rouen', *The crown and local communities in England and France in the fifteenth century*, ed. J. R. L. Highfield and R. Jeffs (Gloucester, 1981), pp. 146–61

Bossuat, A., 'The re-establishment of peace in society during the reign of Charles VII', *The recovery of France in the fifteenth century*, ed. P. S. Lewis (New York: London, 1971), pp. 60–81

Chevalier, B., and Contamine, P. (eds.), *La France de la fin du XVe siècle: renouveau et apogée* (Paris, 1985)

Lewis, P. S., *The recovery of France in the fifteenth century* (New York: London, 1971)

INDEX